Best Practices in University Teaching

Second Edition

CENTER FOR TEACHING EXCELLENCE
UNIVERSITY OF NORTH CAROLINA WILMINGTON

1

Published by Center for Teaching Excellence
University of North Carolina Wilmington
601 S. College Road
Wilmington, NC 28403

Printed in the United States of America

First edition Spring 2006

LIBRARY OF CONGRESS CATALOGUING-IN-PUBLICATION DATA

Best practices in university teaching: essays by award-winning faculty
at the University of North Carolina Wilmington
edited by Caroline Clements and Diana Ashe.— 2nd ed.

ISBN 978-1-312-21321-0

1. College teaching. 2. Effective teaching. I. Clements, Caroline. II. Ashe, Diana. III. University of North Carolina (System)

Acknowledgments

We would like to acknowledge the importance of a healthy and enthusiastic community of teachers—and of willing and sometimes even eager students—in creating a collection like this one. Each of the authors of the essays collected here faces a challenging climate in higher education and has chosen to respond with deepened commitment and greater energy. Thank you all!

This double-blind, peer-reviewed, second edition of *Best Practices in University Teaching* was funded by **an anonymous donor**. What a wonderful gift this is! We are thrilled to share this generous gift with all of you and to spread the ideas in this book through this benefactor's good will. We hope and believe that our benefactor, and you, will be as excited about the content found in this volume as we are.

We also appreciate **Provost Denise Battles** and **President of the Faculty Senate Gabriel Lugo** and for providing material for the volume as well. Their endorsement of the project, and of the power of transformative teaching, is very important to our success.

In the making of this book, we are deeply indebted to so many talented people who have offered their skills: **Drew Walker**, for designing the new CTE and CFL image; **Michael Wadkins**, for design work; **Elizabeth King Humphrey**, for the book design and layout; **Shirley Mathews**, for her incomparable editing; **Emily Boren** and **Kirsten Leaberry**, for their facility with APA style; **Holly Lynn**, for editorial assistance; and **John Crawford**, for saving the day with his astounding design talents. We also appreciate the dedication of **Dianne Bass**, making sure that our accounts are balanced and that we are staying out of trouble (no easy task!).

We owe a tremendous debt of gratitude to the members of the Center for Teaching Excellence and Center for Faculty Leadership Advisory Board and our graduate assistants who graciously agreed to review essays for us, and reviewed them with thorough professionalism. Our stellar cast of reviewers includes **Tim Ballard, Madeleine Bombeld, Emily Boren, Michelle Britt, Theodore Burgh, Don Bushman,** Super-Reviewer **Marsha Carr, Don Furst, Russ Herman, Diane Levy, Kae Livsey, John Lothes, Michael Maume, Brandy Mechling, Anne Pemberton**, and **Colleen Reilly**.

We'd also like to thank our families for their support as we compiled this volume and handled the hundreds of documents and messages involved. **Henry Dworkin, Craig Harris,** and **Donovan Harris**: We cannot imagine making our way through this work without your love and support. Thank you!

Contents

DENISE BATTLES

PROVOST

Foreword

I write this foreward exactly one year to the day since the start of my UNCW appointment. My campus interview – necessarily brief, as such visits always are – provided me some strong impressions about the university, its people, and values. Having been an official member of the Seahawk community for the past twelve months, I have had the opportunity to refine those first impressions through interactions with campus personnel and other stakeholders. Some of my impressions were mistaken; others were incomplete. However, the sense of UNCW as a community that embraces quality teaching and truly prizes the student-faculty relationship is unchanged.

That dedication to instructional excellence is evidenced in this book and its collection of essays. Through their contributions, the authors – representing a diverse array of disciplines and instructional interests and approaches – share their passion for teaching and strategies for success in the classroom, to the great benefit of the reader. Whether one is new to the role of instructor or a seasoned hand, all with an interest in continuous quality improvement as an instructor can find herein thought-provoking techniques and practical tips in support of that end. I appreciate the authors' willingness to share their expertise, and I hope that others will also find inspiration in their words and practices.

GABRIEL LUGO
PRESIDENT OF THE FACULTY SENATE

Recipient of the Dr. J. Marshall Crews Distinguished Faculty Award,
the Distinguished Teaching Professorship,
and the Chancellor's Teaching Excellence Award

Preface

The words of wisdom you hold before you are tangible proof of UNCW's commitment to provide the most powerful educational experience to our students. This cross-disciplinary collection of essays exemplifies the dedication and creativity of professors seeking to deepen and strengthen the keenness of students to perceive and engage in the world around them.

Learning—and teaching—must be more deliberate now than ever before. These contributions expand on how to balance excellent teaching and experiential involvement against competing distractions. The insightful ideas shared in this second edition of *Best Practices in University Teaching* will bring you into the classroom and demonstrate what has worked for numerous educators—and what could work for you.

The Center for Teaching Excellence faculty often reach out to offer resources, including this book, to professors across the disciplines. It is just one way the Center for Teaching Excellence engages us in the learning process to ensure that the joy of learning endures for all of us at UNCW.

CAROLINE CLEMENTS
CENTER FOR TEACHING EXCELLENCE AND CENTER FOR FACULTY
LEADERSHIP / DEPARTMENT OF PSYCHOLOGY

Why Faculty Matter

In writing this book we focus on at least two audiences, which is a departure from our first edition. The first edition in 2006 focused on junior faculty. The intent was to give new faculty a resource, gleaned from their award-winning teachers, which would serve as a guide as they developed their own teaching practice. In reading those essays, I realized that we had targeted another audience, too. It was the audience of teachers who were always beginning anew, who had reinvented themselves over and over, sometimes as a result of institutional mission, and often in response to the students they were teaching. These teachers reinvented themselves for deeply personal reasons as well. In fact, reinvention is the hallmark of the essayists in the first edition, and is so in this book.

What seems to distinguish these essayists is their desire to keep their material fresh, their openness to new practice, and their enduring willingness to learn from their colleagues. In a sense, these teachers are never "done." Their classes are not quite perfected, their approach not set in stone. After a decade working in faculty development, I recognize that quality and applaud it. These teachers, and others like them, approach each semester with a new sense of wonder, imagine it as a time when everything is possible, when a willing heart and hard work will result in something special and transformative, for the student and for themselves (Bain, 2010). It is that quality I would like to explore in this essay, the process of being engaged in teaching, and staying engaged. When we cultivate that engagement in our teaching, and with our scholarship, we are to some extent always new faculty.

Umbach and Wawrzynski (2005) said it best; "Faculty do matter." The real essence of teaching is the relationship faculty form with students (Christenson, Reschley, & Wylie, 2012). That relationship has changed over the years. When Socrates taught, the outdoors was his classroom and his questions were his pedagogy. His philosophical approach embodied the belief that all learning comes from within, that the students know the answer and must only be asked the right question to achieve knowledge (Wegeriff, 2013). His method of Socratic questioning is delightful to practice and astonishing to watch in someone gifted in the method.

For hundreds of years after Socrates, the professor as teacher grew ever more remote from students and roles and responsibilities for each became more rigid and codified. Imagining the "father" of psychology, Wilhelm Wundt, striding into a psychology lecture hall in full regalia, accompanied by obsequious research assistants is quite a contrast to today's American teaching styles but that is how he taught. Wundt lectured for about an hour and brooked no questions, not that students in his lecture halls would have dared to interrupt. Students were considered far beneath the learned professor, and considered themselves lucky to study with such a master. Questions were best self-answered through rigorous autodidactic practice so that Herr Doctor Professor would not notice shortcomings.

Remnants of that teaching style can be seen today. I experienced them in China, where high school students study ceaselessly to be granted admission to the more prestigious universities (Arnov, Torres, & Franz, 2012). Once admitted, these same undergraduates work hours unfathomable to their American counterparts. It is not unusual for them to be in class and studying 16 hours a day, most days of the week. They do so for good jobs for the most part, jobs available only to the best of the best. Some do so, only to re-experience the same mind-numbing pace as graduate students. They endure hours that their American colleagues could not imagine, some for jobs but still others to enter the Academy, which is fairly well compensated.

The Chinese approach is uncommon in the Westernized world, and the Chinese have begun to question its usefulness. While Chinese students score dramatically better than Americans on many measures, studies show that exhaustive rote memorization may result in decrements in innovative thinking, cognitive flexibility and the ability to think outside the box that is so richly rewarded in our global knowledge economy (Li, Whalley, Zhang, & Zhao, 2011). Right now the Chinese Full Professor is more similar to Wilhelm Wundt than Socrates in approach, but that is changing as China is recognized as an economic super-power and more Socratic methods are being taught to a new generation of Chinese teachers (Tweed & Lehman, 2002).

As beginning teachers, junior faculty often struggle with balancing their "inner Wundt" and their "inner Socrates." As newly minted Ph.D.'s they have high expectations for themselves and for their students, leading them to difficulties with career balance (Swoboda, Davidson, Keiler, & Oglensky, 2011). One of my favorite anecdotes as UNCW's Director for the Center for Teaching Excellence (CTE) came when I was asked to consult with a first-semester professor whose entire class had failed her first midterm. She felt the test was fair; when she was their age she would have studied hard and passed it handily. She did not understand what had happened and her assessment of her students was rather harsh. They were "lazy." They wanted to be "spoon-fed." They didn't care about the material. They were "unmotivated."

I had worked with enough beginning teachers to know that her Wundt was out of balance with her Socrates. She was teaching herself, not her students. I asked her to go back and ask her students what they thought happened. Her students did what all American students do in this situation. They blamed her.

When she got this feedback she was puzzled, and more than a little angry. It was "proof" that her class did not care about learning. She had worked hard, and her students' test results confirmed that they were unwilling to reach her standards. This faculty member knew that her position was untenable. Unlike Wundt's students, or my students in China, American students have a voice, and that voice can considerably affect a faculty member's job security (Lee & Egan, 2007). More than that, though, this teacher was miserable. She cared about her students and obviously wanted them to do well. That they did not despite her best efforts confounded her.

What to do? I suggested she go back to her students for suggestions, and that she do so genuinely and without rancor. This technique, known as midcourse correction, is a well-studied method of getting a course back on track (Bonnstetter, 1998). In fact, I recommend it to all teachers as a mechanism for not getting off track in the first place. I worked with her to develop a feedback protocol that would give her the information she needed to see the problem from their eyes.

It may seem obvious that what was wrong was that the test was too hard. While I certainly thought that was the case, I wanted her to learn more than how to pitch a test. I wanted her to learn how to teach a class, and by that I mean a class of students. Far too many junior faculty focus on conveying content, at which they are no doubt experts, without reflecting to whom they are conveying the content. This results in frustration and anger in students, and cynicism and burn-out in faculty.

What this faculty member learned through that feedback is that her students did not feel as if they were in a teaching relationship with her. They felt that she valued the content more than she valued their understanding. To use their language, "she just doesn't care." This feedback was, of course, devastating to the faculty member, because she did care very much. In terms of external contingencies she cared about keeping her job. More importantly, though, she cared passionately about her subject matter and truly believed that her students' education would be all the better for conquering it.

The thing she lacked was a bridge to the students, a mechanism by which she could bring the material to them and have them engage with it in ways that were meaningful to *them*. For all her hard work in the course, she had been thinking about the content through her own passionate love for it and had failed to ignite the same connection to the material in her students. This to me was the good news. She had everything she needed but the relationship, and she could be mentored toward that. She just needed to get out of the graduate classroom and into the undergraduate. As a tool for establishing the relationship she needed to bring what colleagues in the Watson College of Education might call scaffolding into her assignments, starting with what they knew and giving them bridges to what they needed to learn (Pol, Volman, & Beishuizen, 2011).

The library at CTE and CFL is liberally sprinkled with books on this topic and many of our workshops focus on aspects of it. In fact the tentative title of the first edition was *Only Connect* and that essay is one of the few that is repeated in this second edition of the book. Whether describing Millennial generation characteristics (e.g., Winograd & Hais, 2011), student motivation, or just good, sound practice, the fact that teaching starts the first day with the building of a foundational relationship has been a characteristic of best practice since students upended the college classroom on the 1960s. The need for this relationship is not "new." It is not because our current generation is lazier, more entitled, or unable to think independently or have helicopter/lawnmower parents. It is as true of that first junior faculty member as it was of me when I was an undergraduate 30 years ago.

My junior colleague had only to recognize this responsibility to create the relationship to create the bridge. She needed to see that someone, at some point, had *seen* her as she was and recognized that she should be taken to another place in her learning. The minute someone did that, she became much more actively engaged as a learner. She began to see connections between disciplines and within her own discipline that heretofore had been fragmented chaos to her. She began to look at her world differently, and to benefit from those new eyes. In today's language she became an "engaged learner" (Coates, 2013). Her job was to pass along the favor and of course she did. Some day she will be writing her own chapter in a later edition of this book. I hope she includes what happened with her first midterm.

There are others who take a more cynical route. They "dumb the class down" because the students "won't" work and they have to achieve tenure. I usually inform them that research shows that teachers who do this receive worse evaluations than students whose initial expectations are far too high; at least students respect the latter (Love & Kotchen, 2010). Students know they are receiving less than they should in the former. It is the rare teacher who gets away with manipulating academic expectations, and the foundational academic relationship, to meet their own narrow needs. Our students may not know as much as we do but they are not stupid. They know the difference between a quality education and manipulation.

Equally disturbing are those individuals who give everything to the teaching relationship at the expense of their own scholarship and eventual tenure. For them the relationship is endlessly reinforcing. It is the short-term, immediate reward that lets them burn brightly as that "special" teacher; the one who "truly cares." Psychology is rife with studies showing that most people will choose a smaller, immediate reward over a delayed, larger reward (Dalley, Everitt, & Robbins, 2011). In my career I have known a number of such junior colleagues. Their students love them. Their teaching is typically extraordinary. But one of two things happens in these cases. In some cases the person has difficulty getting tenure because their teaching/ scholarship balance is far too heavily weighted toward teaching. In more difficult scenarios, boundaries are crossed with students that should not be crossed, resulting in ethical and fiduciary dilemmas that fundamentally alter and undermine the teaching position. This is such a common beginning faculty pitfall that there is actually a large literature on it (Aultman, Williams-Johnson, & Schutz, 2009). This is an instance in which mentoring can be tremendously helpful.

More positively, most junior faculty do well. They garner the considerable resources available in the teaching literature, through faculty development and mentoring, and find themselves by their third year or so reasonably comfortable in the classroom environment, adapted to a teaching style that fits their personality. After reappointment, faculty gain their first public validation of their teaching effectiveness. I typically see more creativity in the classroom, a relaxing into the teaching relationship, and the beginning of genuine enjoyment of the classroom experience.

After reappointment, faculty tend to think of students in more complex ways. They understand through direct experience multiple modes in ability and motivation likely to be present in every class. Rather than fighting those modes, they develop mechanisms of engaging the entire classroom so that students who are on fire with the learning process are not hampered in their learning by students who may be less content in the classroom. They know their boundaries and are less likely to fall for Grandmother problems or to cut some students an extra break they don't cut others. In short, they have learned the lesson that clarity and consistency are the currency of the realm in a well-run classroom (Svinivki & McKeachie, 2011). Their students thrive in this environment, as do their department Chairs!

Then comes the challenge of tenure. In order to attain tenure, faculty must build a portfolio in which their effectiveness as a teacher is documented through student perceptions, evaluations by senior colleagues, and materials demonstrating years of course development and refinement. Mastering the content of a discipline took most of us 5-7 years. Why should mastering teaching of the content take any less? (Bain, 2010). The task is daunting, and it is meant to be. Tenure is not given; it is earned. Tenure is when one's status in the community of scholars is publically affirmed. The essays in this volume are deliberately designed as one resource junior faculty may tap, among other professional development opportunities at CTE and CFL, to achieve teaching excellence.

Faculty members have the opportunity to challenge themselves further in teaching after tenure. Some begin to look at the teaching enterprise itself as a scholarly activity and publish in the area. Others edit textbooks or journals on teaching. There has been a dramatic increase in the scholarship of teaching and learning and the scholarship of engagement in the past two decades. In part I think this reflects the seriousness with which the ability to demonstrate teaching effectiveness is taken in an era of externally-driven accountability structures. The increase also reflects the fact that faculty members are pursing with great seriousness the mastery of teaching for their own professional development and, quite rightly, are sharing that mastery with others through scholarship.

I challenge you to read any of the essays in this book and find one writer who is not in a state of continuous renewal of their teaching. Indeed, it is my impression that all faculty do this on at least some basis. Course material becomes outdated. New texts, new literature and new technologies have to be mastered. At its most basic, teaching the same course in the same way over many years becomes less challenging, and faculty as a group thrive on challenge.

The perception of intellectual laziness is the bane of tenured faculty. It is how we are stereotyped by legislators and others who know nothing about the rigor of our days. We engage in it at our own peril and to the peril of the academy itself through the one student who remembers the one teacher who phoned it in. We have an obligation that is greater than ourselves to guard against such complacency, even as increased demands and stagnant wages make it a somewhat attractive alternative to working ever harder to just stay afloat.

How does one fight complacency? I encourage the reader to circle back to the example of the junior professor with the unfortunate midterm outcome. In order for her to become the teacher she so wanted herself to be, she had to learn to bridge a relationship between her students, herself and he subject matter. This teacher, and all faculty, serve as catalysts for knowledge, much like Socrates and not at all like Wundt (although one could argue that Wundt's approbation was catalyst enough). So too must we act as continuing bridges as that relationship is formed in every class we teach.

The cynics among you may wonder if it is enough to adopt and perfect a teaching persona, to develop a few "tried and true" techniques that will accomplish this purpose with less effort than that our junior colleague expended. I have seen this approach tried by colleagues who for whatever reason are stuck or stagnated in their professional development. There is only one problem with it. It doesn't work. Those who wind up relying on such gimmickry become caricatures of the teachers they once were. This happens through student disengagement, changes in their discipline, institutional mandates in teaching practice, and cohort shifts in the students themselves.

One need only look at the changes in the college classroom in the last 30 years to understand why this position becomes untenable in one to three years after it is attempted. It is Moore's Law applied to teaching. The classroom environment is changing at an ever-accelerating pace and faculty who do not work rigorously at staying up with these changes do so at their own peril.

The positive news is that what works in teaching has stayed the same even while its conveyance has changed rapidly, and that is the student-teacher relationship. If we are to help raise an informed citizenry who have the ability to deal with a world ten years from now that we cannot even begin to imagine, we have the obligation to be the catalysts we enjoyed in our undergraduate experience. And those catalysts had a relationship with us. Because of that relationship, we worked hard. Our motivators may have been grades, or money, or grad school or simply fear (in the case of my undergraduate experimental psychology professor) but we worked hard because that person saw us and that person motivated us until we began to motivate ourselves.

At that point the relationship comes full circle. The student becomes the scholar her teacher saw in her. This is why learning without relationship has failed so far. It is the central dilemma of massive open online courses. Without that relationship between teacher and student, learning suffers. People aren't catalyzed by paid course assistants. They cannot be seen by a teacher who cannot see them. I suspect at some point individuals who are trying to monetize MOOC environments might figure this out and, perhaps, we will all be the better. A far worse scenario would be a bifurcated educational experience in which that relationship is offered only to those paying premium prices to the few faculty left while the rest of the students learn what they can while experiencing the same frustration (and hunger) as individuals traveling in the ever-shrinking world of economy class on airlines. The difference here is that airplanes eventually land at their destination, regardless of passenger comfort. What we lose when we super-economize education is the relationship, and that is everything.

So whether you have taught Abnormal Psychology one time or, as I have, over 100 times, your job is essentially the same. The information is there and you either know it or you have the skills to gain it. Someone was a catalyst for you. They built a bridge; they developed a relationship with you and you became a scholar. Forgoing all financial sanity you elected to enter the academy, because for you passing that gift on, in your scholarship and your teaching, means everything. That means that if you stop building yourself, and your relationship with your students, you have forgotten why you came here. When that happens, and it will at times, let us hope that there are opportunities for faculty development still out there. Let us hope that there are mentors, and faculty and students for that matter, who you can rely on for renewal, who can remind you of why you came here, how lucky you were the day *your* relationship with knowledge first started.

REFERENCES

Arnov, R., Torres, C. & Franz, S. (2012). *Comparative education: The dialectic of the global and the local.* Lanhan, MD: Rowman and Littlefield Publishers.

Aultman, L. P., Williams-Johnson, M. R., & Schutz, P. A. (2009). Boundary dilemmas in teacher–student relationships: Struggling with "the line". *Teaching and Teacher Education, 25,* 636-646.

Bain, K. (2010). *What the best college teachers do.* Boston MA: Harvard University Press.

Clements, C. (Ed.) (2006). *Best practices in university teaching: Essays by award –winning faculty.* Asheville, NC: Blair Publishing.

Bonnstetter, R. J. (1998). Inquiry: Learning from the past with an eye on the future. *Electronic Journal of Science Education, 3*(1).

Chang, L.T., (2013, March 20). Why the one-child policy has become irrelevant. *The Atlantic.* Retrieved from http://www.theatlantic.com/china/archive/2013/03/why-the-one-child-policy-has-become-irrelevant/274178/

Christenson, S., Reschly, A. L., & Wylie, C. (2012). *Handbook of research on student engagement.* New York, NY: Springer.

Coates, H. (2013) *Students Engagement in Campus-Based and Online Learning.* London, England: Routledge.

Dalley, J. W., Everitt, B. J., & Robbins, T. W. (2011). Impulsivity, compulsivity, and top-down cognitive control. *Neuron, 69,* 680-694.

Kuh, G., Kinzie, J., Schuh, J., & Whitt, E. (2010). *Students success in college: Creating conditions that matter.* New York, NY: John Wiley and Sons.

Lee, M., & Egan, M. (2007). Understanding the millennial generation: Pedagogy for tomorrow's leaders. In J. M. Bissell (Ed.), *Proceedings of the 38th annual conference of the environmental design research* (pp. 165). Edmund, OK: The Environmental Design Research Association.

Li, Y. A., Whalley, J., Zhang, S., & Zhao, X. (2011). The higher educational transformation of China and its global implications. *The World Economy, 34,* 516-545.

Love, D. A., & Kotchen, M. J. (2010). Grades, course evaluations, and academic incentives. *Eastern Economic Journal, 36,* 151-163. doi: 10.1057/eej.2009.6

Parker, P., Zajonc, R., & Scribner, M. (2010). *The heart of higher education:*

A call to renewal. New York, NY: John Wiley & Sons.

Pol, J. V. D., Volman, M., & Beishuizen, J. (2011). Patterns of contingent teaching in teacher–student interaction. *Learning and Instruction, 21*, 46-57.

Svinicki, M., & McKeachie, W. J. (2011). *McKeachie's teaching tips: Strategies, research, and theory for college and university teachers* (13th ed.). Belmont, CA: Wadsworth, Cengage Learning.

Swoboda, D., Davidson, E., Keiler, L., & Oglensky, B. (2011). Creating space for scholarship of teaching and learning: Transforming the meaning of academic work. In J. Summerfield & C. Smith (Eds.), *Making teaching and learning matter* (pp. 125-143). New York, NY: Springer.

Tweed, R. G., & Lehman, D. R. (2002). Learning considered within a cultural context: Confucian and Socratic approaches. *American Psychologist, 57*, 89-99.

Wegeriff, R. (2013). *Dialogic: Education for the Digital Age.* London, England: Routledge.

Winograd, M., & Hais, M. D. (2011). *Millennial momentum: How a new generation is remaking America.* New Brunswick, NJ: Rutgers University Press.

RICK OLSEN
DEPARTMENT OF COMMUNICATION STUDIES

Some Touchstones for Teaching Excellence

I come from a family of teachers. My mother taught art at a nearby high school. My father taught theatre at the college level. I didn't always want to be a teacher; the desire to do so did crystalize in a public speaking class in college. Just a few years later, while earning my Master's degree, I was teaching my own public speaking class as a graduate TA. My first semester, after a midterm, much of the class was upset with their grades. They whined, they wanted to bargain question by question. By the end of the class session I was exhausted. One student who had been rather stoic all semester in the back of the class wandered up after most of the folks had left and said "You don't need to apologize for being hard. You told us what was going to be on the test . . . they just didn't believe you." And then he shrugged his shoulders and left.

I, along with my convictions, had been shaking in my boots until he offered that affirmation. It wasn't that my standards were unreasonable. It was that I had not convinced those students that my standards were reasonable. Since that class, part of my quest as an educator has been to find ways to present rigor as a believable and reasonable expectation in my classes. Ideally, they then embrace higher expectations for themselves. In this quest I am, of course, always "in process" and often rediscovering something I once did and had forgotten. I have occasionally come across an old assignment description or lecture note while cleaning and thought "Wow, that's good! Why don't I do that any more?" One of the documents I more intentionally revisit is my teaching philosophy.

Share Your Compass. Students often have many questions when they sit down to take a class with an instructor. Some of them are related to class focus, class workload and the like; others are related to the instructor. The rumor mill may have "answered" some questions but not all. I try to answer some of these questions the first day of class. I offer a 1-page abstract of the class to help clarify the topical focus and workload issues. A more detailed syllabus and set of assignment descriptions is available online but I think a tangible take-away from day one is helpful.

On the back of that course summary is my teaching philosophy (see Appendix A). I use this as the catalyst for sharing my passion for teaching and for my discipline. I also use it to put a positive frame around the rigor they will encounter in the courses I teach. I will take this up in greater detail in the last section of this essay. For now, let me say that revisiting my teaching philosophy almost every year for the last twenty years or so has been a very helpful exercise. Some statements have gone away and new ones have been added but for the most part, it is like renewing my vows. The words I wrote as a passionate, young lecturer still ring true and remind me of my calling. This is helpful when over-familiarity and burnout begin to singe the edges. I would encourage taking time to articulate a philosophy of teaching designed to share with your students that explores your aspirations, motives, and understanding of your role as a teacher in their lives. I have occasionally been encouraged by students and even parents who have found my teaching philosophy helpful. It was especially impactful when a non-traditional student came up and said "I wish I had read this as a freshman. If I had known this was what college could be about, I might not have dropped out." The advantage of an articulated teaching philosophy that is actually referenced in the class is that it can provide clarity and a foundation for excellent teaching which can sometimes be uncomfortable for some of your students.

Manage, Don't Solve. One of the challenges I personally face as an instructor is that I am never going to "get it right." I'm never going to create a curriculum or set of slides or assignments, etc. that nails it for evermore. Instead, it has been helpful for me to approach my job as one of ongoing management of the organic process of growing students into engaged citizens and informed practitioners of their major. One of my colleagues calls himself a "brain farmer" and that is an apt if not fully complete picture of our challenge. This organic/management approach is further enriched for me by the concept of "dialectics." Dialectics as I use it here is the idea that there are productive tensions between opposites that must be managed rather than statically solved. For example, there is a productive tension between structure and creativity. I must manage this tension by being clear enough to provide direction but not so clear as to eliminate any need for critical thinking, problem solving, meaningful collaboration among group members, etc.

So what are some additional dialects, additional productive tensions, that must be managed as I strive to teach with excellence? Law and Grace is one that comes up. I require APA style, I have an attendance policy, I have a host of other "laws" that students must strive to keep to do well in my classes. But there are circumstances that warrant grace. However, it is important to have your values in place before the crisis of a student at your door. Academic dishonesty in any intentional form is an issue I hold fast on. Submission deadlines is an area where occasionally some flexibility may be justified. However, whenever I deal with such a case, I take the student through my decision process. "Could I explain this situation in front of the class and have most of your peers agree with my decision?" That often helps students gain perspective. What I will often do is allow an exception to the policy IF an effort is made to address the root of the problem that led to the infraction. For example, I have had students miss excessive classes because of difficult life issues. I will replace an absence if they visit the counseling center and the center sends proof of the visit. If poor time management was the issue, I will take the paper past the deadline if the student takes a computer-based training module on time management or personal decision making. This "root cause" approach has helped me manage exceptions to policies with a bit more transparency and allowed students to truly feel like they participated in their return to "good standing" in the class. It has also expressed that I care about them as human beings without such care devolving into simply "cutting them slack" at a crucial time in the semester.

Another way I show my ongoing management of key classroom issues is to show student feedback comments that speak to both sides of an issue. Our university has student evaluation forms and students can offer narrative comments. I have collected useful comments over the years that ask for more or less of a particular strategy or more or less point values on a particular assignment. I share some of these during the first few class sessions as a way to say "I understand that this class is not perfectly tailored to your preferences and expectations but notice that there are many of you in this room and I've tried to find a defensible balance point on these issues."

The key takeaway here is to anticipate and reflect on the tensions you manage in your approach to teaching. Sometimes it may seem (?) they are competing goals or values or . . . but wrestling with them ahead of time and clarifying the process by which you manage them will help when addressing issues in real time.

Use Technology to increase Humanity. There are some teachers who seem to embrace technology and others who see it as a barrier to connecting with students. My position on educational technology has evolved over the years to the following position: educational technology is valuable and appropriate when it facilitates accountability, engagement and the quality and quantity of human connection between teachers and students. What can technology do better than I can so I have more time to do only what I can do? With this perspective in mind, it has been easier to wrestle with the challenges of new software, course management systems, maintaining a website, etc. It has also provided the rationale for me to have a Facebook page with which I do "friend" students if they request it. So, what technology have I found particularly useful? I have found PowerPoint useful in that I am able to keep myself on track, offer images that support my verbal illustrations and facilitate active learning in my classes.

A weakness I have if left unchecked is that I can lecture from buzzer to buzzer. My slide deck is designed to minimize that tendency. I begin most sessions with a quote of the day. This often establishes the social or historical significance of the topic or connects with another scholar's perspective on the importance of the topic. I then offer a preview slide. While lecturing I put key content in brief bullets and rarely have a slide without a reinforcing image. The image is sometimes an abstract representation of what I'm talking about or a reminder to offer a particular illustration. But, to address my weakness, I have designed slides that remind me to ask questions, leave time for a comprehension check activity, etc. I appreciate the reminder, the students appreciate having the discussion question up on a slide to contemplate.

I also use TurningPoint, which is one of the "clicker" vendors, and find this a valuable addition to my teaching technology tool kit. With 110-140 students in my class, even basics like taking attendance need an efficient system. I have an "on time" bonus question as my first slide each day. The question is typically a review question from the prior session, a question about an upcoming assignment ("What is the minimum number of sources required . . .") or a question from the worksheet. For each chapter I have created a review worksheet. I also have them read a selection of journal articles. Again, there is a worksheet for each one. Given the high numbers, I can't collect the worksheets, but I do ask questions from them with the clickers and that fosters accountability and class preparation. I have set the software to reward correct answers with 2 points and any answer with 1 point so that a 0 means someone was absent. Thus I efficiently take attendance. I have questions throughout the lecture and especially after short in-class activities. Because these quiz points are, in many ways, the easiest points to earn in the class, students see them as a reward for attending—and for an 8:00 a.m. research methods class, that's no small thing!

Finally, I do have an established web presence through my website and on our course management system, Blackboard. I keep my syllabus and assignments on my website because I want them to be available to students and colleagues who are not in the class. Within Blackboard, I use the gradebook and online exams feature. Giving online exams frees up two class periods to do active learning. That is consistent with my approach to technology: freeing up class time to do community things because technology can help with the individual things. Using technology to assess recall and comprehension and basic application allows me to take up writing assignments that help me assess analysis, evaluation and creativity.

The key takeaway here is that the integration of appropriate technology is an evolution, not a revolution. I did not begin teaching with all of these (and others) in place, nor did I have a "summer of miracles" where my courses were transformed. I slowly addressed key issues and then built on my small successes. The summary above is in rough chronological order because my urgent issues were getting some active learning in, getting some daily accountability in despite large numbers and finally, harnessing Blackboard to address grades and some testing.

Frame it Forward. One of the rewards of clearly articulating your teaching philosophy and being transparent about the ongoing management of teaching challenges with students is that you have the opportunity to frame issues in positive and healthy ways. I try to frame most course challenges as a necessary means of cultivating an outcome we can all agree is worth celebrating.

For example, most students would like to think of themselves as confident or grow in their self-confidence. I point out to them that a key path self-confidence is overcoming challenges and that true self-confidence is tied to self-efficacy. I typically say something like "If I could help you grow more confident without the fear of failure, I'd do it. I'm just not sure how to create confidence without such challenges." Or, "Most of us want to say we're critical thinkers and problem solvers on our resumes and cover letters. I'm not sure how to help you grow in this area without some ambiguity and challenges to the assignments. If I make them checklists, then all you can say about yourself is that you follow directions well. You can't really say you're a problem solver. I want you to be able to say you're a problem solver and that requires ambiguity." By putting positive frames around some of the challenges of the course, I'm able to assist students in understanding the rationale for the challenges and having a healthier frame of mind as they approach the challenges. Similarly, even when setting up class policies, it is important to put developmental rather than punitive frames around things. My attendance policy rewards attendance and encourages responsibility. It does not punish absences. The penalties are an unfortunate consequence of irresponsibility. My policies for electronic devices in the classroom reward engagement and civility. It was liberating to me when I realized that because of the structure of the classroom and the university system, I have a tremendous amount of authority granted to me. I need not be heavy-handed with that authority.

As a final example of how I intentionally frame my role, I let them know that I am their "coach" until a specific date in the semester and after that I am their "client." Any excuses, unresolved issues, questions, etc. must be addressed while I'm still their coach. Once I become their client, then my focus is on results and whether or not they satisfied the contract we agreed to at the beginning of the semester. I say it with a smile but they typically "get" that transition and how it relates to the world beyond the classroom.

The key takeaway is to review your language choices in your syllabus, policies, assignment descriptions and classroom elaboration on such things and see if you are establishing a framework of ideals and aspirations or punishments and consequences.

Still in Process

As I continue to strive to be an excellent teacher I, of course, look to use relevant examples, humor, enthusiasm, etc. But that is not enough. The strategies above help to underpin those more superficial behaviors and choices. But the key is to keep the process going. I will often solicit student help even more intentionally than that when trying to manage issues that vex me as an instructor. I have done this on a number of levels of formality. First, with one of my exams which requires students to work in groups to master secondary research and the university library, I also ask them to review my website and offer one very specific improvement or correction. They are not allowed to offer a global comment or say "change the colors." This has helped me catch typos or conflicting statements about due dates and much more. I also offer an extra credit question in the final exam, which is an in-class exam. I ask them to create a question that they thought would be asked but wasn't and to tell me which question it should replace. This helps me in two ways: 1) I get the exams back so they don't end up in circulation, 2) I sometimes do get a great question and some sense of an unclear one to get rid of. Students can even be of greater help in managing teaching challenges.

My father taught theatre for many years and his least favorite part of teaching the introductory class was the history of theatre sections. One day as we discussed his frustration it became clear that he just wanted students to take away "something!" from the discussion of each era. So we created an assignment where groups of student would be assigned an era/chapter and simply have to make ONE key insight come alive through some form of a group presentation. What had been a series of droning lectures and low-level discussion became a fun, interactive assignment that yielded sitcoms, panel discussions, videos and more. I had a student, who was a late bloomer and wanted to go to graduate school, help me with some videos that summarized her group's approach to each assignment. They are now on my website as resources for my students.

My father was in his 60s when he made that change to his class. I'm now 20 years into teaching and I'm still making changes. And I guess that's the real lesson. Continue to grow and learn about yourself as a teacher and the craft of teaching in addition to keeping up with your discipline. Both are changing and it is our responsibility to stay current and intentional in both the content and skills of our disciplines and how we help our students master them.

APPENDIX A

SOME NOTES ON MY TEACHING PHILOSOPHY
(OR, "WHY THIS IS, AT TIMES, A DEMANDING CLASS")

DR. RICK OLSEN

I like my job. I want to be here. I assume that you like your job and want to be here too. I believe that college is one of many options after high school. I assume that you are here because you made a choice to pursue your personal development through the opportunities provided by formal education. If you only want to be hired as a worker, go get trained. If you only want to socialize, go home. If you want to grow as a person, then embrace your education and then take personal responsibility for it.

You are a student, not "the customer." Education is far more significant than a business transaction. The student-teacher relationship is much richer than the customer-merchant metaphor could ever capture. If there are customers at all, they are the citizens of this state and country, and your children. Tax dollars make this education affordable and your children and fellow citizens will be direct beneficiaries, or sufferers, of the person you become. Become legacy minded—it can change your perspective in wonderful ways.

I as an instructor, and we as a department, ask that you develop your whole person. We expect and will work to cultivate the following traits: confidence, intellectual curiosity, responsibility, collaboration, critical thinking, problems solving, civility and praxis. We also will expect and keep you accountable to a high ethical standard.

Learning how to learn is as important as learning itself. My role is to act as coach. The course content is our common challenge. I understand that my expectations are fairly high. View that as a compliment to what I see as your potential. I want each of you to succeed in mastering the course content. I hope you will look back with pride at having achieved positive changes within yourself through this course.

Learn to enjoy the striving for excellence. Excellence is pursued because it is, of itself, a right thing to strive for. Do not be intimidated into mediocrity by your peers or your own ability to be "good enough" without much effort. I make the assumption that we are creatures of habit. A goal of this course is to develop good habits. Look for ways that this course material—and your efforts to master it—can change the way you perceive, think, feel, respond and act. Look for ways to turn information into knowledge and knowledge into wisdom. Turn your education into action. To a large extent, you are what you do.

Many of you ask college to prepare you for a career. That request comes with some clear implications: In a career you will be asked to put in a 40-hour week (or more) and be at work by eight or nine in the morning. You'll likely be allowed about 30 minutes for lunch. A career will not allow for daytime TV, late night TV, or skipping work without being fully prepared to make up for the time you lost. A career is not conducive to habitual mid-week partying, late night web surfing, X-box addictions, or any other activity that would undermine your ability to perform to your highest potential the next day. If you strive to act intentionally as a student, you could likely be done studying by 8:00 pm., enjoy the weekends and still get solid grades. The "40-hr.-week-approach" is both demanding and liberating! I don't have two full-time jobs. I don't expect you to have two full-time jobs either. If you work full-time, don't expect to go to school full time. I don't say this to be mean, but to save you from the trap of the "you can have it all" myth.

Active reading, attendance, curiosity, participation, efforts to personalize the material, assisting your classmates and asking questions are not required . . . but then success in this class, or in life, are not required either. Grades are not a statement about your potential or a denial of the equality offered to everyone in the eyes of God or the Constitution. Grades reflect an assessment about your performance according to agreed-upon standards for a given assignment or course.

I realize many of you work and we all have lives outside of the classroom. However, college is a special and short season in your life. College is ideally a time to immerse yourself in the life of the mind and create or refine the compass that will guide you on your life-journey. Work to find ways to focus on your studies, knowing that these efforts are what is called for, for now.

RICHARD L. OGLE
DEPARTMENT OF PSYCHOLOGY

Teaching As A Dance: Collaborating to Create What Ought to Be

"If you treat an individual as he is, he will stay as he is, but if you treat him as if he were what he ought to be and could be, he will become what he ought to be and could be."

—**Johann Wolfgang von Goethe**

About five years ago, a professional request that I create a written statement of my teaching philosophy landed me in an uncomfortable state of anxiety and rumination. "I don't know my teaching philosophy," I thought. And worse, "What if I don't *have* a teaching philosophy?" To quell my anxiety and stop the rumination, I did what I always do in a teaching context when I am stuck: I asked my students. When I told them of my quandary, my students jumped to my aid – as they always did and always do. I received numerous emails with long and detailed descriptions and heartfelt comments about who I am as a teacher. One email in particular struck me; that one contained only the above quote by Goethe. I laughed a long time after reading it. The quote is one that is very dear to me. It is the very quote that I gave to the student who emailed me, the very quote that I give to all my graduate students. Reading that email helped me realize why I was stuck. I understood then what I understand and believe now, even more strongly, five years later: *I don't have a teaching philosophy.*

I honestly mean that last statement: I don't have a teaching philosophy per se. I do, however, have a philosophy of life. As a dyed-in-the-wool existentialist, to me, life is defined and made meaningful through authentic relationships and interactions with others. We are social creatures, and life is a collaboration with other human beings toward the goal of becoming.

As an individual, a dad, a psychotherapist, a clinical trainer, a mentor, and a teacher, I am guided by Goethe's advice in all domains of my existence. Even as a student and an employee, I resonate with those who live through this stance in their molding and mentoring of me. As I read this quote, it says to me that one's stance in life should be that of acting to create an environment in which those around you can maximize their potential. The use of the word "ought" in that quote, to me, refers to what the individual believes he or she ought to be, not what I necessarily believe he or she ought to be. In this sense, the "ought" is based in the other person's perspective and values. Those whom I teach, train, and guide are **autonomous** individuals, not passive vessels, and they have at least as much to offer me as I have to offer them. My goal is to look through their eyes and find their "ought" — and then to create an environment where they can move further along in becoming that "ought." In this sense, the process of teaching is *always* about guiding behavior change. As a psychotherapist, this is the environment I attempt to create in the therapeutic relationship. As a father, I do the same thing (although the techniques are somewhat different), and in the classroom, as an instructor, or a clinical trainer, I attempt to do the same, as well. As this is an essay on teaching, I'll explain my life philosophy as it applies to that domain, and I'll expound a bit on some of the specific techniques I use to manifest that philosophy.

As a teacher, I live through this stance in the environment I create in the classroom and in the objectives that I have for the learning experience. I teach a variety of courses at both the undergraduate and graduate level; in all, these two things remain constant, regardless of the material or the audience. The environment that I strive to create in classes is that the course is not simply mine or simply the students', the class is mine *and* the students'; it is ours. Given this, the environment is one of **collaboration**. In this way, the course plays out like a dance. A dance is a coordinated effort of creation in which individuals work together to display, express, and transfer a meaningful experience and a message to others. When dancing with a partner, there is definitely a leader, but without the partner, there is no collaborative creation. Although I consider myself the leader in this dance, I am reminded of an insightful bumper sticker I have seen a number of times: "Ginger Rogers did everything Fred Astaire did, only backwards and in high heels." That statement captures the idea that the role of partner is often more difficult, and, in the end, the partner's role is the stronger and more impressive part of the creation. In this environment, the lectures, discussions, and activities that I plan are the lead, but after that, it's all improvisation, and it only works with a partner. In this case, it's a matter of partners — plural — all of my students.

My objective for the experience of learning is to help students *become* something rather than merely to learn something. Accomplishing this objective takes different forms, depending on the course. In undergraduate survey courses, I strive to help individuals become more intelligent consumers of the media output concerning the psychological and behavioral content relative to the specific course. The techniques I use in these courses include modeling, reinforcing, and expecting critical thinking skills; practicing the practical use of scientific thinking; and delivering content through the students' perspectives. I tell stories, I invite and encourage discussion, and I make great use of reflective listening skills (more on this later). Telling stories that reinforce our shared experience and creating discussions that allow the students to share their perspectives and reflect their insight and concerns in a way that lets them know they are being heard helps students join in the experience and clarify their "ought." There is an idea in social psychology that asserts that people come to know what they truly believe when they hear themselves speak. People do not come to know what they believe when they hear others speak about what those others think should be believed, or what is "fact." In this sense, learning comes as much from **evocation** of experience as it does from installation of information, as much from the practice of empathy as it does from the professing of expertise. Practically speaking, it means that if we want students to learn, they must talk or write as much as they listen to lectures. Whether this is carried out in my Drugs and Behavior class, toward the objective of creating an individual who is more flexible and sophisticated in his or her understanding of the social and political complexities of drugs in our society, or in my Health Psychology class, where I strive to create this flexibility in thinking and have students apply it to their daily life activities in the areas of diet, exercise, and behavioral health, the overarching goal remains the same. By focusing on transferring my enthusiasm and passion for the content by delivering it through the language, perspective, and life concerns of my students, I believe that the actual content will stick, students will learn, and, most importantly, behavior will change.

The graduate courses that I teach are very much in line with what I outlined above in that the environment of autonomy, collaboration, and evocation is the same, but the objectives are somewhat different. My goal is again to be part of the creative processes of an individual becoming something. In this case, that "something" is a professional psychologist. At the graduate level, I teach courses on psychopathology, clinical interviewing skills, and psychotherapy. These classes are geared toward training the skills of diagnosis, reflective listening/interviewing, and the delivery of psycho-therapeutic interventions, respectively. Again, the atmosphere I attempt to create is one where the dance involves taking informational content and technical skills and empathically delivering them through the students' perspective, language, and life experience. In these courses, students take a much greater role in the creative aspects of the experience through teaching each other, skill practice, and role-play. My graduate courses are the most fulfilling because the courses are truly collaborative: They are truly a dance.

At this point, it may seem that I am arguing that all you need in order to be a successful teacher is an impassioned philosophy of life and a catchy metaphor. Although I believe that those two things will certainly ease a person into a comfortable spot on the dance floor of higher education, there are a few basic steps a teacher will need in order to create the more complex dance. These are natural human communication skills that have been described, defined, and empirically validated as best practices in the context of a number of counseling and psychotherapy styles (Miller & Rollnick, 2013; Rogers, 1980). I have found through experience that these skills also transfer quite well to the teaching context. The skills are: **o**pen questions, **a**ffirmation, **r**eflection, and **s**ummary, or, as they are known in the literature, OARS.

Open questions are questions that invite narrative and conversation and allow the individual to provide perspective, rather than information. They differ from closed questions, which are questions that either have a simple correct answer or that can be answered simply with a "yes" or "no." Closed questions serve to halt discussion processes. Closed questions do little to encourage elaboration, and they squelch the opportunity to listen for elements of a student's perspective that can be used to facilitate learning.

Affirmation is the skill of accentuating the positive. It comes from the belief that there is something of value in each answer, in each perspective, and in each level of engagement. In practice, affirmation means that you avoid saying something that is untrue, trite, and/or shallow (*a la* Stuart Smalley from *Saturday Night Live*), while engaging in a manner that demonstrates that you are stretching to hear, understand, acknowledge, and affirm another person's perspective and contribution.

Reflection, also called active listening, is the process of repeating what you hear in the responses given to you by your students — much the same as the concept of mirroring within a dance. A reflection is a hypothesis (a statement, not a question) about what you believe the person is saying; this reflection can be delivered at a number of levels. At the simplest level, you can simply parrot or paraphrase what is said. As simple as this seems, research shows that this type of reflection leads a person to feel heard and motivates that person to continue speaking. At a deeper level, you can reflect the meaning of what is heard. Reflection of meaning demonstrates to the speaker that, beyond being heard, he or she is also being understood. Being understood increases an individual's willingness to collaborate, to be vulnerable, and to engage. The deepest level is the reflection of the unspoken emotion in the words of another. This not only leads to the sense of being heard and understood, it leads to the potential of a transformative experience — experiencing something in a new light or from a new perspective.

Summarizing is a versatile skill used to collect, link, and transition in the course of an interaction. Collecting summaries can be used to restate content, perspective, and sharing. Linking summaries can link content, perspective, and discussion between points in a lecture or across lectures. Transitional summaries can be used to wrap up a point within a lecture in order to move on or to wrap up a lecture itself. Importantly, each summary allows students and the instructor to hear again what has been delivered or discussed — often in a different, more integrated light.

Bringing this back to the metaphor of a dance, let's take the example of choreographing a lecture on anxiety and anxiety disorders with four main sections: defining anxiety and fear, describing various anxiety disorders, theories of anxiety disorders, and treatment of these conditions. Within the four sections, the basic steps (OARS) are followed within a larger pattern that Miller and Rollnick (2013) call the elicit-provide-elicit strategy (think "1...2...3, 1...2...3"). First, *elicit*: Use an open question or series of open questions to generate student comments (e.g., "Tell me about what you fear the most."). As you listen to student responses, you will reflect, affirm, summarize, and even ask more open questions. Based on discussion and responses from students and using the stories and words of the students, you will *provide* content that delivers information, affirms accurate understanding, fills in gaps, and gently corrects misperceptions. Then, you will *elicit* reactions to what you deliver, and you'll assess understanding and the degree to which students related to the content. When appropriate, you will use a transitional summary to move on to the next section and begin the elicit-provide-elicit process again. When you have finished, you will provide a linking summary to end the lecture. You create the best summaries when you reframe as much as possible of your student comments and experiences into the important parts of the delivered content.

As mentioned above, this style and these techniques have been empirically validated through controlled research and are best practices in the context of counseling and psychotherapy (Miller and Rollnick, 2013). The literature showing the effectiveness of this overall approach is vast, but only recently have we begun apply it directly to an academic setting. However, as it turns out, most of the elements of this perspective (e.g., autonomy, collaboration, and evocation) have deep roots in educational theories and philosophies, such as transformative learning (Mezirow, 2000), radical pedagogy (Friere, 1970), and constructivism (Fosnot, 1996). In addition, I have found more recently that this perspective is highly consistent (as are the above-mentioned theories) with the learner-centered approach to college teaching (Weimer, 2002; Weimer, 2013). Specifically, Weimer (2013) outlines five key practices that define the learner-centered approach: 1) instructor as facilitator (evocation), 2) instructors and students as partners (collaboration), 3) use of content to develop skills (change behavior), and not just to develop a knowledge base, 4) student responsibility in learning (autonomy), and 5) using evaluation and assessment to promote further learning. What I have stumbled across, over the years of my learning this dance, is that the approach I outline in this essay turns out to be highly resonant with all five practices advocated by the learner-centered approach. The techniques that I discuss here are behavioral-level strategies that I have found to be well-suited to instantiate these key practices. From a practical point, this is not difficult, and there is no one correct way, but it does take practice. When mastered, however, it leads to a vibrant and engaging organic experience.

As a case in point, my former graduate student who sent me that quote so long ago is now an instructor in my department. Over time, I have watched her practice the dance and transform from partner to leader in her own classes. Almost weekly, she comes to me with new ideas she has tried — ideas always steeped in OARS and elicit-provide-elicit, ideas that always allow students to speak or write as much as they listen. In these conversations, I see that she has found her "ought," and I realize what every teacher should hope to realize in his or her career — I have taught someone to dance, in many ways better than I can.

As I try to live out this life philosophy and practice these skills in the domain of teaching, I realize that I am not at all unique. I developed this philosophy from teachers and mentors who chose to dance with me, as well as from my philosophical heroes (existentialists like Viktor Frankl and Rollo May and humanists like Carl Rogers), and I learned these skills from my doctoral mentor and others who provided my clinical and teaching training. I have seen it in many of my colleagues over the years, and I now see it in newer approaches to college teaching. As I imagine is the case with most people, I am not always successful at maintaining this environment or implementing these skills, but that is part of the dance — when I flub a move, I laugh, I move on, and from that mistake, I keep creating something new. Oftentimes, that something new is something better than what I had planned. For me, this is the way it *ought* to be.

REFERENCES

Fosnot, C.T. (1996). Constructivism: A psychological theory of learning. In C.T. Fosnot (Ed.), *Constructivism: Theory, Perspectives, and Practice.* New York: Teachers College Press.

Friere, P. (1970). *Pedagogy of the oppressed.* New York: Herder & Herder.

Mezirow, J. (2000). *Learning as Transformation: Critical Perspectives on a Theory in Progress.* San Francisco: Jossey Bass.

Miller, W. R., & Rollnick, S. (2013). Motivational interviewing: Facilitating change (3rd ed.). New York: Guilford Press.

Rogers, C.R. (1980). *A way of being.* Boston: Houghton Mifflin.

Weimer, M. (2002). *Learner-centered teaching: Five key changes to practice* San Francisco: Jossey-Bass.

Weimer, M. (2013). *Learner-centered teaching: Five key changes to practice, 2nd edition.* San Francisco: Jossey-Bass.

TRACY HARGROVE

DEPARTMENT OF EARLY CHILDHOOD, ELEMENTARY, MIDDLE,
LITERACY, AND SPECIAL EDUCATION

Teaching as Gardening: A Metaphor for Reflection

"The way we think, what we experience, and what we do every day is
very much a matter of metaphor." (Lakoff & Johnson, 1980, p. 3)

Metaphors can be powerful tools of reflection that deepen our understanding of the world and portray our experiences in ways to which others can relate. As Lakoff and Johnson (1980) acknowledge, metaphors can help us make sense of our experience and shed light on what we believe. As educators, we see and interpret the world of teaching in many different ways, and there are a number of metaphors that have been used over the years to describe the teaching experience. Some of the more frequently cited comparisons include teacher as architect, teacher as coach, teacher as gardener, and teacher as travel agent. In reflecting on my own teaching career and what has been most meaningful for me and for my students, I, too, turn to metaphors. While there are connections that I make to each of the comparisons mentioned above, the one that resonates with me the most is teacher as gardener. In this essay, I will describe why the gardener metaphor best characterizes my views on teaching and how such an analogy can provide a meaningful way of reflecting on the craft of teaching.

Friedrich Froebel, the German educator who founded the first "kindergarten" in the early 1800s, saw the value in the garden metaphor for young children. Froebel coined the term "kindergarten," meaning "children's garden," as a way to capture his vision for best practice in teaching our youngest students. In Froebel's words, "Children are like tiny flowers; they are varied and need care, but each is beautiful alone and glorious when seen in the community of peers" (n.d.). As I reflect on my own career, which spans the past twenty-four years, I also find that my work as a teacher parallels that of the gardener. My career began as an elementary school teacher and has evolved into teaching pre-service and in-service teachers at the university level. While Froebel used the garden metaphor to capture the essence of teaching and learning for the young, I believe this metaphor also holds potential for describing effective practice in higher education. These connections help me frame my work as a teacher and highlight the elements of my craft that are most essential to success. There are many elements shared by gardeners and teachers. I have selected three to discuss here: environment, diversity, and a shared community.

First, in the garden and in the classroom, environment is everything! A great gardener, like a great teacher, recognizes the importance of creating surroundings that are optimal for growth. Gardeners don't make plants grow any more than teachers make students learn. Instead, the plant (or the student) does this on its own. What master gardeners or master teachers do, however, is provide the best conditions for growth. Great gardeners and great teachers seem to know almost intuitively what conditions are needed to help their plants, or their students, flourish. In the garden, essential nutrients including soil, water, and sunlight help to create an environment that promotes life. In the classroom, teachers provide nutrients in the form of encouragement, support, respect, and trust. These nutrients help create an environment for the student that promotes life in the form of motivation.

What makes their work complicated, however, is that gardeners and teachers alike must know the precise amount of each nutrient and the combination of nutrients that will allow those in their care to thrive. A plant cannot grow without water, but if fed too much of this life-sustaining nutrient, the plant will die. The gardener, as well as the teacher, must also recognize and combat factors that inhibit growth, factors often out of their control. Gardeners don't control the weather, but the gardener can help create a set of conditions whereby the plants are most likely to prosper, whether that means providing additional water or protecting the plants from the sun. Likewise, teachers may not control the curriculum, and they certainly don't control their students' backgrounds, yet great teachers are able to put into place a set of conditions that will optimize learning in spite of these barriers. The potential for a rich and fertile environment is there, just waiting for the master gardener or the master teacher to provide the right conditions.

In a speech to California teachers, Dr. Ken Robinson, Professor Emeritus at the University of Warwick, challenged teachers to look for this potential in their students and create conditions that would enhance student success. He explained that Death Valley, considered the lowest and driest area in North America and one of the worst environments for plants to thrive, came to life in the Spring of 2005 as an unusual seven inches of rain fell on the desert terrain "creating the right circumstances for a carpet of bright yellow wildflowers to blossom, bringing the valley of death to life." (Robinson, 2013). This demonstrated that Death Valley wasn't really dead at all. "Right beneath the surface [were] seeds of possibility waiting for the right conditions to come," said Professor Robinson (2013). A good gardener sees the potential that exists in the worst situations and works with care to provide the conditions that are needed.

A second way that gardening and teaching intersect is through the diversity that they share. Diversity allows for a richer, more inclusive experience. Gardeners strive to achieve a balanced, healthy ecosystem by intermingling different types of plants. A classroom rich in diversity is also more balanced as it will have many perspectives on which to draw. In a vegetable garden, some believe that certain combinations of plants result in crops that are more flavorful. It is also true that different combinations of students working together produce different outcomes, some of which are more desirable than others. Students in diverse settings are afforded the opportunity to examine their own perspectives more deeply and to consider new perspectives as possibilities. This creates opportunities for more complex thinking. Master gardeners, like master teachers, work to establish a culture that not only tolerates, but celebrates, diversity.

Gardeners, like teachers, must carefully monitor the progress of those in their care to ensure maximum growth. They must observe the various interactions that occur to determine if a different configuration must be implemented. The gardener must pull weeds to make sure that these plants don't inhibit the growth of those which are productive. In the classroom, modifications may be needed to help each individual reach their full potential. In the words of Ralph Waldo Emerson, a weed "is a plant whose virtues have not yet been discovered." Just as contemporary gardeners are finding uses for plants previously designated as "weeds," the teacher must find the best use of the talent that each student brings to the classroom. What appears to be a weed is really an individual, teeming with possibility and just waiting for the right someone to unearth their unique gifts.

A third way that teachers can be seen as gardeners is through the community that they create. If you've ever sat in a garden and observed the various forms of life all around you, it is clear that there is a complex system at work. All of the diverse elements in this system work in concert to create a breathtaking scene. One cannot help but marvel at the harmony that exists in such a setting. When students are engaged in learning that is truly purposeful, the same kind of harmony exists in the classroom. As Froebel noted, while "children are each beautiful alone," they are also "glorious when seen in the community of peers" (n.d.). What makes this setting so meaningful is that the group is focused on a common purpose, a vision that is shared by all. Groups build communities when individuals work together to create and sustain an environment in which all feel safe and supported. In such an environment, diverse experiences are shared and respected. All perspectives are valued, and no individual is marginalized.

It has been said that "as the garden grows, so grows the gardener" (Author unknown). Just as a garden takes many years to mature, so it is with teaching. Reflecting on my craft through the lens of a gardener gives structure to my perspectives and allows me to capture more vividly the complex work that is done in the classroom. To share this work in a community of scholars contributes to a shared understanding of best practice.

REFERENCES

Lakoff, G. & Johnson, M. (1980). *Metaphors we live by.* Chicago, IL: The University of Chicago Press.

Robinson, K. (2013, April). Ken Robinson: How to escape education's death valley [Video file]. Retrieved from http://www.ted.com/talks/ken_robinson_how_to_escape_education_s_death_valley.html

RUSS HERMAN

DEPARTMENT OF PHYSICS AND PHYSICAL OCEANOGRAPHY
DEPARTMENT OF MATHEMATICS AND STATISTICS

The Challenges of a Veteran STEM Professor

"I believe that our own experience instructs us that the secret of Education lies in respecting the pupil" (Emerson, 1884, p. 141).

How do you know if you are a good teacher? It is hard to look at yourself and determine the answer, though you might recognize a good teacher if you saw one. Students certainly think they know a good teacher when they see one. When we evaluate our peers, we bring our own perceptions of what an individual has to demonstrate. Being a good instructor is about the whole teaching experience. It is not just what we do in the classroom, it is how we extend the learning environment beyond those walls through interactions, virtual or real, with students and faculty, which lend to the perception that an instructor stands out. Perhaps, this is what we took away from Russell Crowe's portrayal of mathematician John Forbes Nash in the film *A Beautiful Mind* (Grazer & Howard, 2001) who exclaimed, "Classes will dull your mind, destroy the potential for authentic creativity," as the reason he did not attend classes as a graduate student. It is a combination of what we do both inside and outside the classroom that contributes to our impact on student learning. These interactions provide a feedback loop, which in turn makes for a better instructor and leads students to take part actively in the learning process.

While I consider classes important in the learning process, and recognize that real learning takes place outside the classroom, there are other challenges one faces. In this essay I will describe some of my thoughts and experiences about my challenges in teaching mathematics and physics classes.

What is My Reality?

From the age of thirteen, I knew I wanted to be a physics professor.

In junior high school, I found that I enjoyed reading about math and got hooked on the strangeness of relativity. In eighth grade I asked, "If planets traveled in ellipses and the sun was at one focus, then what is at the other one?" I proceeded to draw the orbits by hand and found that the foci did not match and could not be due to some invisible body. Thus began my personal excursion into science. I taught myself algebra and calculus long before I saw them in classes and enjoyed explaining physics to others.

By tenth grade, I did a project on relativity as Einstein had become my idol by then. A five-minute presentation turned into over an hour and the science teacher even invited the department chair to see the second half of my talk. In twelfth grade I repeated this with a talk on quantum mechanics. In Physics class, when asked to put problems on the board with everyone else, I actually went to the board and explained the problems to the other students.

As a freshman in college, I collaborated with my calculus teacher to teach his class how to use FORTRAN, a scientific programming language, to enhance the course material. This was a decade before the first personal computers were available! Already, I was not only forming the foundations for my profession as a teacher, I was also involved in instructional technology at a time before personal computers were ever envisioned.

Unlike many who recall the influences in their lives, I cannot say that I was inspired by any particular teacher, or that I adopted a teaching style of any of my professors. At the core of my teaching is a deep belief that anyone who desires can grasp the fundamental ideas in mathematics and physics at some level.

Students enter my classes with varying abilities, levels of preparation, needs and goals. Learning the concepts involved in mathematics and physics is not easy for many students, especially since many have developed some level of math anxiety.

I strive to engage and encourage students by providing an environment in which they feel comfortable communicating with me both inside and outside the classroom. I make myself available both virtually through email and online course material, and physically in my office for discussion of homework, course material, and advising. I want students to feel at ease enough to talk to me as early as possible in the semester. I encourage this by emailing students before classes begin, learning every student's name within the first few weeks of class, and providing a balance of humor and seriousness in my classroom. I also provide feedback, and grade exams and homework in a timely manner, for which students have commended me. I do my best to return materials the first class after the work was due and often hold long review sessions before exams. To further the students' coursework, I offer samples of past exams, and assign project work to explore topics at a level not covered in class. I have explored many types of pedagogy, as I have observed from my countless encounters with other instructors across campus through my experiences with the Center for Teaching Excellence.

I feel that I get the most from students when my expectations are high, but realistic. Students are expected to come to class prepared, listen, participate, ask questions, and interact with others and then go back to reread and rethink the material. Attendance and participation in the classroom are only a small part of getting students to begin to internalize the subject matter and develop critical thinking skills. Just as important, I provide them with a role model - I come to class prepared and on time, respond to their emails, and meet with them when the need arises.

Many years ago, I adopted the philosophy that "learning takes place outside the classroom." So, I routinely provide homework assignments and projects that engage and challenge their understanding of the material presented in class. Students are required to do the homework problems, get down and dirty with the details, and work on the subject material every day. In this way, students are presented with a variety of opportunities that encourage and challenge them to explore, learn and question the subject matter that I place before them.

I provide information through various forms of media: course web pages, multimedia materials, coursework, and organized lectures. Different media permit students to develop different tools and skills. Technology plays an integral part in the students' learning environment from mathematics software to videos. Also, I have worked with many students on special topics not usually covered in their course work.

I enjoy teaching and I enjoy explaining things to my students. I am especially excited when my students appreciate both my efforts and the subject matter. I have been known to go out of my way to work with students and find the students appreciate my efforts. I strongly believe that students can learn whatever they want if they put their minds to it. My perception of my job is that I was hired first and foremost to teach, and it is this aspect of my job that brings me the greatest satisfaction, particularly when I learn that I have made a positive influence in a student's education.

The Challenges of Teaching in the Sciences

Richard Feynman once said in an address to the National Academy of Sciences:

It is our responsibility as scientists, knowing the great

progress which comes from a satisfactory philosophy of ignorance, the great progress which is the fruit of freedom of thought,
to proclaim the value of this freedom; to teach how doubt is not
to be feared but welcomed and discussed; and to demand this
freedom, as our duty to all coming generations (Feynman &
Leighton, 1989).

When I was in junior high school, we were taught that there were two
competing theories of the evolution of the universe, the steady state model
and the big bang model. The discovery in 1965 by Penzias and Wilson of an
afterglow of a big bang had not yet made it into the science books. Over the
next 50 years our knowledge of the large-scale structure of the universe has
greatly changed and has excited young minds to think about black holes,
wormholes, and multiverses. Advances in understanding the make-up of
matter has led to terms like quarks, strangeness, charm and the Higgs Boson.
The World Wide Web, which was invented so that high energy physicists
could share this information, has led to unprecedented access to information,
including online texts, video lectures, and current breakthroughs in science
and technology. The world has changed quite a bit in the last several decades
and we can only imagine what the ubiquitous access to information will lead
to in the decades to follow. In this global and mobile environment, we have
many challenges in the classroom. Reading popular books, exploring the
Internet, or watching Discovery and Nova on a Roku box, can bring students
into the science classroom, but they eventually have to learn to dig into the
details and apply critical thinking. This is where we come into the picture.

How is teaching science and mathematics different from other disciplines? Contrary to popular belief, we do not just teach facts, though one
does need a basic set of fundamentals on which to build our models of
reality. In physics, we aim to teach, or transfer, concepts. Students want to
memorize facts and formulae but not actually understand them. In physics
we aim to understand the physical world in the simplest terms by distilling
the rules behind how the universe works. Feynman, in his famous *Lectures
in Physics* (Feynman, Leighton, & Sands, 1970), provides an analogy of an
observer watching two chess players. The observer tries to determine the
rules for how the chess pieces move through observation. We do not want
students to memorize every possible game, but want them to internalize
the principles and processes that can be used to progress to the end game
given a particular alignment of the pieces on the chessboard. They need to
see the bigger picture. There is a balance that needs to be found between the
abstract big picture and the concrete single move. This is not always easy.

There are several challenges that we face when teaching STEM disciplines. The first challenge is that of teaching non-majors. These students often are not as motivated or prepared as we would want them to be. Not every instructor is adept at catering to these students. In fact, as Physics Education Research (PER) has shown in the past several decades, it is not so clear that the way science has been taught over the past two hundred years is effective even when presented by the most gifted of instructors. There are more students going to college and fewer students taking science classes are eager to be there. According to Redish (2003), "The task of physics today is to figure out how to help a much larger fraction of the population understand how the world works, how to think logically, and how to evaluate science" (p. 7). Redish (2003) goes on to say:

> Many of our students dislike physics; many feel that it has no relation to their personal lives or to their long-term goals; and many fail to gain the skills that permit them to go on to success in advanced science courses (p.7).

Even if we get interested students into the classroom because they are enticed by the Hollywood version of recent theories of the universe, they tend to leave with little understanding, or even become discouraged.

A key element of teaching physics and applied mathematics is problem solving. This is how one applies the knowledge. Problem solving is a challenge because there is not just one way to solve a problem and one needs to practice and build up one's own bag of tricks. Students just want to be given a set of specific steps that always work, but this is not the way the world works. As teachers, we have to present several methods. Students need to learn to go from formulating problems to identifying simplifying assumptions and interpreting the results. They learn that we are always using models which are only approximations of reality. Students must also learn to question these models and modify the misconceptions that they bring with them.

Another challenge in physics is finding balance between teaching quantitative and qualitative reasoning. PER has shown that students do not pick up concepts by only solving problems. Students come in with many physical misconceptions and they need to learn how to reason with the principles of physics and not just do the mathematics or memorize a bunch of facts and equations. This lack of understanding, which extends well beyond the classroom, means that students do not see how the information they get in the classroom has anything to do with the real world.

Overcoming these misconceptions becomes a challenge to instructors. They need to then take the time learn about recent research into new active learning techniques, such as peer instruction. However, these new techniques are not readily accepted by their peers or even students. This leads to further challenges of adopting what has been discovered about the way students learn. One way to lessen the pushback by the students who think they want lecture-only classes is for all of the sciences to work together to bring about similar approaches to learning in which the information is discussed in the classroom by students as opposed to just regurgitating the text.

Recent studies have shown that while there can be significant gains in conceptual knowledge using what has been learned from PER about active learning practices, instructors who adopt such practices soon abandon a full implementation due to a variety of reasons (Dancy & Henderson, 2010). One finding is that instructors often cut out the most essential part of the best practice, such as allowing for student-student interaction. Also, their environments often do not allow for faculty the time to develop and implement the new pedagogy. For example, this interactive teaching is hard to carry out in the large class sections which we often have to teach in times of dwindling resources.

Another challenge is that each course is not an entity unto itself. Science and mathematics courses typically build on each other and it takes several years to build up the toolkit and an understanding of what has taken civilization thousands of years to develop ... from Aristotle to Newton to Einstein to Hawking. In mathematics, one needs algebra and trigonometry in order to learn calculus and calculus to continue on to advanced mathematics. In order to fully understand the current models of cosmology, one needs a grasp of classical physics (mechanics, thermal physics, electricity and magnetism) and modern physics (relativity, quantum theory, nuclear physics), which all require a number of courses in applied mathematics well beyond calculus.

Mathematics classes are also a challenge to teach. Students come to class with a weak algebra background even though there are record numbers of students taking AP calculus in high school. Our students rely heavily on calculators but do not know how to add simple fractions in their heads. They do not know simple identities involving trigonometric functions. Why should they? They have calculators, computer algebra systems like Maple, and they can go to Wikipedia or Wolframalpha.com to look up facts. One reason students should have immediate access to such information in their heads is so that they can follow arguments in calculus, physics, and higher level mathematics without wondering at every step, "Where did you get that?" This is part of the reason these disciplines are challenging. It takes time to dispense with misconceptions and to internalize a working knowledge of the basic techniques needed to learn to solve problems and not merely memorize facts, or just look them up on the Internet, without understanding.

Summary

With all of these challenges, the best practices discovered across disciplines are equally valid for the sciences. I have recently thought about what makes for a great professor and had written an essay for *The Journal of Effective Teaching*, which outlines important ideas on what are good practices in teaching (Herman, 2011). I do not always follow best practices, but I would hope that what I actually do comes from a deep belief in what I do. I provide opportunities for students to see the world through my eyes and have high, but realistic, expectations for their success. They need to learn that they own their education, need to continually practice what they have learned, and even learn from their mistakes. Students should see some of the same qualities in their teachers, who serve as role models. They should also see that there is more to learning than what they see in a single classroom. As a result, students will develop a lasting intellectual curiosity. Excellent professors accomplish this and more by showing students that professors care about their students' learning.

REFERENCES

Clements, C. (Ed). (2006). *Best Practices in University Teaching, Essays by Award-Winning Faculty at the University of North Carolina Wilmington.* The Publishing Laboratory of UNC Wilmington.

Dancy, M., & Henderson, C. (2010). Pedagogical practices and instructional change of physics faculty. *American Journal of Physics, 78,* 1056-1063.

Emerson, R. W. (1884). Education. *Lectures and Biographical Sketches.* Boston: Houghton, Mifflin and Company.

Feynman, R., Leighton, R., & Sands, M. (1970). *The Feynman lectures in physics.* Reading, MA: Addison Wesley Longman.

Feynman, R. P., &. Leighton, R. (1989*). What do you care what other people think?: Further adventures of a curious character.* New York, NY: Bantam Books.

Grazer, B. (Producer), & Howard, R. (Director). (2001). *A beautiful mind* [Motion picture]. U.S.: Universal Pictures.

Herman, R. (2011). Letter from the editor-in-chief: What makes an excellent professor. *Journal of Effective Teaching, 11*(1), 1-5. Retrieved from http://www.uncw.edu/cte/et/articles/Vol11_1

Redish, E. F. (2003). *Teaching physics with the physics suite.* Hoboken, NJ: John Wiley & Sons.

MEGHAN SWEENEY
DEPARTMENT OF ENGLISH

You Don't Have to Be Here

At age eighteen, Maggie Doyne left her home in New Jersey in order to spend a gap year traveling the world. She had been an over-achiever in high school, consumed with SAT scores, grades, her boyfriend. While trekking through the Himalayas, her life changed. She encountered children whose lives had been brutally disrupted by war and poverty. Many were orphans; many were forced to work for a living, breaking rocks to sell as gravel or acting as caregivers to smaller children. Galvanized, Doyne called her parents and asked them to wire the money that she had earned babysitting to Nepal. With this $5,000, she bought her first piece of land and began to build a home for orphaned children (Doyne, 2013). Now, Maggie Doyne, at 26, spends her days serving up bowls of rice, changing diapers, and battling lice, worms, rotting teeth, floods, and droughts (Kristof, 2010). She runs a home for 40 children as well as a school for over 300 children and has recently begun both a high school and a women's center. Throughout the year, she gives lectures all over the world (including at the Forbes 400 Summit in 2012), fundraising and acting as an advocate for children in need.

She has never been to college.

I sometimes share Maggie Doyne's story with my students as a reminder that college is not the only path. They know this, of course: they have friends or family members whose jobs did not require college or whose life circumstances did not permit it. But Doyne is something else altogether: a middle-class, high-achieving girl who had every intention of going to college and then, one day, decided not to. Many have never considered this an option for themselves. Going to college immediately after graduating from high school is what they are expected to do, what they have been led to expect since kindergarten.

The last time I talked with my students about Doyne, one of them came up to me afterwards. "That's it," she said, "I want to do something like that with my life. But my mom would kill me." I talked with her a little while, asking her what her mother expected, suggesting that maybe she would support her, but she shook her head. She knew her mother.

It can be hard for college students to feel as if they are adults who can choose their own paths. Their parents often have very strong ideas (bolstered by offers of financial assistance) about what their sons and daughters should be doing with their lives. Often, this means not just directing them to go to college but also determining what they should study.

I believe that one of the most important things we can tell our students is that they do not have to be here. They do not have to be in college, they do not have to be at UNCW, they do not have to be in our class. These are choices that no one else should make for them. If you want to take a year to volunteer or go hiking in the Himalayas, work to make that happen. If you want to go to college and major in English or psychology or math, do that instead. But make sure that it's not just a way to spend four years because you couldn't think of anything better to do.

Reminding my students that coming to class is their own choice is an important part of our class dynamic. Sometimes, I begin class by asking students to think of all the mind-numbing, soul-sucking things they could be doing instead. Aren't you glad you're not doing that? I ask. You're here, in this classroom, surrounded by people who are willing and even eager to listen to you. Listen back, I urge them. Learn everyone's name. Engage with the material. If you've made the choice to be here, try not to be miserable.

Recently, a colleague of mine, Chris McGee (2013), a professor in Virginia, posted this to Facebook: [I] have two wishes for the people in the room - smile and nod. It isn't that I want you to agree or blindly accept what I am saying, but at least try to look like I am not torturing you. Smile and nod. These are really my greatest wishes. Spread the word.

I tell my students that, too. Imagine you're standing where I am, and you're surrounded by a room full of blank faces, open mouths, and glazed eyes. How would you respond? Would you ignore it? Joke about it? Make everyone do jumping jacks? (I have resorted to this once or twice.) While the outward signs of the body do not always match the processes that may be going on internally, facial expressions and body language are key forms of communication. So I give them, only half in jest, a series of facial expressions that they might use if the standard smile and nod combo doesn't fit their current mood. Try "Thoughtful, yet skeptical," for example. Or incredulous. Enthusiastic. Unconvinced. Remember, I ask my students, when you were in high school or middle school and you got excited about something in class and your friends made fun of you because you were supposed to be bored because being bored is the same as being cool? Ok, remember that, and know that that's the opposite of what's going to happen here.

In the last few years, I have noticed a shift in attitudes about learning. Being smart and curious (I would argue) is becoming noticeably cooler. While being cool isn't the goal of education, this attitude fuels students' resistance to the pervasive anti-intellectualism of contemporary America. It makes being an active participant in class seem like something that might be worth doing.

I take the Nerdfighters as one sign that attitudes are shifting. Nerdfighters are the almost 90,000 fans and followers of the "Vlog Brothers": John Green (a bestselling young adult novelist) and his brother Hank (from Ecogeek, an environmental technology blog) (Green, 2013). Their mission is to celebrate traditionally nerdy pleasures or, as the website bluntly puts it, to "increase awesome and decrease suck" by engaging in debates about politics, education, and literature; raising money for charities ("Project for Awesome" is a charitable movement the brothers started); and encouraging followers to share art and music. The Vlog Brothers also launched Crash Course, an educational channel on YouTube; Hank is doing a yearlong series on chemistry and John on American history. Last week, when I asked my Literature for Young Adults students about nerdfighting, more than a third of them knew about (or were themselves) fighters.

Nerdfighting offers only one example[1] of the way that popular media can help foster dynamic intellectual exchange, but it has some important lessons for teachers. It's a rare teacher who doesn't integrate some form of popular culture into the classroom (a comic strip, an advertisement, a video clip), but I'd argue that we also need to be aware of the ways that our students consume culture and are active creators of it. In their nerdfighting lives, students engage with a blend of what used to be called high and low culture; they are also learning to combine a snappy kind of irony with earnestness. They learn about harnessing mass media to enact change. By becoming aware of the new and sometimes novel ways our students exchange knowledge outside the classroom, we are not capitulating to the latest trends. Rather, we are reminded that students may live lives that are more intellectually rich than we might at first think, a good starting point for building a classroom rapport. (I'll admit that my faith in this crop of students begins to wither when I find—as I did recently—that Yahoo Sports was one student's go-to source for "world events" and that another had never heard of NPR. Often,

---

1 PBS Digital Studios' "It's Okay to be Smart" and the PBS Idea Channel (both on YouTube) are two others.

though, I'm impressed to find that students are adept at seeking out ways to enhance their knowledge of the world: listening to podcasts, reading smart web comics like XKCD, and watching documentaries on Netflix.)

By engaging with students in this way, we emphasize that our class is part of a broader culture of curiosity. How might what we learn outside of class inform the classroom experience, not just what we know but how we learn? How can we as teachers think about the ways that knowledge is presented and performed in popular culture in order to borrow from it? How can we use it to help us create a narrative arc for the semester that is intelligible and accessible to our students?[2] It's not enough just to have our students write blogs or give presentations using Prezi. We have to think about how to use all of our resources (old and new) to create classrooms that draw students in, allowing them to be active creators as well. I'm still grappling with how best to do this.

One of the biggest challenges in creating a culture of curiosity comes from students who are beset by a fear of failing—which, for some, means getting a B on a paper or saying something wrong in class. This fear may lead them to resist experimentation in the classroom or to take only courses that they believe will offer them the quickest path to success. I understand that: I can be fairly risk-adverse myself.

Still, I have tried to emphasize the ways that failure can represent an opportunity. Recently, the power of positive failure has been popping up in the news frequently. An article in The Atlantic emphasizes that parents need to let their children fail and that suffering setbacks and dealing with the consequences will make them both more resilient and more successful (Lahey, 2013). Paul Tough's (2012) book, How Children Succeed, similarly emphasizes that success depends not primarily on cognitive skills but on character, which is formed when we encounter and overcome failure (xii). In an example that may seem more relevant to students, author J.K. Rowling (2008), in her commencement speech at Harvard, maintained that "[f]ailure gave me an inner security that I had never attained by passing examinations. Failure taught me things about myself that I could have learned no other way." Both Steve Jobs and Bill Gates[3] have touted the virtues of failure, emphasizing

2 Gerald Graff (2003) makes a related point in Clueless in Academe when he emphasizes that the link between academia and the popular media is frequently obscured. He argues that this "habit of defining academic culture by contrasting it with popular culture" "contributes to the mystification of academia" (p. 37) and to students' lack of motivation and feeling as if they don't belong.

3 Steve Jobs maintained that getting fired from Apple was the "best thing that could have ever happened to me. The heaviness of being successful was replaced by the lightness of being a beginner again, less sure about everything. It freed me

that devastating failures can lead to periods of tremendous creativity.

It's one thing for a Rowling or a Jobs to talk about their failures: we know what became of them. According to Gregory (2001), students caught up in their own struggles need pragmatic teachers "who can help them view each failure as merely interim, as merely a halt in forward progress, not as a terminal judgment on their abilities" (p. 76). We all need to learn how to fail gracefully, students and teachers alike.

Fear of failure grips every teacher at one time or another, coming to us in the standard "I'm teaching a class and none of my students are paying attention" dream.4 I haven't revealed my dreams to my students yet, but I do tell them a story that, I hope, shows how I take on the fear of failure.

When I was interviewing for academic jobs, I came upon a young woman dressed in a crumpled gray suit, curled up on the loveseat of a hotel bathroom and biting her nails. She was obviously a job candidate, and either her interview had gone so poorly that she was reduced to the heap I saw in front of me, or the sheer anticipation of the event was too much for her. She made everyone in the bathroom visibly uncomfortable, and they scurried around her, averting their eyes.

It was something of a wake up call for me, and I think about this poor woman often. Maybe she had received some devastating news moments before. Maybe she had eaten a bad chicken salad. But, given the circumstances, I doubt it. She had, more than likely, gotten caught up in the madness of the job search, blowing it out of proportion. Years later, I'd like to thank her, because after seeing her unraveling, my own interviews went pretty well. Really, did my performance matter that much? I wanted a job, sure, but if I didn't get it I'd try again or do something else. I didn't have to be here. No one would live or die because of the way I answered the question "And where do you see your research going in the next five years?" It really was that simple.

Fear of failure can be crippling. But, I tell my students, if the B minus you got on your 6-page paper analyzing depictions of divorce in children's picture books makes you want to curl up in a ball and weep, take a step back. Reconsider assuming the fetal position and come talk with me about what you can do next time. We'll get through this.

Confronting these fears calls up a more basic challenge to the cultivation of curiosity: how do I characterize the relationship I have with my students

---

to enter one of the most creative periods of my life" (Yarrow, 2011). Bill Gates has said, "Success is a lousy teacher. It seduces smart people into thinking they can't lose" (Tugend, 2011).

4 Jane Tompkins (1996) talks about these anxiety dreams in Life in School; so does Elaine Showalter (2002) in Teaching Literature.

in the first place? Am I a mentor? A curiosity coach? Friend? Ally? I suspect that much of my own uncertainty about how best to articulate it stems from an experience I had my first semester at as a newly minted PhD, when I ran into a student at a bar. Or, I should say, she ran smack into me, squealing, "Meghan!" and engulfing me in a hug. I was (almost literally) floored. Not only was this student calling me by my first name (hadn't I told them to call me doctor or professor?), she was also hugging me. I chalked it up to alcohol and surprise, but it made me wary. I became much more insistent on reminding students that, just because I was younger than some of their professors, I was not there to hang out with them, or to be, as they put it (using a word that drives me nuts) "relatable."5 I was intent on avoiding what Marshall Gregory (2001) calls a "disquieting and flabby kind of friendliness devoid of rigor or sharp edges" (p. 81). I remembered (although I didn't necessarily always follow) what one of my undergraduate professors said to me as I went off to teach my first class in graduate school: wear shoes that make you feel powerful and don't smile for the first month. How, after all, do you let students know that you won't put up with bullshit if you're not a little bit distant, a little bit tough?

What are the alternatives? Gregory (2001), who writes about teacherly ethos, supports a model he calls the "befriending model of teaching." It is, he is quick to assure his readers, not "touchy-feely" and does not require sharing tastes or secrets. It requires creating an atmosphere of trust by pursuing such qualities as curiosity, honesty, unpretentiousness, humor, and even, when necessary, indignation. Gregory (2001) writes that teachers create a "context of feeling" that "turns curricular content into a burrowing force that gets under our skin, that irritates our natural self-satisfaction and by so doing turns it into the kind of dissatisfaction that only real learning can salve" (p. 74). Teachers act as "messengers" of this content—whatever it may be. As Gregory (2001) notes, "It's never just for the sake of the skill or idea alone that the learner learns it, but for the sake of the life that is heightened, vivified, intensified, and enriched by means of the skill or idea" (p. 77).

Writer and teacher bell hooks similarly argues that we need to be "willing to be a witness to our students of how ideas change and shape us, how something affects us so that we think differently than we did before" (National Council, 2004). The language of witnessing may seem off-putting—too

---

5 This is a term of approbation that I beg students not to use. First, because it suggests not that a particular someone is relating to someone or something else, but that the quality inheres in that thing or person. Second: why should being able to relate to something necessarily be a good thing? Might it not be beneficial to be alienated from, bemused by, or disconnected from something, too?

personal, too pushy, perhaps because contemporary witnessing can take on an evangelical zeal that is inappropriate in secular contexts. But what we do is attest to the ways that our own lives have been shaped (transformed, even, to use another dramatic word) by ideas. This is not the same as saying, "This idea should shape you as it has shaped me." It is, rather, acknowledging that such shaping is possible and can be pleasurable. Sharing what excites us about our research is an important part of this. Modeling enthusiasm for the texts we're reading is, too. (I remember reading novels I hated in college but thinking, well, if Dr. L. loves it so much, I probably should give it a shot. His passion for the text made all the difference.)

An academic life is complicated, as we know, and we have to "witness" to that, too: to the ways that writing irritates us and research drives us nuts. I think of it as a kind of witnessing when I make the process by which I analyze texts and construct arguments transparent to my students. I sometimes show my students a very early draft of an article I'm writing. It is, inevitably, full of ///////s and ???s and sentence fragments. It has comments like "move paragraph" "need quote here" sprinkled throughout. Students are surprised to see ideas that haven't emerged, arguments that go nowhere, convoluted sentences. They see that writing is messy, that it is (as we've been telling them all along) very much a process, and one that requires hard work and persistence.

It may not be the kind of persistence that Maggie Doyne requires when she raises money to build a school for hundreds of Nepali children. It may not seem very important at the time. But if we—and I definitely include myself here—recognize that each activity (paper or test or discussion) is a small part of a larger culture of curiosity, we remember why we're here.

As I made my way through graduate school, I frequently asked myself, "Is there something else I would rather be doing?" Through my first year of classes, early teaching experiences, and dissertation, the answer was always the same: no, at least not right now. I told myself that, if I ever found something I wanted to do more, I would do it. I gave myself an out. We can give our students the gift of this "out" as well. Then, when we meet in class each day, we can say (without too much exaggeration) that there is nowhere else we would rather be.

REFERENCES

Doyne, M. (2013). *FAQ.* Retrieved from: Blinknow.org.

Graff, G. (2003). *Clueless in academe: How schooling obscures the life of the mind.* New Haven: Yale University Press.

Green, H. (2013). *Nerdfighters.* Retrieved from: nerdfighters.ning.com.

Gregory, M. (2001). Curriculum, pedagogy, and teacherly ethos. *Pedagogy 1.1,* 69-89. Retrieved from: http://muse.jhu.edu/journals/pedago gy/v001/1.1gregory.html

National Council of Teachers on Leadership. (2004, Septemeber). Bell hooks urges 'radical openness' in teaching, learning. *The Council Chronicle.* Retrieved from: http://www.ncte.org/ magazine/archives/117638

Kristof, N. D. (2010, October 20). D.I.Y. Foreign-aid revolution. *New York Times Magazine.* Retrieved from: http://www.nytimes.com

Lahey, J. (2013, January 29). Why Parents Need to Let Their Children Fail. *The Atlantic.* Retrieved from: www.theatlantic.com

McGee, C. (2013, January 25). Facebook post. Retrieved from: facebook. com

Rowling, J. K. (2008, June 5.) The fringe benefits of failure, and the importance of imagination. *Harvard Magazine.* Retrieved from: harvardmagazine.com.

Showalter, E. (2002). *Teaching Literature.* Oxford: Wiley Blackwell

Tompkins, J. (1996). *A life in school: What the teacher learned.* New York, NY: Perseus Books

Tough, P. (2012). *How children succeed: Grit, curiosity, and the hidden power of character.* New York, NY: Houghton Mifflin.

Tugend, A. (2011, August 2). You need to make mistakes to get ahead. *Cable News Network.* Retrieved from: CNN.com

Yarrow, J. (2011, October 6). The full text of Steve Jobs' Stanford commencement speech. *Business Insider.* Retrieved from: *Businessinsider.com*

PETER W. SCHUHMANN
DEPARTMENT OF ECONOMICS AND FINANCE, UNCW

KIMMARIE MCGOLDRICK
DEPARTMENT OF ECONOMICS, UNIVERSITY OF RICHMOND

Motivating Student Learning and Preparation through Mastery-Based Incentives

One of the challenges of college instruction is finding the appropriate level of rigor. Too little rigor, and the best students may become bored or may not be sufficiently motivated to think and learn. Too much rigor, and students at the lower end of the distribution may become frustrated and disengaged and turned off from the class or field of study. We know that it is our job as instructors to push our students, but we don't want to push them over. The challenge associated with finding the appropriate level of rigor may be especially daunting for instructors at public universities or community colleges where there is a great deal of variation in students' academic abilities. Regardless of the size and focus of the institution, the task of attaining a suitable level of rigor is germane to all instructors at the start of each semester and may be particularly important in introductory classes. Foundation courses often provide the only exposure students will ever receive to a particular set of topics and ideas. Success in these initial courses can be an important catalyst in students' choice of major, and, by extension, their academic careers and lives beyond the classroom. The readers of this volume can likely recount a story of the first course in their major where something clicked. A part of that story is most certainly the degree of challenge afforded by the instructor.

Conversations with your colleagues will likely reveal disparate opinions on the issue of rigor. One perspective is to maintain rigor no matter the consequences: "If the lower-level students can't keep up, then it's too bad. They should find another major/class/instructor." Another viewpoint is to cater to the lowest common denominator: "It is our job to ensure that all students achieve a baseline level of knowledge. Quality is more important than quantity." In addition to variation of opinion on rigor among your colleagues, you may find that your own opinions on the matter change over the course of your career or even during a particular semester. In particular, obtaining tenure may release instructors from the inclination to make concessions for the sake of teaching evaluations.

The authors of this chapter both maintain high standards for learning and know that most students appreciate being challenged. At the same time, we understand that many students arrive in the college classroom unprepared for the demands of a rigorous course load. This balancing act leads us to adopt several classroom techniques that fit under the umbrella of mastery learning. Mastery learning, largely initiated by Bloom (1971), is based on the idea that students must demonstrate sufficient knowledge of a set of ideas before moving on to new topics (Kulik, Kulik, & Bangert-Drowns, 1990). This approach differs from the traditional method of teach-assess-review in that it is not assumed that students will learn from their mistakes. Instead, students who do not demonstrate mastery of a set of concepts must complete additional assignments until mastery is shown. In the purest form of mastery learning, additional assignments are provided after learning difficulties have been identified and remedied with personalized remedial instruction (Bangert-Drowns, Kulik, & Kulik, 1991).

Mastery learning has its pros and cons. The obvious downside is the extra time and effort required on the part of instructors to provide supplementary instruction and assignments. There are also equity considerations. Students who perform well on initial assessments may feel that it is unfair to grant second chances to students who did not. Further, as suggested by Covic and Jones (2008), there is also the potential for a moral-hazard problem. If students know that they will have additional opportunities to earn a grade, they may be less inclined to adequately prepare for the initial assessment. Mastery learning may also be criticized on the grounds that it can distort the evaluation function of assessment by permitting students multiple opportunities to move into the higher end of the grade distribution.

The principal benefit of mastery learning is that by providing students additional learning opportunities, they are more apt to achieve a standard level of knowledge before moving on in the curriculum. Empirical evidence supporting such gains is mixed, but generally favorable. Test results from a mastery learning application in an undergraduate operations research course by Armacost and Pet-Armacost (2003) show grade improvement with subsequent examinations. A survey of students by the authors revealed a preference for this form of learning. Using Blackboard facilitated quizzes in an undergraduate genetics course, Marshall (2009) finds that allowing students to retake quizzes as many times as they wished yields no significant improvement in overall course grades, but students were very positive about the approach. In a meta-analysis of 108 studies of mastery learning across an array of disciplines, Kulik et al (1990) find that 93% of studies that included examination results indicated a positive impact, with 70% reporting a statistically significant difference. Of the 18 studies that included an evaluation of student attitudes, 89% found a significant positive impact, and 86% found a significant improvement in student attitudes towards the subject matter.

Mastery learning also grants instructors latitude with regard to rigor. Knowing that students can be granted additional opportunities to master a set of material allows the instructor to establish and maintain a firm standard for the quality of student work with less trepidation that students at the lower end of the distribution will become frustrated, disengaged, or disenchanted. Those students may have to work harder or longer to achieve the standard, but the additional opportunities to demonstrate mastery can serve to mitigate some of the pressure. As instructors, we should understand that not all students learn at the same pace. If true learning is our ultimate goal, then this aspect of mastery learning should be appealing.

The effectiveness of mastery learning techniques will vary with instructors, students, level of remedial instruction, and the format of the formative assessment. Armacost and Pet-Armacost (2003) argue that the content associated with each successive assessment should be more difficult, and the last examination taken should provide the grade that students receive, rather than allowing students to take the highest grade from a set of assessments. Our own experience with mastery learning supports this notion. Indeed, employing a mastery-learning process without consequences for students who fail to exhibit effort may undermine the learning process. We have also found that the structure and timing of the assessment tools are critical elements of the mastery-learning process, but the assessment can take many forms, including traditional written essays/papers, examinations, and quizzes.

Below, we highlight three alternative assessments based on mastery-learning principles that we have found to be effective in stimulating student interest in our courses. Moreover, these methods provide an incentive for additional study, motivate the adoption of more advanced study techniques, and allow students to improve their grades on a scale that maintains fairness and minimizes grade distortions. Importantly, our approaches have the potential to increase student learning without placing an onerous burden on instructors. Each of these methods can be adapted to suit the needs of different classes and assignments. We hope you find them to be productive additions to your classes.

Exam Rebates

Tests and quizzes commonly comprise a majority of student assessments in college courses. It is often the case that a series of exams are administered over the course of a semester, with a comprehensive final exam given at the end of the term. Because exams often carry a significant weight, poor performance on an exam can have adverse effects on student grades and motivation. To incorporate the tenets of mastery learning into course exams, students who perform poorly on a test can be given another chance to improve their grade by demonstrating improved mastery of the material using exam rebates.

After the exam is returned, students are given the opportunity to "earn back" a percentage of lost points by replicating incorrect portions of the exam in detail. There are several ways to facilitate the replication process. As a take-home assignment, students can be instructed to write a short paragraph detailing why each incorrect or incomplete response was deficient, as well as provide a complete description of the correct answer. We typically instruct students to consider the idea or principle that the exam question was designed to test, and to construct their responses from the "ground up" as if they were attempting to teach someone the correct answer to the question. To capitalize on the positive benefits of peer-learning, students can be allowed to perform rebate tasks in small groups. The benefits of small-group learning are well-documented and include improvements in academic achievement and attitudes toward learning, as well as reductions in course and program attrition (Springer, Stanne, & Donovan, 1999). To offset free-rider effects, we recommend that each student be required to submit his/her own exam rebate if a peer-learning approach is used. The exam rebate can also take the form of an in-class exercise where students are provided with a blank exam, their exam grade, and instructions to re-take the exam, using their books and notes. Again, this can be a collaborative effort, but each student should be required to submit his/her own work. Because this process typically takes longer than the original exam, we often use this approach for selected parts of the exam. For example, directing the in-class rebate effort toward concepts or question formats where students were most deficient.

This format of mastery testing is amenable to any type of exam format and motivates students to consider the underlying concept that exam questions were written to test. So as to remain fair to students who did well on the original exam and to avoid the moral hazard problem, we do not allow 100 percent rebates, and we do not announce the rebate opportunity until after the exam has been returned. Typically, we only grant one exam rebate per semester (often on an unexpectedly poor exam) and allow students to earn back up to 50 percent of lost points. Students are also told that the provision of exam rebates will depend on the performance of the entire class, and future rebates are by no means guaranteed.

It is important to put a firm timeline on take-home rebates (we suggest a week or less) and conduct in-class rebates in a timely fashion, so that students are motivated to master the material before the class moves on to more complex topics. Students should be instructed that rebate responses will be graded very critically, and that a clear demonstration of content mastery will be required to earn full rebate credit. We have found it useful to require the referencing of text and/or lecture materials in their written responses, so that students are motivated to access primary source material.

The revise-and-resubmit method for written assignments

Written assignments, such as research papers and reflective essays, can be an important element of undergraduate courses and, in many cases, are necessary to accomplish course learning goals. Indeed, at UNC Wilmington, "writing intensive" courses are a significant component of the University Studies Program. In our experience, writing assignments come with several pitfalls for students and instructors. First, students may be unfamiliar with discipline-specific writing styles and may find it difficult to adapt their writing to instructor expectations. For example, in economics it is common to write in a style that is devoid of opinion, emotion, and subjective language. Students often have no experience writing in this way and struggle to adjust. Further, despite reminders and advance due dates, students will often procrastinate, putting off writing until a due date is near. It is important to teach our students that good writing takes time, and the first draft of a writing assignment is often substandard. Moreover, if students are not given the opportunity or incentive to improve their writing, a valuable learning opportunity may be wasted.

When course content calls for a major research paper, the combination of these pitfalls often makes for disastrous results. In order to help our students learn to write in the style of our discipline and to motivate our students to begin writing well in advance of due dates, we require that research papers be constructed in sections with each section due independently during the semester. We provide detailed comments and suggestions for changes to each section and return the draft sections to the students for revision. When the draft of the next section is due, students are required to resubmit the edited draft of earlier sections. This process continues until the final paper is submitted as a compilation of the individual sections, each of which having been revised and resubmitted multiple times during the semester. To motivate timely submission of the individual sections, a portion of the final grade (e.g., 25 percent) is based on meeting draft due dates. The drafts are graded on a pass/fail basis, and we provide rubrics for each section to guide expectations.

This method has proven to significantly improve student writing in our classes, and we find that considerably less editing is necessary for latter sections of the papers. In other words, during the process of revising early sections, students improve their writing and submit more effective drafts. While there is a nontrivial grading burden during the semester, grading the final papers at the end of the term is often relatively easy since each draft has been revised according to our suggestions.

The Challenge Quiz

Another method for mastery-based learning that we use in our classes is the "challenge quiz," which is a blended formative/summative assessment tool designed to allow students the opportunity for grade improvement in a format that requires more preparation and explicit demonstration of analytical ability. In many of our courses, students are given a series of quizzes, which carry less weight and require less time than the more substantial exams. Rather than adopting a policy of dropping the lowest quiz grade, we instead employ mastery-based incentives by allowing students to replace a limited number of quiz grades by taking more difficult quizzes covering the same topics. Students are given an incentive to master material by the summative component of the challenge quiz and may be motivated to modify their methods of preparation by the formative nature of the challenge quiz.

The second optional challenge quiz comes with a set of restrictions. First, students are only allowed to challenge a subset of the original quizzes, typically one-third. Second, challenge quizzes must be taken prior to the exam that covers the same material. Third, the student receives the grade earned on the challenge quiz, regardless of whether the new grade is better or worse than the original quiz grade. Finally, the format of the challenge quiz requires more preparation and explicit demonstration of content mastery than the original quiz. Specifically, while typical in-class quizzes may be composed of short-answer questions, challenge quizzes are composed of open-ended essay questions. These parameters are designed to motivate students to carefully consider how they prepare for the original in-class quiz and in choosing whether to take a challenge quiz. Again, in addition to the incentives provided by the structure of the assessment, it is important to clearly convey to students that success on the challenge quiz will require mastery-level knowledge of content. More information on challenge quizzes can be found in McGoldrick and Schuhmann (2012).

Conclusion

The mastery-based practices outlined in this chapter serve to bring students' objective of quality grades in line with instructors' objective of quality learning. Each of these methods was designed to motivate student learning and preparation while limiting the burden placed on instructors. These methods were also developed to minimize the risks and inequities that may be associated with mastery learning, such as distortions to the evaluation function of assessment and the moral-hazard problem associated with providing too large of a safety net. Each of these procedures allows us to set high standards for quality, maintain rigor, and preserve fairness. We have found that students appreciate this balance. While these methods are amenable and adaptable to any course or curriculum, they may be particularly important in introductory classes. Exam rebates, writing through revision and resubmission, and challenge quizzes all foster the mastery of basic knowledge. Retention of foundation knowledge is essential if students may never again be exposed to our field of study. Further, acute comprehension at the introductory level can enhance the probability that students will be persistent in a field of study and be successful in advanced classes. Finally, these methods motivate students to develop effective learning habits and processes, which can be transported to all of their academic endeavors.

REFERENCES

Armacost, R. L., Pet-Armacost, J. (2003). Using mastery-based grading to facilitate learning, 33rd Annual ASEE/IEEE Frontiers in Education Conference: T3A-20-T3A25.

Bangert-Drowns, R. L., Kulik, J. A., & Kulik, C.-L. (1991). Effects of frequent classroom testing, *The Journal of Educational Research*, 85, 89-99. Retrieved from: http://www.jstor.org/stable/27540459

Bloom, B. S. (1971). Learning for mastery. In B. S. Bloom, J. T. Hastings, & G. F. Madaus (Eds.), Handbook on formative and summative evaluation of student learning (pp. 43-53). New York, NY: McGraw-Hill.

Bloom, B. S. (1971). Mastery learning and its implications for curriculum development. In E.W. Eisner (Ed). *Confronting curriculum reform*. Boston: Little Brown and Company.

Bransford, J. D., Brown, A. L., and Cocking, R. R. (Eds.). (2000). *How people learn: Brain, mind, experience, and school*. Washington DC: National Academies Press.

Covic, T. & Jones, M. K. (2008). Is the essay resubmission option a formative or a summative assessment and does it matter as long as the grades improve? *Assessment & Evaluation in Higher Education*, 33, 75–85. doi:10.1080/02602930601122928

Kulik, C-L, C., Kulik, J. A., & Bangert-Drowns, R. L. (1990). Effectiveness of mastery learning programs: A meta-analysis. *Review of Educational Research*, 60, 265-299. Retrieved from: http://www.jstor.org/stable/1170612

Marshall, P. A. (2009). Mastery learning in a sophomore level genetics course using the blackboard course Shell. *Journal of the Arizona-Nevada Academy of Science*, 41, 55-58. doi:10.2181/036.041.0204

McGoldrick, K., & Schuhmann, P. W. (2012). Challenge quizzes: The impact of a unique assessment tool on student performance. *New Zealand Economic Papers*, 1-12. doi: 10.1080/00779954.2012.689746

Springer, L., Stanne, M. E., & Donovan, S. S. (1999). Effects of small-group learning on undergraduates in science, mathematics, engineering, and technology: A meta-analysis. *Review of Educational Research*, 69, 21-51. Retrieved from: http://www.jstor.org/stable/1170643

JOHN FISCHETTI
SCHOOL OF EDUCATION,
UNIVERSITY OF NEWCASTLE, AUSTRALIA

The Student Engagement Paradox

An urban legend related to former President John F. Kennedy goes something like this:

"Jack," as he was called, came to hand deliver a paper in one of his undergraduate government classes to his Harvard professor's office. Back in the day, it was the custom to bring papers to a prof's office during office hours, particularly in upper-level classes, for which a due date might fall between class lectures. Before accepting the paper, the prof looked at Jack and straightforwardly asked him if this draft of the paper was representative of his best work. Kennedy sheepishly admitted that, in his hurry to meet the deadline, he may not have proofread the paper as well as he would have liked or taken the time to verify his references. The professor and Kennedy agreed to meet at the same time the next day, so that Jack could submit a revised version of the paper. That next day, prior to accepting the paper, the professor again asked Jack if this was his best work. Kennedy was embarrassed to admit that, now that he had redone some of the ending, the beginning needed some additional work. The professor told Kennedy to bring the paper back tomorrow. "Why would you give me something that wasn't your best work?" he asked. The following day, Kennedy returned once more, revised paper in hand. Before the professor could ask him the same question, Jack said, "Professor, please accept this version of the paper. It is my best work."

Whether this story is just an unsubstantiated anecdote or based on some historical occurrence is unknown. I use the story to help us understand how important it is for K-12 teachers, community college instructors, and university professors to find ways to motivate students to care so deeply about their academics that they want to prepare and submit their best work. Only when we are dealing with a student's best work, can we attempt to give the extensive feedback and mentoring that is our role, so that students might master the knowledge or skills we are teaching them. Unless we know that students are giving us their best effort, we can only surmise that the work they turn in is short of their best work, and we may then hold back on our own best efforts to help them through mentoring, encouragement, and motivation.

The Engagement Paradox

For the past 25 years, American public school teachers and college/university professors have been cajoled in professional development sessions to move from didactic, teacher-centered pedagogy to using classroom activities that foster student engagement. Educators have been sold on the notion that "engagement" is the key to motivating students to do their best work. They are told that, based on the work of John Dewey (1997), education must be connected to real experiences. This chapter is about unraveling the engagement paradox. Student engagement, while a positive attribute, does not necessarily lead to student learning. It may be one of the stages on the way to helping students do their best work, but engagement alone does not guarantee learning. When engaged, students may be having fun, collaborating with each other, participating in a lesson, and behaving actively in the classroom, but there are other prerequisites to real learning — mastering the knowledge or skill taught beyond regurgitation for a test, so that they will continue to use it throughout their lives. And all of us educated in the 20th century know (or think we know) that we have learned from great lecturers as much as from fun classroom activities.

This idea of the engagement paradox triangulates the overlapping work of John Dewey (1997), Phil Schlechty (2011), Daniel Pink (2009), Eric Jensen (2009) and Robert Marzano, Debra Pickering, and Jane Pollock (2005). I connect the dots between the importance of student engagement, the crisis of the testing nation, and the natural instinct of intrinsic motivation and research-based curriculum design.

Today's college students are a test-weary group, having come from K-12 schools that rated and sorted them by our over-preoccupation with building testing centers at the expense of learning centers. Many of the students we typically see in college and universities survived that system, were on the upper end of the proficiency scale, and have been fooled into thinking that scoring a "3" or "4" on a state test equated with intelligence, aptitude, or college-readiness. Most of those high-stakes achievement tests were put in place to help assess teacher and school performance, not to promote rigor and mastery for students. Few state tests to this point have emphasized writing, creative problem solving, collaboration, defending a position, etc. Those are skills we strive for at the post-secondary level and skills that our graduates must master in order to become future leaders.

The Collaborative, Global, Innovation Age

As we define the skill sets needed for professional and personal success in our modern era, we must reframe why we need schools and colleges to begin with. High school and college classrooms are still too often places students go to watch teachers work. Most knowledge and skills are assessed in examinations. Through that paradigm, we prepare students to be passive learners and to tell us what they think we want to hear (or read). What if, instead, we framed this era as the collaborative, global, innovation age? That is, what if we centered our education system on preparing people to work together to solve problems or to create knowledge that helped improve the human condition? Nurses do that on a daily basis. So do artists, philosophers, plumbers, engineers, and teachers. By focusing on the collaborative, global, innovation age, we might reconsider how we define "good" in the classroom. And we would not rely on the assumption that "fun" or "cute" activities lead to real learning.

Student Engagement

When you observe a colleague's classroom, what are the top one or two most important components you look for to assess that student learning might be occurring?
  1. Great command of the content by the instructor
  2. Well-designed lesson
  3. All students are actively involved
  4. Positive tone/culture/atmosphere
  5. Physical layout of classroom
  6. Effective classroom management
  7. Strong content emphasis
  8. Clear assessment of learning
  9. Other
In most college classrooms, the student learning emphasis has been an assumed result of the instructor's skill in sharing knowledge.

Then, in the last 25 years, instructors at all levels were told that they must get students "actively involved" in the learning process.

The assumption was:

Student involvement in the lesson = student learning.

But how do we know that assumption is correct? My view is that student engagement is a prerequisite to other phases of the learning process, but that these other phases must also be present in order to foster learning. There are many types of student engagement. Schlechty (2011) defined engagement as:

1. The student is attentive
2. The student is committed
3. The student is persistent
4. The student finds meaning and value in the tasks (p. 14).

In other words, engagement trumps lecture. Schlechty's use of engagement is a powerful reminder of the importance of capturing students' attention, and keeping them active learners instead of passive bystanders, which is the first prerequisite to learning. Teachers at all levels are using engagement in a variety of ways.

Robert Marzano, Debra Pickering, and Jane Pollock (2005) developed a renowned curriculum-design method to promote student engagement. Their work has transformed curriculum in K-16 classrooms across the United States. They included research-based strategies that deepened the learning experiences, or opened opportunities for learning:

- Identifying similarities and differences
- Summarizing and note taking
- Reinforcing effort and providing recognition
- Homework and practice
- Nonlinguistic representations
- Cooperative learning
- Setting objectives and providing feedback
- Generating and testing hypotheses
- Cues, questions and advance organizers

Their blueprint for design has created tangible ways to plan lessons for student engagement.

Multiple strategies abound for engaging students. For example:

Flipping is a way to have students watch a lecture or read the lecture notes prior to a class in order to use the class time for a laboratory, simulation, discussion, performance, etc., … something that applies the learning from the didactic "homework."

Blogging, using wikis, or embracing other online tools is used by some as a way to motivate students to apply their knowledge and to communicate beyond their tendencies to be passive learners.

Publishing products, submitting a paper, project, or arts project to an online source can offer an immediate posting/publishing opportunity right. For example, a book review can instantaneously be posted on Amazon.com and directed toward an audience that would share interest in the topic. The availability of a real audience for the project can engage students far more than just submitting it for grading to the instructor.

Service learning can allow a real-world application of a course topic. Studying the environmental impact on runoff to a creek and presenting the collected data to local leaders brings the curriculum alive; tutoring young people at a town shelter confronts the social, political, economic, and personal tragedies around homelessness.

Facebooking can be a new way to do a traditional report with a template on, for example, Abraham Lincoln. Would John Wilkes Booth have been creeping on Lincoln's "wall" to know he was headed to Ford's Theatre? Would haters from the passage of the 13th amendment have sent inappropriate timeline postings?

Tweeting can be an excellent way to review for tests — summarize the main plot or the key takeaway of a reading in 140 characters or less.

There are countless other ideas for encouraging active student involvement in the lesson, rather than listening to faculty talk. But do those approaches ensure learning at any higher level than the traditional lecture? Or, are they gimmicks that keep students happy without necessarily promoting learning?

Doing Your Best Work: The Case for Effort

The recent emphasis on student engagement has been misleading to teachers and faculty and has oversimplified the learning process. Think of an example of something you learned during your lifetime, something that has been important for you to know and be able to do. Is it tying your shoes (Velcro does not count), driving a car, leading a meeting, hiring or firing someone? There are any number of critical skills we exercise in our professional and personal lives on a daily basis that we, at some point, learned and absorbed as knowledge.

When you did learn that specific knowledge, skill, or disposition? How did you learn it?

1. By figuring it out on your own with no help?
2. Listening to an expert explain it, and then it just "clicked"?
3. Watching an expert model it?
4. Practicing it individually with a teacher, coach, or mentor?
5. Practicing it in a group or team?
6. Practicing it on your own with notes, videos, etc.?
7. Many/all of the above?

Most likely it was a combination of many of these learning approaches and styles, and it is also likely the skill and knowledge was reinforced over time with continued practice and usage. Engagement or active involvement is just the first prerequisite for learning. The focus on the importance of student engagement imbedded in current professional development and teacher evaluation practices overlooks other cognitive and affective elements required for learning to occur. I propose that the steps between engagement and learning include excitement, hopefulness, and effort.

Engagement gets students cognitively excited – keeps them "awake" and prepares them to do good work. But engagement alone does not guarantee learning. Cognitive excitement is the launching pad for the potential for "hopefulness." Jensen (2009) discussed the work of Seligman, who proposed that hopefulness is the academic endorphin of sorts for learning excitement. Hopefulness is the sense of great anticipation, edge-of-the-seat focus on the possibility that stops everything around us. This is the feeling we get when someone has captivated us with an activity so compelling that we are right there in the moment. Bottom of the ninth, two out, two on, two strikes with Barry Bonds (back in the day) at the plate. The kind of focus that comes when great theatre has reached its climax, or there is a box with your name on it under the gift tree. Or, the first time you learned that the Civil War started in the front yard of the McLean family home in Manassas, Virginia, and later ended in their parlor at Appomattox Court House. How could that be? Tell me more? While fostering that same feeling in a college classroom in philosophy or math seems unusual, for learning to be facilitated, students should be engaged in something meaningful, excited about the opportunity, and hopeful that this is a learning event. That brain chemistry is what we strive for, the epitome of why we do what we do. Sadly, even then learning is not always the result. The hopefulness should next facilitate a student putting forth his or her best effort.

Student effort is the prerequisite to learning. Without the confidence that students have put forth their best effort, any faculty feedback comes up short of the mark in guiding students forward. Best effort is the key to stretching ourselves to reach our potential – not just to be compliant or "wanting an 'A.'" Pink (2009) proposed that intrinsic motivation research was buried in favor of extrinsic motivation as the impetus to get students to perform to their best. It is time to focus on getting students to care so deeply about their work, they do their best.

Identifying and Assessing Best Work

Most of the professional development and center for excellence activities in high schools and on college campuses are about ways to apply learning, get students involved, and promote engagement. Harmin and Toth (1996) discussed hundreds of methods that pedagogically enhanced lessons to promote active learning or engagement. Less is written about how we might connect effort to pedagogical practice with the ultimate goal of learning.

One of the most important ways to promote effort is the framing of a clear rubric for each assignment, project, lab, etc. A rubric is a fancy education term for a set of criteria and a scoring guide. Many assignments from professors are vague. "Prepare a three- to five-page response to Marx's view of capitalism." That assignment may connect to a learning objective in the syllabus and may directly relate to a reading in the course, but how does one do his or her best work in response to this? A faculty member could have students do a Webquest, cooperative activity, or interview each other to get ideas — all forms of "engagement." But will any of those approaches lead to a "better paper"? If the assignment includes specifics in a table called a rubric, students will better understand what is expected of them and include those aspects in the assignment. A statement such as, "Please include specific quotes from three different primary sources referenced in MLA, two quotes or passages from your course text, and one contrary source from the supplemental readings provided in the course Blackboard module" would help students understand that the major goals of this assignment include being able to use primary sources accurately. If writing style is important, additional criteria for length, font, grammar, style, and overall writing quality can be included. One way to improve student effort is to have them self-assess based on the criteria prior to submission — or after a performance in a different discipline — to allow the student to own their own work. Becoming intrinsically motivated to become a best learner is a key component of the college experience.

Another approach that improves student work quality is to use real audiences for the work. Students take more seriously assignments that are part of preparing to deliver a presentation to experts, to apply their knowledge in real-world settings, to publish their work online, or to showcase their work in an exhibition, which occurs as standard practice in the visual and performing arts and athletics. The professor, then, is the guide to help students become so facile in their mastery of knowledge and skills that students can apply that new knowledge or the new skill in a setting beyond the classroom.

If our goal is learning, then the step prior — effort — should be the pedagogical emphasis. Engagement keeps us excited. Excitement gets us hopeful. And cognitive hopefulness gets us ready to do our best work. Finally, employing our energies and efforts into producing that best work enables us to truly learn — and use for a lifetime, not just for a final exam grade.

Intellectual Curiosity

The real motivation for learning is intrinsic (Pink, 2009). Incentives that might work for very young students to comply create a passivity of learning as we move to the upper grades and college, and that defeats the intent of a liberal arts education to create proactive and open-minded scholars.

The key to success in college is intellectual curiosity. Students who come ready to learn get engaged, excited, and hopeful and, therefore, do their best work. And they bring the attitude that "I have not learned it all yet. Bring it on, teacher." Working with those students and planning engaging lessons that trigger excitement and hopefulness makes teaching an honor. What college profs who are discouraged must remember is that it is the system that has taken that curiosity out of students through constant inane testing and a lobotomizing high school experience. Under those circumstances, hopefulness comes rarely and more likely in extra-curriculars and Facebook, rather than through the formal curriculum.

If we emphasize that we expect students' best work, even when it comes up short of the learning bar, we can re-teach, remediate, or suggest a change of majors. Without best work, we are "going through the motions" of the college experience. And, as faculty, we are going through the motion in our own professional lives, as well.

What does best work look like? How do we judge and measure it? While the answer to those questions varies by discipline and individual faculty expectations, it starts with a conversation: "Jack, are you confident this is your best work?"

REFERENCES

Dewey, J. (1997). *Experience and education.* New York: Touchtone Press. (first published in 1938 by Kappa Delta Pi).

Harmin, M., & Toth, M. (1996). *Inspiring active learning.* Alexandria, VA: Association for Supervision and Curriculum Development.

Jensen, E. (2009). *Teaching with poverty in mind: What being poor does to kids' brains and what schools can do about it.* Alexandria, VA: Association for Supervision and Curriculum Development.

Marzano, R., Pickering, D., & Pollock, J. (2005). *Classroom instruction that works.* Upper Saddle River, NJ: Pearson Education.

Pink, D. (2009). *Drive: The Surprising truth about what motivates us.* New York: Riverhead Books.

Schlechty, P. (2011). *Engaging students: The next level of working on the work.* San Francisco, CA: Jossey-Bass.

Weimer, M. (2013). *Learner-centered teaching: Five key changes to practice, 2nd edition.* San Francisco: Jossey-Bass.

MARK BOREN

DEPARTMENT OF ENGLISH

Furthering the Discussion: Forging Rapport and Cultivating a Learning Disposition

This past semester I taught a class on lyric poetry, from the Middle Ages to today (talk about a potential snore!), and we spent the semester doing scansion exercises every class meeting (analyzing the metrics of poems—feet, trochaic pentameter, acatalytic), in addition to talking about literary terms and tools, questions of genre, poetic content, historical moments, and the greater significances of the poems. The students—all 25 of them— nevertheless had a blast, and by the end of the course were scanning their favorite songs on their own. Universally the students ended the course appreciating poetry and their music on a level they did not conceive of at the beginning the term. And I let them teach me about their favorite artists, their favorite songs and their own incredibly complex cultural moment. The key to the rapport within the classroom was tying what we were doing in class to modern concerns about their music, so from day one on, we compared the poetical forms of the poems with current forms that mirrored them and then talked about their effects. Alexander Pope's "Epistle to Dr. Arbuthnot" (reading the title aloud will cause student heads to plunk upon tables) is, remarkably like most of Run DMCs lyrics, iambic pentameter, heroic couplets (every two lines rhyme)—and in his verse Pope complains about his fame making his venturing out in public in his fancy car (short for carriage even then) an impossibility, about his being blamed for the commission of local crimes, and for leading the youth astray; he notes how all the ladies fawn on him and the husbands blame him for their wives cuckolding them—oh, and by the way he notes his rhymes have made him very, very rich. The students get it immediately, and every day we met I had examples for them from contemporary lyrics from a range of genres until I handed that aspect of the class over to them. When it comes to establishing a rapport and opening up discussion, finding a connection is the key.[1] I thus try to discover a connection with them outright individually, and through the content of the course, and I also—and this is very important in teaching different kinds of classes to different majors—focus my energies on teaching critical methodologies so each student is empowered.

So how do you connect with students? These may seem like no brainers, but they warrant mentioning. First off, learn your students' names. Make eye contact with every student during a class. Call on them for their ideas and thoughts, and then genuinely listen to what they have to say. Read your students' body language and level of interest. If someone in the back of the class appears to be bored, then he or she is not at that moment learning anything—and you are the one failing. That's the student that you should engage, and precisely at that moment.[2] Boredom is contagious and one yawn will turn into several. And if other students see a student disrespect you or not engage, then they will lose respect for you as well. Modify your approach, and watch your own body language and rhetorical signals. An authentic discussion is an exchange between two or more people. Like any conversation, that exchange should vary, have pauses, rhythms, occasional silences, and, perhaps most importantly, a mood. You can't expect any student to be excited about something that you yourself are not. Remove everything that interferes with the conversation you're having between you and your students—put the lectern in the corner, take off the tie if you like, trash the "I'm the expert" demeanor, as well as your past disappointments in student engagement, and for heaven's sake, jettison any idea that your class will contain even the hint of apathy. If you go into the classroom prejudging your students' abilities, then you are not allowing that everyone in the room is capable of learning, and you are accepting that you yourself are unwilling to rise to the occasion to teach. I'm not saying be falsely excited—I'm not one of those teachers that one would call a flurry of encouragement or gushing enthusiasm—but my interest is genuine and the students sense it. And finally, it's your responsibility to teach everyone who signed up for your course, like it or not.

If you're showing up expecting only to hand off knowledge to the small percentage of your class already primed for that transmission—the As and Bs as it were—then, well, you're not teaching; you're delivering information like a machine and partially. If that were effective—and what our students, their parents, or society wanted—we'd long ago have been replaced by books and programs. Teaching is about individuals developing, and everyone in the class is capable and in need of cultivating his or her skills and knowledge (including the teacher). Knowledge is acquired by the students; it is not passively received. Thus cynicism and close-mindedness on the teacher's part about anyone's learning potential only conveys cynicism and close-mindedness to the student. My students often joke (in class, on student evaluations, and I've just learned on blogs and in tweets) that I will entertain any observation a student makes or any idea, no matter how crazy—and there is some truth to that. I'll let a student run with his or her idea—even if tangential, even if facile, but then I steer it back towards the developing discussion, help make it become contributive. The student who offered the thought—if unused to risking or otherwise insecure—learns he or she can participate and will be taken seriously.[3] And even the at-first-odd idea may indeed add to the conversation if indulged a bit—that's the nature of thinking outside the box. In the odd case that a student is intentionally sabotaging the conversation for laughs, he or she will learn such interactions will fail in my class and the student will end up being a positive member of the class. Of course at times a student will say something obviously dumb—recognizably to the other students and to the student who said it, but if I have a rapport established with that student I can just say, "Gee, that's kind of a dumb thing to say? Isn't it?" –but I do this with a sense of humor in a nonthreatening way, and then—and this is the important next move—ask for a better response because (I tell him or her) I know he or she is capable of it. I never simply shut a student down, deny a student's response and move on. In my experience, rare as they are, students find even these types of responses, if they are honest and carry no attitude of hostility or condescension on my part, refreshing and ultimately respectful of them as intellectual humans.

Of course all of this will make you have to rethink your grading expectations because as your engagement increases, students will learn and that will distort the "natural" classifications that students are funneled into by their second year. When I first began teaching as a teaching assistant in graduate school, I realized that it was relatively easy to grade students at the end of the semester because they had already learned what to expect of themselves and thus they tended to engage at their "grade level," to write papers that predicted certain grades. Classes have a tendency to sort themselves. I played my role; the students played theirs and with some minor wiggling and a couple exceptions, they left the class as they arrived, having more or less successfully completed a course, "earning" a grade. Although I saw I could easily perform such a job throughout my whole career, doing that just that did not sit easy with me. The more I thought about it, the more I became convinced that such an approach was professionally unethical, even immoral.

This struck home particularly with me as I had been raised with the idea that I would, if lucky, go to a local community college if I graduated from high school and learn a trade. My father thought I would make a fair auto mechanic, and it was years before I realized that I could learn whatever I wanted to learn (as long as I was willing to do the work to learn it. Hell, I found I was even capable of abstract thought). Now that I'm a professor at a university (still a bit unbelievable to Dad who now distrusts higher education more than ever), I know my students are limited to a great extent only by what they've come to expect of their own abilities, and thus I look for ways to engage them and to help them raise their own expectations. If the class seems populated by students who appear to be underachievers or those reticent to engage, I share parts of my own life with them from time to time: the fact that my family lived in a trailer for awhile (hey, it was a doublewide), and that my first job was crewing on a crappy shrimp boat, working for a fingerless drunk (the result of repeatedly running a winch when inebriated) who had no learning curve (he lost his fingers one at a time). The students will be inclined to respect you (you are a professor after all), but they often don't realize that they can achieve or rise from their own expectations, so I often mention, when the conversation leads in that direction, elements of my own life that serve to humanize me—often these are some of the stupid things I've done. They need to hear they can achieve from someone they respect (which basically means someone who listens to them and takes them seriously), and they need to see they can achieve—and this goes for everyone in the class, especially those who undervalue their own talents.

At the same time, I think it important to raise your own expectations for the entire class—make the syllabi and the requirements harder, not easier, but be sure and make the class more human at the same time that you raise the intellectual expectations.[4] Look for ways to have spontaneous exchanges, and connect as often as possible the discussions of materials and skills to everyday life, to the students' existence, and to your own. Have very high demands for student performance, for students respect that, but at the same time they need to know that you respect their efforts to achieve those demands, and they need to develop the skills to reach them. Sure, many students will go into a research-oriented class expecting to be bored, but a teacher need not confirm expectations. The teacher's job is to teach, and if that means teaching students to be interested in learning in the first place, then that seems to me to be the place to start. I purposely begin to forge connections with the notorious "back row students" the first day of the semester, for if you can connect with them, you can find a way to connect with everyone else. On the way out of class I always draw one or two students aside for a minute, make an observation, ask a question. To foster empathy generally, I begin off-handedly mentioning those minor incidents of my own family life from the first, such as a surprising lesson I just learned as a father, how I am trying to explain "dreams" to my four-year-old, and answer questions like, "How does your brain make you think?" I don't recommend you cross any professional boundaries, or invade personal space, but you should also realize that the professors are often the first non-family related adults beyond their years that students have conversations with about ideas, and thus you are in a unique position to cultivate the idea that they are taken seriously by other adults. It's a strange position to be in and a responsibility we have as teachers to aid that transition from the spheres of their peers and parents to the sphere of adult citizenry, as well as professional conduct.

Of course one needs to tailor one's approach to each course, and even, if one is teaching different classes of the same course, to the individual class, for the individual make-up of each class is different. Although this kind of rapport-based teaching is transferrable from one topic to another, there are ways to think about building the foundation for it into course designs, as well. Those ways should be subject specific (such as the linking of "back in the day" poetry to contemporary hip-hop lyrics), and methodological if possible.

So far what I've been describing is an attitude towards teaching and a general pedagogical disposition. In higher undergraduate levels, in specialized major-specific classes, and in graduate classes, it's easier to connect with students and forge a rapport, for they're more generally committed to their majors and fields of study, and the connections often easily occur through the materials discussed. But at the lower levels, in core curriculum courses that contain diverse majors, it's often difficult to connect to the students, and for them to connect to you. There are ways to help facilitate this in the structuring and requirements of the class, though of course these ways will differ in different courses and disciplines. But just thinking about these concerns helps me much in planning my courses, and it increases my own interest in my courses, which become idiosyncratic experiments that often change and evolve even as the semester progresses.

Focusing on Critical Skills over Content

The challenge in these student cocktail classes (those with a diverse mixture of students) comes in creating an even intellectual playing field, establishing and sustaining a high level of discussion in which everyone participates daily, and making the course intellectually rigorous for each student in the class. In, say, a theme-based basic studies literature class only a small percentage will be undeclared English majors and few of these will know much of anything about the formal study of literature, but even if they do, I do not want them to have a perceivable, undue edge over the other students, so I frame the course wholly around skills they acquire in the class itself, and I let all the students know this. To do this I try to give students from different disciplines a flexible analytical method they can master for understanding literary works, but also one that they can become passionate about because it empowers them to better understand of the cultural workings of their own respective lives.

I will organize the course around a subject-appropriate analytical method (for example "close textual analysis") that can be taught to first-year students as well as seniors. The chosen analytical method ("close reading" is a highly flexible one in that it can become as sophisticated as a student is able to make it, but there are others) is honed through required pre-class discussion questions, and then extended through a series of textual analysis papers designed to develop students' critical thinking and originality. This same method is eventually used in a lengthy research paper, and augmented with outside scholarship. Class discussions are built upon and reinforced by the approach as well. The idea is to give the wide range of students an archetypal analytical method that is based on analyzing specific details in the texts, so that by the end of the semester every student can confidently and critically interpret any text given them and relate that text to larger issues within his or her culture, and perhaps more importantly to issues outside it. And once the students see that their own observations, many of which they at first dismiss in class as trivial, can be developed into sophisticated arguments, their confidence in their own thinking grows (and this mirrors how those tangential questions in class can lead outside the box only to return to the conversation productivity).

Basically, what I try to do is decide on a flexible analytical method that can be easily learned, teach them that and reinforce it in every way possible (in papers, discussions, homework, quizzes, etc.) in order to empower them. I then let them explore the subject of the class through that methodology. Students then feel they can participate fully in our developing discussion over the course, and that they are not being judged based upon what they actually do not know (a history of the subject), but on their ability to construct knowledge. I make it clear to the students from the outset that we are learning a form of apprehending the texts, and I let the themes, images, motifs, and so forth arise from their own analytical forays into the texts. Many of the students are afraid at first—mainly of getting things wrong—but if they learn all they need to know are the analytical skills that I'll teach them and that their grades depend on their application of those skills, they relax and engage. Of course, you try and make it fun; in the case of teaching close reading skills, I often say something like, "a literary crime has been committed and this class is from now on going to be called "CSI –literary studies." The goal, once you've established a rapport with them through all that stuff you find to connect with them, is to make "What they are finding" their part of the discussion. It becomes what they primarily bring to the table, their side of the conversation.

So, for example, since we've discussed close reading here, in the classes where I use it as the primary methodology, I'll demonstrate day one how one goes about performing one and then we do a few. The class is immediately relieved to discover there is an easily understood analytical process for articulating how literary texts work, one that a chemistry major or an anthropology major can do as well as an English major. Availing ourselves of the Oxford English Dictionary (OED) online and the overhead projector, we discover that there are hidden connotations to the words of a selected piece of text. With the dictionary and our own connections we began to build subtexts to specific passages, often diagramming sentences word by word. This way they see that effective authors reinforce their manifest meanings with the connotations of their words, or subvert them with subtexts. We also discuss how the form of the sentence, the style of the text also reinforces or subverts those subtexts.

In such a class on a daily basis we would continue to write unusual sentences on the board and do associative word chains off each word, subsequently drawing lines connecting the subtexts when words in separate chains associated with each other. Not surprisingly, individual texts will consistently generate their specific subtexts almost anywhere you stop to analyze them. And importantly we go to passages the students choose, as well as a few randomly selected "normal" passages we arbitrarily pick. Of course, you have to be willing to accept a certain Beavis-and-Buttheadian element that will inevitably arise in letting students choose textual material and free associate connotations from it, but even this can be educational and empowering ("Yes, Shakespeare is making a bawdy pun on poor Yorick's fate and the fate of mankind—but why?"), and shared laughter in the class, is well, shared experience. And while they are laughing, students see they are leading the direction of the investigation, and that they can rely upon their skills anywhere they find themselves in a text.

Robert Scholes (2001) claims we neglect to teach reading strategies, even in English departments, focusing more on teaching themes or genres in literature and in culture, stressing too much what a text "means" and not on methods for analyzing *how* it means. He calls for a fundamental change in the approach to teaching texts (Scholes, 2001, p. 213). I think Scholes correct, and I've found that students afraid to engage because they felt they simply didn't know enough immediately engage if given the tools and encouragement. In a recent Honors course on the Gothic in literature, because I focused on analysis over literary history, those majoring in the hard sciences (chemistry, physics, math) found they could be very adept at literary analysis, once they had a critical methodology explained to them and were given some fundamental conceptual tools. This methodological approach is directly translatable across disciplines. After all, you can't, say, walk into a figurative drawing class and say, "draw this person really well," without some inducing panic. But if you give your students an analytical approach (the ability to see and read light values that render form three dimensional), and then the tools to empower them ("this is how you hold a pencil, and this is how hatching works to approximate those values you see, and thus you turn form"), then your students are far more likely to engage and succeed.[5]

So in a literature class such as the one based on close reading as a methodology (even if it's called something like "Madness in Literature" of "Literature of Human Bondage" or "American Literature before 1870"), students are taught a methodology for the class discussion, and this is reinforced by homework assignments ("come to class with a sentence or part of a paragraph of your choosing, analyzed, with implications to provoke intelligent class discussion") and reinforced by their papers, both isolated analytical arguments and research papers that are extensions of that methodology.[6]

With the students thus empowered, I can simply begin class with a greeting and the question, "where shall we go today?" I trust the students, with their self-chosen specific spots for engagement, and their reading skills, will start discussions that lead to the big themes and important issues in the text. At the end of the semester, I have them analyze the progression of the course. This approach, of course, calls for patience and an open-mindedness to pursue what at times initially appear to be unfruitful leads. But it also fosters lightheartedness in the classroom that belies the serious interrogation of texts. We have fun with the discussions, which are very often informal and lively, and often—and this is an important part of it—spill over into discussions of students' own cultural artifacts (films, music, literature), and I let it briefly spill. All of this goes to forging that rapport and earnest discussion we are having in the classroom. It may seem like we are having more fun than a serious subject of study warrants at times, but when students "are in environments where learning is occurring in a meaningful context, where they have choices, and where they are encouraged to follow their interests, learning takes place best" (Singer, Golinkoff, & Hirsch-Pasek, 2006, p. 9). Once students understand they can analyze and no longer fear engaging, they lose their frustration in reading even daunting texts, such as those written by Pope, Byron, Melville, even Faulkner. Focusing on small specific moments instead of having to understand the big ideas—they can do that; and then that leads to, well, big ideas. And thus armed with tools, terms, and a flexible methodology, the students begin analyzing their own worlds, not just the texts we study for class. By the middle of the semester—no matter what the course, students begin staying after class or dropping by my office to ask me if I've ever listened to the lyrics of Led Zeppelin, Die Antwoord, John Lennon, Rakim, if I'd ever read *The Hunger Games*, *Fight Club*, *Buffalo Soldier*, or if I'd seen *Teeth*, *Memento*, *Inception*.

I can count on the fact that my students will respect my expertise, for I don't hide from them my ability to articulate or analyze—that, say, a psychoanalytic reading of a poem can be supported by the poem's metrics to reveal how it induces specific emotional effects in a reader, or that synthesizing research in various manners in a paper to support a sophisticated thesis achieves various rhetorical effects —but I can only count on that respect if they invest and participate in the conversation. In order for them to do so, they have to see that I respect them. Discipline-specific skills, the ability to conceptualize and articulate ideas orally and through writing, the ability to research, self-awareness, critical thinking, common sense, a good sense of humor—and all the other things we want our students to achieve in order to be happy, productive, well-educated citizens—these depend upon their participating in the conversations that we've been entrusted by our society to have with our students about those things. When our students are invited to participate, and we take the time to help them develop the skills to do so, they inevitably rise to the occasion, and before you, or even they know it, they're furthering the discussion.

REFERENCES

Bain, K. (2004). *What the best college teachers do*. Cambridge, MA: Harvard University Press.

Bartlett, T. (2003). What makes a teacher great? *The Chronicle of Higher Education, 50*, 8. Retrieved from: http://chronicle.com/section/Home/5

Boren, M. (2012). Dreaming the gothic: From Dracula to gaga. *Honors in Practice 8*, 85-100. Retrieved from: http://digitalcommons.unl.edu/nchchip/149/

Ripley, A. (2010, January). What makes a great teacher? *Atlantic Magazine*, 36-38.

Scholes, R. (2001). *The Crafty Reader*. New Haven: Yale University Press.

Singer, D., Golinkoff, R., & Hirsch-Pasek, K. (Eds.). (2006). *Play=Learning: How play motivates and enhances children's cognitive and social-emotional gorss*. New York: Oxford University Press.

Wentworth, M. (2006). Only connect: The continuing value and relevance of the liberal arts. In C.M. Clements. (Ed.), *Best Practices in University Teaching* (pp.1-12). Wilmington, NC: The Publishing Laboratory.

NOTES

1   I believe successful teaching depends to great extent upon establishing mutual respect between the student and the teacher, a respect that goes beyond a tacit premise of the student's expected acquisition of skills and the acknowledgement of the teacher's relative expertise in the materials and methods of an area of study. For excellent teaching to occur, the teacher must find a way to connect with each student in the class and cultivate a rapport with each based upon a mutual awareness that the student and the teacher are having a human conversation about things that are important to both the student and the teacher. For this to happen, the teacher always must be actively looking for ways to connect with the student—whether that is directly through interest in the materials at hand (let's discuss, for example, how an author constructs a precise metaphor to convey moral ambiguity) or in conversations about a student's future (even if the student simply needs the course as a requirement for his or her degree, he or she is still invested in that degree or future profession), or more indirectly through other common interests—say, in music, the arts, sporting activities, travel adventures, cooking mishaps—really anything from everyday life that provides a way into genuine conversation. If the student senses a connection in any context, he or she will more readily assume he or she is a participant in the classroom—and that the classroom *conversation* is key.

This is supported conceptually by Thomas Bartlett (2003); and in praxis by Michael Wentworth (2006).

2   I don't accept that one can't connect with all of one's students, for we are part of many overlapping communities and also share numerous hours a week in common. There is—as much as we want to avail ourselves of it—a direct connection between the lives of students and the lives of teachers; and in any case, things outright alien to the teacher's current existence can be learned, if the teacher shows genuine interest—even if that be in an off-handed, brief discussion of the intricacies of growing up in modern suburbia or the lyrical complexities of death metal. In fact, having the students teach you about their interests is one of the easiest ways of opening up an exchange. In short, for a student to actively participate in the pedagogical conversation, he or she must trust that there is a genuine conversation occurring between two people, and the teacher has to do that as well. Our exchange can't be merely performative of pre-established professional academic discourse. If it is, then the student learns to communicate strategically, not interactively.

3   Ken Bain hammers home in *What the Best College Teachers Do* that "knowledge is constructed, not received" (2004, p. 26-33). It may reveal my humanist table linens, but I have never met a student with whom I could not, if I wanted to, have an authentic discussion about something. It takes patience and a predisposition to learn something new, but as the teacher who knows why he is in the classroom (and many of our students do not yet share a similar understanding), it is within my abilities to find a connection. Indeed, it is absolutely incumbent upon *me* to do so, for I am the teacher. If your class is quiet and won't engage, you can't assume that the students are bored, resistant, or just not bright; watch them walk out the door of the building, and you'll see them light up and become downright chatty with their colleagues. They can talk, and they can, even the most apparently sullen of them, become animated when having a discussion with someone they connect to, on a topic of mutual interest. The trick is to find a way of fostering a similar interaction with your students. Bain's text is an excellent source for improving one's teaching. It's clear, concise, and easy to read, with pragmatic suggestions. I recommend it highly.

4   In her analysis of the *Teach for America* teaching effectiveness database, Amanda Ripley notes, "great teachers tended to set big goals for their students. They were also perpetually looking for ways to improve their effectiveness." She concludes, "Superstar teachers had four other tendencies in common: they avidly recruited students and their families into the process; they maintained focus, ensuring that everything they did contributed to student learning; they planned exhaustively and purposefully—for the next day or the year ahead—by working backward from the desired outcome; and they worked relentlessly, refusing to surrender to the

combined menaces of poverty, bureaucracy, and budgetary shortfalls" (2010, p. 13).

5   I'm using the drawing example (as how this conceptually translates into a different discipline) because it serves both the analytical and (importantly for more academically oriented rather than studio-oriented disciplines) the empowering aspects of what I'm trying to teach. In addition to having a terminal degree in English, I also have one in studio arts and teach drawing and painting.

6   For an in-depth discussion of the strategies I developed for a specific course I taught this past year, and an analysis of what worked pedagogically and what didn't, see my essay: "Dreaming the Gothic: From Dracula to Gaga." (Boren, 2012).

STEPHEN J. MCNAMEE

DEPARTMENT OF SOCIOLOGY AND CRIMINOLOGY

Some Principles of Good Teaching*

In this essay, I describe some principles and practices that I think are associated with good teaching. These principles are derived from a combination of my experience as a student and as a teacher. They are neither exhaustive nor mutually exclusive, but represent in summary fashion what I consider to be some key elements of effective teaching/learning. Although I see teaching and learning as reciprocal and mutually reinforcing processes, to avoid redundancy, I will express them here simply as principles of "good teaching." I offer these principles for consideration through the lens of a sociologist using some sociological concepts along the way to illustrate them, but they are applicable to instruction at the university level in general.

Good Teachers are Good Storytellers

Storytelling is almost a lost art form in modern industrial societies. Prior to written and electronically enhanced forms of communication, the primary way to transmit the knowledge of the group was through storytelling. Good storytelling requires good stories and good storytellers. Every academic discipline has a story to tell — about how the physical world works, about how the social world works, and about the nature of the human condition. Good teaching begins with a good story, which is acquired — as it was for our preliterate ancestors — through the passing on of a tradition.

The academic tradition represents a cumulative body of knowledge and an intellectual legacy of scholarship. Good storytellers know the stories and know how to communicate them. For me, telling the story of sociology is similar to sharing a juicy bit of gossip with a friend. I am fond of telling my students that the "stuff" of sociology is the "stuff" of everyday life that people talk about in everyday conversations — how individuals act with and toward one another, how people come together to do things, how we fit into the grand scheme of things, and how society is organized as a whole. I consider myself very fortunate to be able to make a career out of what most people find inherently fascinating and experience in everyday life.

Whatever one's discipline might be, passion for the subject matter is essential to good teaching. Passion for subject matter cannot be "taught"; it must be experienced. We cannot expect our students to be engaged in what we are teaching unless we ourselves are engaged. Enthusiasm is contagious. It is here where stylistic aspects of teaching can make a difference in capturing and holding students' attention. As teachers, we can maintain our own enthusiasm by constantly reinventing ourselves, adopting new techniques, being open to change, and generally being willing to take risks.

Good Teachers are Good Listeners and Good Learners

Good teachers are good at what George Herbert Mead (1934/1967) referred to as "taking the role of the other toward the self." George Herbert Mead emphasized role taking as the key to symbolic communication. For Mead, our ability to symbolically communicate is the secret of our success as a species. We use words and gestures that stand for or represent something else within a shared, social symbol system. This allows us to plan ahead and align our behavior with the anticipated reactions of others toward the self. Through symbolic communication, we can divide labor and accomplish more together than we could alone, making organization and civilization possible as we know it. To do this, we put ourselves imaginatively in the role of "the other" and ask ourselves, "If I was the other, what meaning would I intend to convey to the listener by using particular words or gestures arranged in a particular sequence?" In order to figure out where someone is coming from, we need to try to see the world as he or she sees it. People do not act on the world as it is, but as they perceive and as they make sense of it. Like umpires, we all "call them like we see them."

Good teachers know this and don't just act, but act and react. Good teachers modify and adjust to what students are thinking, saying, and doing. Good teachers "read" student reactions and are sensitive to social cues. Good teachers place themselves imaginatively in the role of student and constantly ask themselves how they would react under similar circumstances. Would this be comprehensible for someone hearing it for the first time? Am I presenting the material in a systematic and organized way? Am I engaging students in the material being presented? Good teachers also continually solicit student input to get a reading on what is making sense or not making sense to them as they see it from their perspective. Teaching is not about impressing students by how much you know. The purpose of communication should be illumination, not obfuscation.

Taking the role of the other to the self, by the way, is not the same as pretending, as an instructor, that you don't know anything. In an attempt to be nonhierarchical and nonintimidating, instructors will sometimes overcompensate in striving to "de-center" their role as expert and bring themselves "down" to the level of the student. We should not come across as the proverbial know-it-all "sage on the stage," but we are the experts in the room — or should be. The university goes to great lengths to hire instructors who are credentialed experts in their field of study and have advanced training beyond the level of instruction offered. It makes no sense to me for those experts to then act as if they don't know anything. I routinely encounter students who are smarter than I am, but I do not encounter students who know as much about the discipline of sociology as I do. We should not expect them to. In short, good teachers are authoritative, but not authoritarian.

Good Teachers Don't Give Students Everything They Want

I disagree with a teaching philosophy that essentially says that, if students don't like it, then don't do it or don't assign it. Everything else being equal, students might prefer a steady diet of "light and lively." But not everything worth knowing is superficially amusing or easy to comprehend. People "like" high fat, high sugar, and high salt food, but a steady diet of the same is ultimately lethal. I believe the same principle applies to higher education. Put somewhat differently, good teachers challenge students both intellectually and in terms of their own lived experience.

It has become fashionable in some circles in higher education to equate good teaching/learning with being able to relate course content to the students' personal experience. The general spirit of this philosophy is sound and, where applicable, works very well. However, I think that it can be overextended to the detriment of students and the learning process. We may know when we are hungry, tired, or hurt, but that does not make us experts in anatomy, physiology, or biochemistry. Similarly, that someone occupies some social space in the context of a particular society does not make that person an expert in social behavior or society. Sociologists contend that our individual experience of society is necessarily out of context (unrepresentative of society as a whole) and out of focus (filtered through various prisms or frames of reference that we experience and interpret the social world – rich vs. poor, white vs. nonwhite, female vs. male, and so on). No one "sees" society in its entirety; instead, we experience society in small fragments of close-up scenes of my family, my friends, my church, my job, and my community. Personal experience may be a point of departure for analysis, but it is not the end point. The small fragment of reality that we experience or observe is not only a small portion of the whole, but it is filtered through the various frames of reference (i.e., bias) that we bring to that experience. As any respectable statistician knows, a sample of one in an American population of over 300 million is a lousy sample. A sample of one in a global population of over 7 billion is even worse. And a sample of one applied to all of humanity among the estimated more than 100 billion human beings who have ever lived is even more abysmal.

Indeed, the job of the sociologist is to systematically contextualize and bring into focus individual experience in relation to the experiences of others. The ability to place individual experience and outcomes in a larger social context is known in sociology as "the sociological imagination," a phrase coined by American sociologist C. Wright Mills (1959). Mills further distinguished between "personal troubles" and "public issues." Being unemployed, for instance, is clearly a personal trouble, but if you are the only unemployed person in America, then your circumstance is unlikely to rise to the level of a public issue. If, however, millions of Americans are similarly socially situated and similarly caught up in larger social forces beyond their own immediate situation, then "unemployment" may also constitute a public issue. The central insight of sociology is that we are who we are largely because of the groups to which we belong, including society as a whole. Although we all experience society as individuals, we do so in a larger social context. Like the forces of gravity that operate among celestial bodies in the universe, social forces act on individuals, given the locations they occupy in the grand scheme of things. That we are not alone in the world and that we are not the center of the universe are important life lessons. Good teachers know this and know how to "connect the dots" and teach their students how to do so.

A corollary to this principle is that it is axiomatic in sociology that you do not have to be one to know one. A criminologist, for instance, does not have to be criminal to be an expert on crime — or, at least, I hope not since half the colleagues in my department are criminologists. A teaching philosophy that would suggest that only by relating everything to one's personal experience can learning be relevant or meaningful is essentially asociological. College students typically have very limited experience of the world. If education is only a reinforcement, a validation, a reaffirmation of limited personal experience, then no value-added learning takes place. People like to be awash with familiarity; it is soothing and comforting. But as Immanuel Kant once experienced for himself, at times we all need to be awakened from our "dogmatic slumber." This necessarily requires us to "see" beyond our own immediate life world. It seems to me that the noble ideal of the academy and the life of the mind is to expand one's personal horizons, not be bound by them.

This journey of discovery is frequently unsettling because it requires us to continually rethink our basic assumptions about what we previously took for granted. We know from "breaching experiments" in sociology that people do not like to have their taken-for-granted assumptions of reality challenged or violated. Using breaching experiments, investigators intentionally violate taken-for-granted assumptions and then observe the ways that people in everyday life desperately try to reconstruct meaning in the situation. This perspective in sociology is called "ethnomethodology" — the examination of the methods (ways) that ordinary people in everyday life make sense of their experience (Garfinkel, 1967). In one classic breaching experiment, for instance, experimenters enter elevators and, instead of following the taken-for-granted norm of turning around and quietly facing the doors of the elevator, the experimenter faces the back of the elevator and stares at the passengers in route as the elevator moves. The most common reaction to such "breaches" is hostility. We do not like to have our life-worlds disrupted, and we do not like being thrown into a state of uncertainty.

That is why learning is hard. Learning forces us to go beyond our "comfort zone" and to reconfigure our sense of meaning in the situation. UNCW's motto embedded on its official seal, "Discere Aude" — dare to learn — captures the essence of this principle: no pain, no gain. We need to take students beyond their own immediate experience and out of their comfort zone of what they think they already know. Students will predictably resist our attempts to challenge them. It is here where we need to let go of the impulse to give in or curry the favor of students as a goal in itself.

This principle applies to all disciplines, but it is a particularly acute occupational hazard for social and behavioral scientists. In social science, because we are what we study, it is that much more of a challenge to get beyond our own individual biases. Students, for instance, are likely to be fairly neutral in terms of how they think chemical compounds are arrayed in the physical world, but they are anything but neutral about how they think society is arranged in the social world. I do not believe that I am doing my job in every class unless I challenge each student's view of the social world as they thought they knew it. For instance, there are many myths about poverty in the United States — that most poor people live on welfare; that if you are working, you are not poor; that people who are poor are mostly African American or Hispanic; that in the United States, poor people live reasonably well, and many others. As part of my debunking instruction, I often have students work in small groups to put together a no-frills budget that would be needed to have a minimally "decent" standard of living in Wilmington, North Carolina, defined by community standards for a family of four, including two children under the age of 18. I provide students with a spreadsheet with categories such as "food," "housing," "transportation" per month and then add up the totals for a year. I then provide students with the current federally defined income thresholds for poverty for such a family. Routinely, students are very surprised to discover that their "no frills" minimum budgets are typically three and four times the federally defined thresholds for poverty and that the income of a single, wage earner working 40-hour weeks year-round earning minimum wage is about 35% less than what would be needed to exceed the minimum poverty threshold for such a family.

Rethinking what you thought you knew is also why reading is such an important and efficient method of learning. By reading, we can get outside of our own immediate experience and frame of reference and do so readily and inexpensively. We can imaginatively travel to faraway places and absorb large amounts of systemic and comparative information that we could not possibly personally experience even in several lifetimes. Research shows that learning by doing is often a superior way of learning than learning by reading. Increasingly, universities are responding to this insight by emphasizing various experiential and applied forms of learning. This is a positive trend in higher education and should be encouraged and expanded. But it should not be a substitute for reading. Applied learning works best when there is something to apply it to. That "something" includes a foundation of cumulative knowledge, part of a legacy of scholarship and body of knowledge most efficiently absorbed through reading. Max Weber, one of the founders of sociology, is widely recognized for both the breadth and depth of his insight and scholarship. In reference to the source of ideas in a lecture on "Science as a Vocation," Weber (1918/1994) wrote:

> Ideas occur to us when they please, not when it pleases us. The best ideas do indeed occur to one's mind as Ihering describes it: when smoking a cigar on the sofa; or as Helmholtz states of himself with scientific exactitude: when taking a walk on a slowly ascending street; or in a similar way. In any case, ideas come when we do not expect them, and not when we are brooding and searching at our desks. Yet ideas would certainly not come in mind had we not brooded and searched for answers with passionate devotion. (p. 283)

Good teachers know that good ideas can come to us at any time at any place, but not without solid preparation and foundation. Good teachers also know we cannot apply knowledge without having knowledge to apply and that there is no quick or easy substitute for concerted time "brooding and searching at our desks."

Good Teachers Teach With the Long View In Mind

Comedian Don Novello does a priest character he calls "Fr. Guido Sarducci." Fr. Sarducci does a hilarious skit about the opening of his "five-minute university." In this skit, Fr. Sarducci explains that five years after graduation from college, what most college graduates can remember about what they learned could be stated in about five minutes. So, in his "Five-Minute University," he skips everything else and teaches students the critical five minutes worth of knowledge that college graduates are likely to remember five years later anyway. Obviously, this was done tongue-in-cheek, but it was funny precisely because there is a grain of truth in it.

Looking back on my own college career (now a distant 40 years ago), I can recall very little detail about the content of courses I took outside of sociology. I remember the sociological content only because it was reinforced and extended in graduate school and because I continue to "do" sociology for a living. The lesson from this, I think, is that process is more important in the long run than content. Good teachers know this. It is more important, for instance, for students to learn how to distill, organize, synthesize, analyze, and interpret information than it is for them to "know" any particular piece of information. This is increasingly the case in a world in which one can "google" practically anything at a moment's notice on a portable iPhone literally attached to one's hip. The rapid increase in the volume and complexity of information and the rapid rate at which new information becomes obsolete, along with the ease of instant electronic access, all drastically reduce the premium on rote recall of content. Good teachers know this and know that, in the long run, process is more important than content.

Content is still important, especially as foundation for further study in a specialized field. But beyond the few students who pursue graduate study among the many who pass through our classrooms, the content of a field of study is not likely to be as essential in the long run as the process. Along these lines, we sometimes make a mistake as teachers in teaching to the top 1% of our students; that is, we pitch the substance and content of our instruction to high-end students who are most likely to pursue advanced study in the field. We then hope that the other 99% will get something of value along the way, but we often see our main purpose as "training" the next generation of professionals in the field. While this is a more appropriate orientation for graduate education, it is largely misdirected at the undergraduate level. The brute reality is that vast majority of undergraduates who pass through our classrooms are not going to become professionals in our own fields of study.

Instead, the vast majority of college graduates in the labor force are working in jobs that have little-to-no direct bearing on what they happened to have majored in college ten, fifteen, or twenty years previously. The longer they are removed from college graduation, the less likely they are to be "doing" whatever it is they were "trained" to do specifically in college. Both professors and students often seem oblivious to this reality. Students often erroneously assume that "major = job for life," and many professors also seem equally susceptible to what turns out to be a demonstrably false assumption. Even in highly technical fields such as engineering, the reality is that after one or two promotions, most college graduates are not "doing" whatever it is they were specifically "trained" to do. In most cases, college graduates end up in various administrative and management positions in a variety of work settings. For the most part, what college graduates "do" in those positions is to manage information, people, and money. It is here were the so-called "soft" liberal arts skills have the most long-term relevance and applicability.

We need to look no further than our own academic hierarchy to see how this process works. In my own academic career, for instance, I have worked directly and indirectly for several academic deans. The list of their disciplinary training includes classics, biology, psychology, music, social work, English, and mathematics. At the provost level, the list includes physics, chemistry, biology, psychology, education, and geology. At the president's or chancellor's level, the list includes engineering, education, military history, English, and biology. In the jobs they held, none of these administrators were "doing" what they were "trained" to do — but they all managed information, people, and money. They all know how to distill and analyze information. They all knew how to effectively communicate. They also all knew how to manage a budget, most having learned how to do so on the job.

Coming to grips with the long-term implications of what we can pass on to our students can make us better and more realistic teachers. For many years, I regularly taught a course called "Organizations in Modern Society." Except for students who are graduate school bound in sociology, the "sociology" of organizations is not as critical as the life lessons that can be gleaned from a general understanding and appreciation of how organizations work. I am fond of telling my students that if they want to "work the system," then they should know "how the system works." Most will, at least, have to navigate their way through an increasingly organizationally dense society; many will be running such organizations. Teaching works best when students can take with them what they learned beyond the next test, beyond the grade, beyond the degree, and beyond the walls of the university.

Along these lines, one of the common complaints from employers about recent graduates is that they do not know how to work in teams. Most of education is focused and evaluated on individual performance. But in the life outside the academy in both public and private sectors, most people work in organizations engaged in collaborative efforts built on an elaborate division of labor. Most academic work, by stark contrast, is a lonely endeavor. As academics, we typically spend many hours in monk-like solitude at the desk. The closest many of us come to collaborative work is through research although that, too, varies by discipline and area of specialization. Even if we are in lonely pursuit of knowledge on our own, we need to be cognizant that life outside the academy is typically more socially engaged. We need to do what we can to teach students how to work effectively in teams and with each other. Having small group discussions is one way of doing this. In upper-division classes, I often have students in the same small groups throughout the semester, and, at the end of the semester, I have them peer evaluate each other's contribution to the group. They are initially reluctant to do so, but this process helps to reduce the "free-rider" effect and rewards individual contribution toward collective goals. This kind of process is also often realized in research labs, internships, and applied-learning settings.

Good Teachers Encourage Students to Think the Really Big Thoughts

It is certainly true that college provides students with practical and concrete skills that they need to compete in an increasingly competitive and global marketplace. But college is more than that – or should be. It is not just about the how-to nuts and bolts, but about the whys and wherefores. It is also about the ultimate questions: What is what is nature of the physical world? What is the nature of the social world? What is the nature of the human condition?

College in many ways is an incredible societal luxury. We take students out of the labor force in the prime of their productive years, and we give them the time and space to think the big thoughts — before they get caught up in the routine of going to work, changing the diapers, and paying the bills. It may be the only time in their lives when they have this opportunity, so they and their teachers should take maximum advantage of it. The spirit of a liberal arts education is in keeping with this intellectual exploration and Socrates' exhortation to pursue the examined life. College may be the last time an engineering major studies art history or an art history major studies chemistry.

Confronting ultimate questions is not the same as resolving them. When I was launching a career as an academic, I was told by a wise advisor that successful academics have both a high tolerance for being alone and a high tolerance for ambiguity. The world is not as definitive and as clear-cut as we would like it to be. Good scholars and good teachers know that "it depends" is usually the best answer to most important questions. Good scholars and good teachers are skeptical of simple black-and-white explanations of the world and, instead, dwell in various shades of gray.

While on a visit to my insurance agent several years ago, I saw a sheet of paper tucked under the glass of her desk facing me which read: "I fully realize that I have not succeeded in answering all of your questions. Indeed, I feel that I have not answered any of them completely. The answers I have found only serve to raise a whole new set of questions, which only lead to more problems, some of which we weren't even aware were problems. To sum it all up: In some ways I feel we are as confused as ever, but I believe we are confused on a higher level about more important things." I have since seen this unattributed quote floating around in various academic circles. Meant as comic relief – at least as applied to the intricacies and nuances of insurance policies – it, nevertheless, captures a wonderfully profound statement about critical inquiry and the life of the mind, befitting any professor's final comment on the last day of class – or as a concluding comment on an essay about good teaching, for that matter.

ACKNOWLEDGEMENTS

I would like to thank Hillary Geen and Christine McNamee and anonymous reviewers for helpful comments and suggestions.

REFERENCES

Garfinkel, H. (1967). *Studies in ethnomethodology.* Englewood Cliffs, NJ: Prentice-Hall.

Mead, G. H. (1967). *Mind, self and society: From the standpoint of a social behaviorist.* Chicago, IL: University of Chicago Press. (Original work published 1934).

Mills, C. W. (1959). *Sociological imagination.* New York, NY: Oxford University Press.

Weber, M. (1994). Science as a vocation. In W. Heydebrand (Ed.), *Sociological writings* (pp. 276-303). New York, NY: The Continuum Publishing Company. (Original work published 1918).

DEBORAH A. BRUNSON
DEPARTMENT OF COMMUNICATION STUDIES

Teaching Diversity: Learning Your Students, Learning Yourself

In considering a title for this essay my first thought was to use the word "knowing" in place of "learning." Certainly, being able to affirmatively claim the stance of "knowing" is a powerful and important quality of the educational process. As an African American woman who is part of the academy, I am often intrigued by the politicization of who gets to determine "knowledge" and what "knowledge" is valued, and under what circumstances it becomes legitimated. This discrepancy has been the basis of much of the multicultural frame within academe and continues to spark debate among higher education's leadership.

In the area of teaching diversity "knowing" has garnered an active and productive field of research and practice from an interdisciplinary roster of scholars. I have been teaching diversity-focused courses at UNCW for over 20 years. I regularly teach Interracial Communication and have also taught Aging and Communication, Introduction to African American Studies, as well as a Diversity in Public Communication course. Along the way I have drawn from the ideas and expertise of some teacher-scholars whose writings have had a profound impact upon the way I teach all of my courses. I am thankful for the insights gained through the work of hooks (1994, 2003); Banks (1997); Frederick (1995); Ladson-Billings (1996); Lowen (2007); Giroux (2003); and Giroux and McLaren (1994). Three volumes that I believe offer an impressive range of research and pedagogical perspective about teaching diversity are *Teaching for Diversity and Social Justice* (Adams, Bell, & Griffin, 2007), *Facilitating Intergroup Dialogues: Bridging Differences, Catalyzing Change* (Maxwell, Nagda, & Thompson, 2011) and *Getting Culture: Incorporating Diversity Across the Curriculum* (Gurung & Prieto, 2009). One of the joys of teaching is finding instructional resources and scholarship that help me to become a better teacher and learner. Common themes across all these readings are an insistence upon the centrality of the diversity dynamic within the academic curriculum, and the importance of supporting this dynamic as we prepare our students to be active and engaged participants in a mulitcultural world.

There are facts that we can know and teach to others, but with what result? For instance, the United States is undergoing major and profound demographic changes; this situates the issue of diversity prominently on the educational agenda. Asian Americans are now the fastest-growing ethnic minority group, and Hispanic Americans represent the largest minority demographic at 17 percent. Almost 50 percent of the nation's population under age five are minority children. Projections indicate that by 2043 white Americans will have fallen below 50 percent of the total population while African Americans will comprise 12 percent. (United States Census Bureau, 2013a [U.S. Census]; Yen, 2013). We can also expect demographic shifts among those 65 and over. By 2015 senior adults will be nearly 15 percent of our population and that age group is projected to reach 21 percent in 2040 (U.S. Census, 2013b).

Those are the facts and figures that are "knowable." However, the classroom that incorporates diversity should encourage participants to move beyond the "knowledge" alone in order to consider the potentialities of that knowledge for themselves, their community, their country, and global society. In order to facilitate that process, I think that learning about self and others will support an environment where diversity education is both dynamic and empowering. I see this "learning" as extremely rewarding because it has the potential to provide our students with the knowledge and the motivation to become engaged in civic issues and affairs far beyond the limited time that they spend with us in our classrooms. For instance, there have been wonderful times over the years when a student will tell me how they shared some resource materials, or points raised in our class discussion with their peers, family members or friends. My efforts to engage colleagues and scholars around the idea of continuous, integrative, and applied learning resulted in a co-edited interdisciplinary book on diversity education (Brunson, Jarmon, & Lampl, 2007).

Learning your students. As is the case with other content areas in most college classrooms, students who approach the topic of diversity do so from different vantage points and with varying, multiple levels of awareness. Clearly, each person's early socialization during their formative years has served to imprint upon him or her a world view of assumptions concerning race, culture, ethnicity, gender, sexuality, social class, age, sexual orientation, and ability/ disability (Harro, 2000). In an earlier essay I co-wrote for the Center for Teaching Excellence with Robert Smith from the Watson College of Education, we addressed these realities of social development. We noted that because diversity is a multidimensional construct, our students will have varying levels of understanding and experiences across its dimensions. For instance, a member of the class may have a well-developed consciousness on race and racism but may have had limited experience about sexual orientation, or may have biases of which they are unaware. It is important for teachers to take the multidimensional nature of identity into account when structuring a diversity-focused course, learning activity, or presentation.

Powerful learning requires multiple levels of engagement and interaction. I believe that knowledge is most powerful when it emerges through interaction. In my teaching, interaction is a vital part of the overall process that contributes to my ability to learn who my students are and how they are experiencing the course. Although Brookfield and Presskill (2005) proposed a synthesis of the terms "discussion", "dialogue", and "conversation", they chose *discussion* as an umbrella term that best reflects the interaction teachers coordinate in the classroom: "...we define *discussion* as an alternatively serious and playful effort by a group of two or more to share views and engage in mutual and reciprocal critique" (p. 6). The concept of dialogue certainly has a great deal of traction both in communication studies and diversity/intergroup work. From my own experience I would visualize these three communication behaviors as two concentric circles, with "discussion/dialogue" at the core and conversation on the periphery. My reasoning for this approach is that discussion and dialogue are truly cut from the same cloth because teachers often use these forms of interaction to support students' thoughtful reflections and deliberations. Brookfield and Presskill (2005) acknowledged that a conversation is sometimes perceived as a low-impact, casual exchange with the potential to provide opportunities for deeper reflection.

When done well a discussion encompasses dialogue that encourages participants to become open and available to the life stories of other persons. For example I usually ask class members this question: Is every student on our campus sharing a common experience when they walk down "Campus Way"? (Campus Way is a major pedestrian path linking the back of UNCW to its center "Commons" area.) The typical answer is that there may be some common connections students share but interactions and experiences may be different based upon age, gender, physical abilities, sexual orientation, nationality and other identity factors. Thoughtful responses often spin out from this seemingly innocuous question because it challenges everyone to suspend "how I see the world" so that "how you see the world" can be examined. The "Campus Way" analogy of seeking to understand how other people experience the world is repeated most successfully within our small group seminars. Over the years students have consistently said that these intense engagements are important spaces where significant learning happens. These discussions are based around assigned readings, but superior learning occurs when everyone is integrating personal experiences into the dialogue. Successful seminars require a high level of trust: trust in the process and trust among participants – including trust in the teacher as facilitator.

As we engage in these discussions I encourage participants to distinguish between interactions that qualify as either dialogue or debate (see Figure 1) and to consider which type of communication holds more utility for our group. Typically, the consensus is that dialogue can best facilitate our learning goals. Although debate is a staple of communication programs it has limited application in the intergroup exchanges in a diversity course, where the primary goal should be structuring activities that build community among participants. Facilitating discussion is probably one of the biggest challenges most teachers face. I am constantly working at strengthening my skills and at forgiving myself when it isn't a successful, seamless process.

Seminars and written journals encourage deeper introspection and offer more opportunities to share ideas, beliefs, and values in smaller, non-threatening venues. They also give me the opportunity to provide immediate feedback to my students in a format that may be more useful to them. Most participants find that within these interactions they are able to comfortably address their questions and concerns to me and to each other about the importance, clarity and accuracy of the readings, lectures, video presentations, or class comments.

As class members are experiencing the class I've also found that they will have preconceived notions and expectations about you as their instructor. Their socialization lenses are fixed upon you, and their expectations of who you should be are initially framed from these perspectives. As an African American woman teaching a majority white student population, I have found that some students may question my teaching abilities. In casual conversations with other teachers of color, we hear stories about students who may struggle with accepting us. At times the challenge may be directed toward our intellect or knowledge of the subject matter; at other times the focus is upon our suitability to lead. The implication here is: are *you* qualified to teach me? This struggle to be accepted often extends beyond teachers of color to students of color, for they too sometimes face institutional challenges as they navigate through the university.

Gaining the respect of students is an issue most teachers must address, but the nuances of that process may be doubly affected when viewed through the lens of race, as well as other diversity dimensions (e.g., gender, culture, or national origin). What I have found in teaching diversity is that some students will question your facilitation of the course. They may wonder, are you presenting the material in an unbiased fashion? Are you treating everyone fairly across the board? This is an important issue for all teachers to consider, but it can be particularly difficult for a faculty member of color to successfully negotiate.

Learning yourself. As scholars we often prefer one type of research tradition over another. I believe that is also the case with my teaching and has led me to consider the question, what pedagogies align or link/interface with my philosophy of teaching? I quickly migrated away from the conventional mode of perceiving teaching as a linear enterprise (e.g. information transmitted to students which they passively receive). Freire (1970) rightly used the "banking" metaphor to describe this form of instruction that limits the potential for a student to create the learning in a way that is most accessible to her or him. From that tradition I moved toward thinking about teaching that promotes collaborative learning and that remains an important part of my philosophical base. What is created in the classroom, we – my students and I – create together.

These days I am migrating toward and wish to more fully employ a critical pedagogy-a transformative pedagogy-to my teaching. I believe that critical pedagogy is an important framework for my teaching because this approach seeks to transform the academy and the wider community. Here, the writings of Bell Hooks (1994; 2003) and the edited volume *Teaching for Diversity and Social Justice* (Adams, Bell, & Griffin, 2007) have been very influential in my learning. These works have challenged me to learn more about who I am as a teacher, what I believe, and how to best construct the learning environment for my students. In *Teaching to Transgress: Education as the Practice of Freedom,* Hooks (1994) states that accomplishing transformation of academic teaching will be a lengthy endeavor that at times may be frustrating and disheartening. Her comments remind readers that transformation is a courageous act:

> To commit ourselves to the work of transforming the academy so that it will be a place where cultural diversity informs every aspect of our learning, we must embrace struggle and sacrifice. We cannot be easily discouraged. We cannot despair when there is conflict. Our solidarity must be affirmed by shared belief in a spirit of intellectual openness that celebrates diversity, welcomes

dissent, and rejoices in collective dedication to truth (p. 33).

It has been wonderful to work in a university that supports my efforts to become a better teacher. I continue to learn valuable lessons about teaching and about teaching diversity. These lessons are often the most powerful when developed through the relationships with my students and the learning we do together. I also learn a great deal from my colleagues who also teach diversity-focused courses by sharing resources and swapping teaching tips.

I hope that as UNCW implements revisions to its curriculum that diversity is a clear, sustained, and unequivocal requirement. This requirement would demonstrate visible, proactive support for the university's efforts to offer an expansive range of educational opportunities to our students. Opening up the diversity dialogue has the potential to create multiple methods of teaching and learning among faculty and with our students. Perhaps one outgrowth of our colleagues' interest and commitment could be the creation of a Faculty Learning Community that focuses upon fully integrating and sustaining diversity in our classrooms, our curricula, and among our faculty ranks. Prieto (2009) explained the importance of high-impact faculty involvement with diversity-focused learning outcomes: "If our ultimate goal is to cultivate a widespread understanding and accepting environment for cultural diversity in our students, we must engage in a joint, unified effort in which academicians from both majority and diverse cultures do their part" (p. 26).

It's an exciting time to teach, and it's always a good time to learn.

REFERENCES

Adams, M., Bell, L. A., & Griffin, P. (Eds.). (2007). *Teaching for diversity and social justice: A sourcebook.* (2nd ed.) New York, NY: Routledge.

Banks, J. A. (1997). *Educating citizens in a multicultural society.* New York, NY: Teachers College Press.

Brunson, D.A., Jarmon, B., & Lampl, L. L. (Eds.). (2007). *Letters from the future: Linking students and teaching with the diversity of everyday life.* Sterling, VA: Stylus Publishing, LLC.

Frederick, P. (1995). Walking on eggs: Mastering the dreaded diversity discussion. *College Teaching, 4,* 83-92.

Freire, P. (1970). *Pedagogy of the oppressed.* (M. B. Ramos, trans.) New York, NY: Continuum.

Giroux, H. A. (2003). Spectacles of race and pedagogies of denial: Anti-black racist pedagogy under the reign of neoliberalism. *Communication Education, 52,* 191-211.

Giroux, H. A, & McLaren, P. (Eds.). (1994). *Between borders: Pedagogy and the politics of cultural studies.* New York, NY: Routledge.

Harro, B. (2000). The cycle of socialization. In M. Adams, W. J. Blumenfeld, R. Castaneda, H. W. Hackman, M. L. Peters, & X. Zuniga (Eds.), *Readings for diversity and social justice* (pp.15-21). New York, NY: Routledge.

Hooks, B. (1994). *Teaching to transgress: Education as the practice of freedom.* New York, NY: Routledge.

Hooks, B. (2003). *Teaching community: A pedagogy of hope.* New York, NY: Routledge.

Ladson-Billings, G. (1996). Your blues ain't like mine: Keeping issues of race and racism on the multicultural agenda. *Theory into practice, 35,* 248-55.

Lowen, J. W. (2007). *Lies my teacher told me: Everything your American history textbook got wrong.* (2nd ed.). New York, NY: Simon and Shuster.

Prieto, L. R. (2009). Teaching about diversity: Reflections and future directions. In R. A. R. Gurung & L. R. Prieto (Eds.) *Getting culture: Incorporating diversity across the curriculum* (pp. 23-39). Sterling, VA: Stylus Publishing, LLC.

United States Census Bureau (2013a). Table 6. Percent distribution of the projected population by race, and hispanic origin for the united states: 2015 to 2060. [Data file.] Retrieved from

http://www.census.gov/population/projections/data/
national/2012/summarytables.html

United States Census Bureau (2013b). Table 3. Percent distribution of
the projected population by selected age groups and sex for the
united states: 2015 to 2060. [Data file.] Retrieved from http://www.
census.gov/population/projections/data/national/2012/
summarytables.html

Yen, H. (2013, June 13). U.S. whites falling to minority in under-5 age
group. The Big Story. Retrieved from http://bigstory.ap.org/
article/us-whites-now-losing-majority-under-5-age-group

EMILY BOREN
GRADUATE STUDENT,
DEPARTMENT OF PSYCHOLOGY

A Student's Perspective on Effective Teaching: Breaking Down Barriers for Student Learning

"A teacher who is attempting to teach without inspiring the pupil with a desire to learn is hammering on cold iron" (Mann, 1867, p. 225).

Professors face many barriers with students in the classroom, such as large class sizes, unappealing topics (as in, let's say, statistics), and tough students who just want a grade. Nearly all of these barriers can be overcome with the enthusiasm and vigor of passionate professors who care about their students. Having a professor stand up in front of a class and truly enjoy teaching the material, regardless of how interested the students are in the subject, will inspire students to want to pay attention; it drives them to search for the same joy in the subject that the professor finds. It is impossible to make the class "interesting" according to every student's criteria, but making it interesting for yourself will undoubtedly make it interesting for the students. Similarly, if the professor does not enjoy teaching the class, then it is unrealistic to expect the students to enjoy it. In a positive teaching environment, learning thrives, ideas spark, and passions for future careers bud.

Professors who are excited about their subject and who genuinely care about their students are those professors who make an impact on students' lives and are the most effective teachers. To genuinely care entails, but is not limited to, getting to know your students on a personal level by challenging them and giving a little extra to your students. "Just as in the case of an overweight person who is an expert in weight loss, knowledge is not always sufficient for action" (Weinstein, Meyer, Husman, McKeachie, & King, 2011, p. 301). This analogy, written in McKeachie's Teaching Tips, reminds us that most students know how to learn, but it is not just the knowledge that is important, it is the motivation to learn that cultivates learning. One of the few ways teachers can increase student motivation is by taking a little extra time and providing feedback about their performance in the classroom (Weinstein et al., 2011).

A few professors whom I was lucky enough to have had at UNCW not only affected my life at that point in time, but also my future career goals. Throughout this chapter, I want to share with you my experiences that I've had with professors of general education courses and major courses. As I take you through my journey as a student at UNCW, I think you will begin to see the common threads of effective teaching practices that are apparent across all course levels and types of classes.

Making an Impact in General Education Courses

Contrary to most students' beliefs, my basic studies courses were extremely influential on my academic future. It was not necessarily the specific content of those classes that I remember; it was the professors, especially the professors of philosophy and biology. It was not that my professors who taught in my major-studies departments (Criminology and Psychology) didn't also affect my life (a topic I will speak to later in this chapter), it was the notion that the professors of some of the largest and seemingly most unappreciated courses still went above and beyond expectations. Those professors cared enough and took the time to recognize the hard work I was putting into their class and gave me additional, positive feedback about my class performance, not just through my grades in the class.

I still have an e-mail saved from my introductory biology professor a few years ago when I was an undergraduate at UNCW. This particular professor took the time to e-mail me and let me know that I made the highest grade in the class on the final exam, and I earned one of the highest overall grades in all of her course sections. She continued to tell me how great of an accomplishment it was to have achieved this standing and that she was always available to me if I need help with anything in my time at UNCW.

I would have known my grades at the end of the semester. However, this professor chose to make an extra effort and look at her class distribution (of more than 100 students) and let me know, not only my ranking in the course, but how great my performance was. That professor took the extra few minutes to give me positive feedback and acknowledge my success in her course, going above and beyond just giving me a grade. Little does she know how tremendously important that e-mail has been to me over the years and what a major motivator it has been academically. To this day I still go back and read her e-mail whenever I feel discouraged and need a boost to get back on my feet, all thanks to a basic studies professor who took a little extra time and effort to reach out to one of her 100 students one fall semester.

Through my student experiences, I have found that teachers who are most effective take a little extra time for their students and challenge them, as well. A teacher should challenge students to be the best they can be, both academically and in every aspect of their lives. They should not challenge students for the sake of making a "hard class," but to create a challenge that is attainable, a little push. An effective teacher is someone who genuinely wants his or her students to learn, understand, and grow to appreciate—or even grow passionate about—the subject.

When I was in my senior year at UNCW, I took a philosophy class online. At this point, I had decided what I was going to do with my future studies and was just finishing up my basic studies courses. I have to admit, at this point in my academic career, I actually wanted to learn, but the passion I had for learning had to grow in me throughout my undergraduate years. The passion for learning, or lack thereof, is also a barrier that professors of basic studies (courses typically taken by first-year students and sophomores) have to overcome. Even with my enthusiasm for learning, I didn't find the subject quite as appealing as my major studies classes (another barrier for basic studies professors). Nevertheless, this particular philosophy professor was able to completely change my view of the subject and was able to do so online, at that. It is necessary to go into a little detail about the class in order to show you how this professor was able to achieve such a daunting task and impact my life to such a high degree.

The exams for the class were multiple choice and essay. For the essays, we were given real-life examples of ethical issues, and we were asked to explain our ethical standpoint and support it with concepts we had learned in class. Essays are notably more difficult for both the professor to grade, as well as more challenging for the student to write. However, this professor not only read my essays (typically at least 4 or 5 pages for each exam for each student), but also gave me very thorough (both positive and construc-tive-negative), nonjudgmental feedback on my conceptual understanding in the essay. The main point is that this basic studies professor was not just teaching or challenging me for the sake of knowing particular theories or findings; this professor tested my ethical beliefs, and then challenged me intellectually by making me support my ethical beliefs with complex class concepts. Through these essays the professor was able to get to know me as a person and my understanding of ethics, and through nonjudgmental feedback, I was able to grasp a deeper understanding of ethics. A professor described this process of effective teaching in Ken Bain's book What the Best College Teachers Do by saying: "It's sort of Socratic… you begin with a puzzle—you get somebody puzzled, and tied in knots and mixed up. Those puzzles and knots generate questions for students, then you begin to untie the knots" (Bain, 2004, p. 40).

I was able to develop a greater understanding of philosophy by having clear comments from an expert in the field specify where exactly my understanding of the topic was clear and where it seemed to go astray. This professor was able to motivate me to want to learn more (further increasing my joy for learning), and made me excited to learn philosophy. By actually seeing the effort my professor put forth and the passion he had in his subject, he was able to spark excitement for his subject in me that I did not once have. The feedback the professor gave me (via e-mail) turned almost into a philosophy discussion that we had throughout the semester. I wanted to take another class of his just to delve further into philosophy, but I was graduating and going on to graduate school. I still get e-mails from this professor inviting me to talks on campus and to things that may interest me pertaining to his subject; to this day he is still taking time out of his schedule to reach out to students and help them enjoy learning.

My philosophy professor was able to challenge me academically, motivate me, and stimulate my interest in philosophy, even though I had other career goals that were in a different subject. For a professor to be able to spark so much interest and excitement in a classroom, let alone an online classroom, is a daunting task. But showing interest in your own subject, as well as your students' learning of that subject, can be extremely beneficial to the students. My philosophy professor may very well have changed my future career goals if I had taken his class during my early undergraduate years (also supporting the argument of how important basic studies are). I have been fortunate enough to have other professors who impacted my career goals, as well, not in a direct subject impact, but more of a motivational impact, such as my biology professor.

The Power of Mentoring Students

All professors have the same basic underlying goals in their classrooms—motivating learning and instilling knowledge in students—though the obstacles that professors face in reaching these goals may be slightly different. For example, basic studies courses in particular encounter students' lack of interest in the subject. Professors of upper-level courses may not have this obstacle (we hope) or the challenge of an incredibly large class size, but these professors have the same impact on their students' learning and future. Therefore, in order to be effective teachers, whether at the basic studies level or at upper-level courses, being enthusiastic about your subject and caring about your students by challenging them and giving them a little extra effort, still applies.

We have all had those major-studies professors who come into the classroom as if they were walking in for jury duty; they seem to have no passion for their subject. When teaching students who are actually interested in the topic, teaching the class as if it were a chore completely deters students from pursuing that field and drains their passion for the subject. Even more detrimental, the students will most likely not feel comfortable approaching these types of professors with questions about the subject or their career goals that may be beneficial to that student's future. Even in upper-level courses, being a passionate professor, both inside and outside the classroom, challenging students, and going above and beyond expectations is vital for students' learning and future.

Hands down, the one person that has had the greatest impact on my life is a professor from my major-studies department, my mentor in my master's program at UNCW. I have never had my mentor as a teacher, but outside of the classroom, the impact that she has had on my academic and personal life is inexpressible. My mentor is not only a professor, but is also a mentor to me and another graduate student, a research lab director, and a director of a universitywide program. Speaking of someone as being an effective mentor may at first seem slightly incongruent with the rest of this chapter as they also have different barriers than teachers in a classroom, but the same methods of tackling barriers to student learning in the classroom also apply to being an effective mentor (and teacher) outside of the classroom. A few examples about my experience as a student with my mentor may help to describe how these methods of being effective teachers can, and should, be applied inside and outside of the classroom.

The first time I met my mentor was in my interview for the master's program. She said to me: "In my lab, we work incredibly hard, but I will get you into your Ph.D. program." Based off of that, I was sold on working with her. My ultimate goal was to get my Ph.D. and work in academia. In my interview she was already challenging me personally; she challenged my motivation and my commitment to my career goals. Since then, she has continued to challenge me and push me further than I have ever thought possible; she trusts and believes in me and my capabilities, and she genuinely wants me to learn.

My mentor uses a type of apprenticeship model with her graduate students, which is not always the norm in master's programs, but it is particularly effective and beneficial for both the student and mentor (or teacher). For example, she has given me various duties and responsibilities. I was put in an authoritative position to undergraduates (some just months younger than me), I was put in an administrative position and ran the day-to-day lab activities, I was given tasks without much direction, which forced me to think for myself, and I was expected to do my best in all of my schoolwork and research; if I failed, it would impact my mentor greatly (no pressure there, right?). When she handed me these challenges (actually, when looking back, they are better described as opportunities), it had only been three months since I was an undergraduate. As you all know, the jump from undergraduate to graduate student can be overwhelmingly difficult for the student developmentally, personally, and academically (and from a teacher standpoint, as I can speak on only from my experience as a teaching assistant and running a lab, the difference between a graduate student and an undergraduate student is tremendous). And here I was, a nascent graduate student being handed incredible responsibility and difficult challenges from a mentor whom I deeply admire and did not want to let down. But it paid off.

Since my mentor genuinely cares about me, my future, and wants me to learn, she took risks and trusted me with important endeavors (emphasize "risk," as I was only an undergraduate three months prior—scary). As Bain (2004) says in his book What the Best Teachers Do, "Highly effective teachers tend to reflect a strong trust in students. They usually believe that students want to learn, and they assume, until proven otherwise, that they can" (p. 18). By trusting me, she challenged and pushed me to my breaking point. As a result, I have confronted and overcome numerous situations and tasks and reached goals that I would never have thought possible for myself.

As if my developmental evolution from the challenges I was given did not have enough impact on my future, the best part about my story as my mentor's graduate student is the infinite knowledge that I have learned from her. She has taken an immeasurable amount of time out of her schedule (that, by the way, looks like three people's schedules combined) to help me with anything that I needed academically, and most importantly, personally. Her making time for me in her exceptionally busy schedule is somewhat analogous to the time constraints that a basic studies professor may have with more than 100 students in their classroom. Nonetheless, my mentor still made time to sit down and meet with me (like a basic studies professor would outside of the classroom), which has been a major contributor to the vast amount of knowledge that I have acquired from working with her.

A good illustration of these teaching methods is well exemplified in the thesis I am doing for my master's program. To begin a master's thesis, you must start with an idea, a question that you want to explore through conducting research. Needless to say, in my first semester as a graduate student I had "researcher's block" and could not even begin to narrow down all of the questions and ideas that I wanted to investigate. So, I scheduled a meeting with my mentor. One main contingency that my mentor has for me is that when I meet with her (if it is about something academic) I come prepared for the meeting by doing all I can do on my own and have pushed myself to my academic limit. (This is quite difficult before some meetings when I'm attempting to do statistical analyses such as binary logistic regressions.) As such, I delved into the literature of my subject and tried to learn everything I possibly could about my area of interest. After countless late nights and early mornings (and an endless amount of Red Bull), I eventually came down to seven thesis ideas that I would present to her, with a very good argument as to why my research question was important. Once I arrived at my meeting, instead of spending our limited time together trying to figure out what I wanted to research, we were able to review what research questions I had already developed. This method was beneficial to both myself and my mentor; I was pushing myself to my limits and acquiring an incredible amount of information on my own, which allowed for my mentor to have extra time during those meetings to share her extensive knowledge on the subject and elaborate and explain theories, findings, and statistical tests. It was the passion my professor had for our field and her desire for me to learn about the subject that drove her to take just a few extra minutes during those meetings to share her knowledge with me.

At this point, only six months since my undergraduate studies, I was no longer the nascent graduate student who was unsure of my academic limits and myself. The academic and personal development that had occurred within me in those six months was mainly due to my mentor's ambitious apprenticeship model and teaching methods. As a result of her pushing me to do all the work I possibly could before our meetings, I studied hundreds of articles that made me quite knowledgeable about my entire area of research and not just my research question for my thesis (which also spawned more ideas that ultimately helped me narrow down my career aspirations). In my experience (which is not by any means extensive), this type of teaching model is not the norm. Some mentors give the graduate students a research question for their thesis, which, in my opinion, robs them of the incredible developmental learning experience that I have been extremely lucky enough to have. As a result of my mentor's teaching (or mentoring) methods, I was able to acquire an incredible amount of knowledge, learn that I can, in fact, achieve extraordinary things both personally and academically that I would have never dreamt possible for myself, and I can think like a scientist, one of the ultimate goals in our field.

Another aspect of my mentor's apprenticeship model includes the principle of voluntary performance feedback. While writing my thesis, the same contingency was held for when I found my thesis topic, in that my mentor challenged me to write all that I could to the best of my ability before I brought it into our writing meetings. It should be noted that, also in my experience as a graduate student in my department, writing meetings for theses are not the norm, either. The majority of mentors will also challenge their students and have them write as much as they can by a certain deadline, but the student then e-mails their thesis to their mentor for them to read over, make track-changes on the document, and then e-mail it back to the student. This is a helpful mentoring practice, where the student can see what changes the mentor makes on the thesis document, and the mentor may even take the time to explain why they changed certain things in the thesis. However, if no feedback is given or there is not an explanation of the edits, then the student has to try to understand why their mentor changed certain things, and the reasons may be ambiguous (this method would be comparable to multiple-choice tests); however, I can only truly speak on the experiences I have had.

My mentor takes time out of her schedule to make meetings with me (even for just 30 minutes) so that I can watch her edit my thesis document, which is incredibly advantageous over and beyond anything that I have learned in any of my classes or readings. She makes the extra effort to explain her edits of my work (anywhere from grammar to theory) and will challenge my knowledge by asking me questions about why I wrote certain things or why I conducted certain data analyses and what those analyses mean (personally, trying to explain statistics both theoretically and practically is just as difficult as herding cats). She does not just challenge me with questions; she gives me feedback (similar to my philosophy professor's essay feedback) on whether I am on the right track or if I am incorrect. Although, just telling a student whether they're right or wrong does not cultivate learning and understanding. My mentor continues to explain why I am wrong (and will even elaborate on the topic when I'm right), so that I can have a complete understanding of my topic. All the while, she is enthusiastic and noticeably passionate about the work we are doing together, which only adds to the motivation that I have to learn. (On a side note, I have never seen statistics bring someone so much joy until I worked with my mentor; inevitably, that joy for research and data analysis is now instilled in me.) This type of teaching method is not as feasible in track-changes, or especially in a large classroom setting, but it is an exceptionally effective teaching method and can be implemented by taking a few minutes out of your day and making the extra effort to meet with students outside of the classroom, no matter the class size.

All of the professors who have impacted my life were enthusiastic about their subject, got to know me on a personal level, took a little extra time to challenge me, and made the extra effort by giving me voluntary feedback on my performance. These professors were effective teachers in the sense that they motivated me to learn, sparked ideas, and impacted my future, whether academically in their subject or in a different area of interest. They were able to do so in ways that did not hinder their time or schedules to a large degree, but impacted my personal and academic life extensively and meant a great deal to me. I have learned that I am capable of achieving the "impossible," accomplishing things I would never have attempted before my mentor and my experiences with my biology professor and philosophy professor. Teaching is a difficult task, especially teaching students who do not want to learn or have interest in the subject, but these students are the ones who need professors' help the most. If you can overcome these barriers and be an effective teacher with these methods, you can change students' lives.

ACKNOWLEDGEMENTS

I would like to thank Dr. Sonja Pyott, Dr. Don Habibi, and, of course, my remarkable mentor, Dr. Caroline Clements, for impacting my current and future endeavors to such an immeasurable degree.

REFERENCES

Bain, K. (Ed.). (2004). *What the best college teachers do.* Cambridge, MA: Harvard University Press.

Mann, H. (1867). *Thoughts selected from the writings of Horace Mann.* Boston: H.B. Fuller and Company.

Weinstein, C. E., Meyer, D. K., Husman, J., McKeachie, W. J., & King, C. A. (2011). Teaching students how to become more strategic and self-regulated learners. In L. Schrieber-Ganster & C. Cox (Eds.), *McKeachie's teaching tips: Strategies, research, and theory for college and university teachers* (13th ed. pp. 292-307). Belmont, CA: Wadsworth, Cengage Learning.

DIANA ASHE
CENTER FOR TEACHING EXCELLENCE AND CENTER FOR FACULTY
LEADERSHIP / DEPARTMENT OF ENGLISH

Truth versus Truthiness: Promoting Habits of Critical Thinking

For more than four years, I have tried unsuccessfully to persuade my son, who is now eight years old, that bagels do not have crusts in the way that a loaf of bread has a crust. I have tried reasoning from every imaginable angle. I have tried showing him the process of bagels being made. I have coaxed him into merely *tasting* the "crusts" of his bagels, hoping that he will see that there is no difference between what he deems a "crust" and the rest of the bagel.

I have pleaded with him on the basis of wasted food. He hates the idea of waste, so his solution was to feed his "crusts" to the dog, until we stopped him (at least while we're looking, anyway).

I have tried not caring about it for a long time and convincing myself that it would stop when I stopped giving it attention. I was good at persuading myself, at least for a while, but not so good at bringing about change in my son's eating habits.

I have tried demanding that he eat the crusts. More crusts went to the dog.

I have tried every persuasive strategy in my arsenal, and yet, four years into this campaign, I am faced with teensy, crescent-shaped rinds smeared with cream cheese nearly every morning. Milhouse, our increasingly over-weight dog, is quite content with the bagel situation at our house, but if I let it, it would drive me to distraction. Pure self-preservation leads me to make pancakes on Saturdays. At least so far, pancakes have not been construed as possessing any offending crusts.

My struggle with the bagel crusts is not a matter of existential crisis, of course, except for one tiny detail: I teach rhetoric for a living. Almost every class I teach can be boiled down to teaching skills in constructing and/or analyzing arguments. I teach writing classes and rhetoric classes, technical communication and document design—all classes in permutations of persuasion, written and sometimes visual. If I can't convince my own child of something as simple as the fact that bagels are the same all the way around, then what is my hope of teaching my students to become strategic and effective persuaders?

The broader form of this question is this: How is it that a person can be faced with what I see as a capital-F Fact, as irrefutable evidence in multiple forms, and not be swayed *in the least* by that new information? If I can't convince my own child that bagels don't have crusts, then what business do I have pretending to have the authority to teach anyone about making convincing arguments? What kind of lousy teacher am I, anyway?

I'm not going to answer that.

I share the bagel-crust dilemma in class now and then, to point out the limitations of arguments. Theories of argumentation are empowering, and I love a well-constructed enthymeme as much as (and probably more than) the next person, but arguments in all forms are, alas, not triggers for automatic effects. Argumentation is wonderful in the classroom because it is omnipresent, adaptable, and readily applicable to students' contexts. I love offering students new ways to make a convincing case for gaining acceptance into graduate school or improving the campus or the community or the planet—or just getting a deposit back on an apartment. All of the confidence we can build by knowing that our arguments are well-structured and thoroughly supported, though, must always be tempered with the understanding that on the receiving end of those arguments dwell human beings—complex, messy, contrarian, unpredictable human beings.

If arguments were totally effective, every college instructor, no matter the subject of the course, could start the semester with the "why this class matters" speech and then spend the next fourteen weeks with a rapt audience of students hanging on his or her every word. We know that our arguments for making our class a priority, preparing for class, studying conscientiously, etc., are sound, for example, so why aren't they getting it? Why do we sometimes ask questions and hear nothing but crickets in a room full of students who, if our words had the desired effect, would be jumping at the opportunity presented by the class?

If it's any consolation, even the people who teach argumentation occasionally face the same blank stares, despite our best efforts at making reasoned or even impassioned arguments to our students about the value of what we're teaching. Recent research by political scientists and psychologists (of which I am neither, but a fan of both) and the favored terminology of a leading comedian (breakthroughs come from all over) may shed light on the conundrum of the argumentative dead end. It turns out that Facts may trigger unexpected responses—and those unexpected responses have ramifications far more serious than wasted bagel bits or even spaced-out students.

When confronted with facts, it turns out, the misinformed often dig in their heels and believe more strongly in their previously held—and wrong-headed—views. We've all suspected this at one time or another, but there is increasing documentation of the phenomenon. Political scientists call it "the backfire effect." And backfire it does: Consider the social and political costs of decisions made by those who are determined to ignore facts that run counter to their predetermined stance on a given issue.

A study by Brendan Nyhan and Jason Reifler (2010), published in the journal Political Behavior, extended some of Nyhan's previous research on this phenomenon and opened with the perfect epigram from Mark Twain: "It ain't what you don't know that gets you into trouble. It's what you know for sure that just ain't so." Because information presented to the public is often couched within a debate-style format that offers both sides of an issue, enough ambiguity is introduced to render it likely that readers or listeners will "resist or reject arguments and evidence contradicting their opinions—a view that's consistent with a wide array of research" (Nyhan & Reifler, 2010). Nyhan and Reifler go on to list four additional studies to add credence to this claim.

Psychologists also document this tendency to favor arguments and evidence that "reinforce their existing views and disparaging those that contradict their views" (Nyhan & Reifler, 2010), listing three additional studies that document the phenomenon. The psychologists' favored terms for this tendency are "motivated reasoning" (Nyhan & Reifler, 2010, p. 22), or "confirmation bias," which has been on their radar since the 1950s (Kuhn, 1989; Sampson, Grooms, & Walker, 2010). Confirmation bias refers to our tendency to believe information that confirms our pre-existing belief systems and disregard information that contradicts those systems. Faced with motivated reasoning, confirmation bias, and the backfire effect, anyone teaching argumentation—or teaching critical thinking in any form—has a steep hill to climb.

Part of what makes teaching critical thinking and argument skills so challenging is the very notion of facts and truth. So many things around us sound or seem to ring true, but which of them are? Now that we can verify so many truth claims in a nanosecond, we seem even less likely to do so. The hard-working researchers at snopes.com, factcheck.org, and truthorfiction.

com, for example, pile up evidence debunking conspiracy theories, urban legends, and simple tall tales. It is a lesson in motivated reasoning to read an online comment section or discussion thread of true believers when faced with a snopes or similar debunking of a closely held belief: The evidence will be dismissed, diminished, denied, ridiculed, or simply ignored.

One of my goals as a teacher is to help my students stay open to new information and ideas, open to contradictory data and confusing facts—and to be challenged to reconcile new information with their existing understanding of the world and their places within it. In the classroom I want to encourage and assist my students as they navigate and interrogate the differences between truth and what comedian Stephen Colbert calls "truthiness" in the messages they encounter—whether those are academic messages or messages from other areas of their lives.

Truthiness, if your bedtime is as early as mine and you've missed Colbert's explanation of the term, was introduced during his "The Word" segment on October 17, 2005, when he promised "to feel the news at" viewers rather than reading it to them. By 2006, Merriam-Webster had declared truthiness its "#1 Word of the Year," offering these two definitions:

1. "truth that comes from the gut, not books" (Stephen Colbert, Comedy Central's 'The Colbert Report,' October 17, 2005)
2. "the quality of preferring concepts or facts one wishes to be true, rather than concepts or facts known to be true" (American Dialect Society, January 2006)

Colbert's term made such a powerful impact—beating even the verb form of "google" and the neologism "decider" for the top spot—because it speaks to a very powerful concept that we needed a word to describe it. It turns out that facts are not so important to us as we form opinions and make decisions.

Those political scientists and psychologists are documenting the tendency of truthiness to overpower truth. If truth were always the most powerful force, we wouldn't have politics or psychology at all. Politics and psychology—along with rhetoric, literature, philosophy, religion, and any number of other approaches to the world—help us to grapple with the gaps between truth and truthiness, between the material conditions of our lives and the individual and social ways in which we cope with those conditions.

We don't always like the truth, but truthiness comes through for us every time. It feels so good. Even though my classes tend to stay firmly within the humanities, this social science research matters in every class I teach, and it matters to all of us who teach. One of our primary responsibilities is to help our students sort out the true from the "truthy," and to give them skills in conveying to others the difference—and the importance of the difference—as well. Maybe most of all, we are here to encourage them to want to know the truth—to lean toward consistent and conscientious inquiry as a method of understanding and navigating their lives.

How do we promote inquiry and discourage the backfire effect in our classrooms and among our students? I can think of six ways, each of which I've tried and, while not perfect, found helpful.

1) **Name it. Declare inquiry a value in your classroom and embed it throughout your materials.**

In 2011, I taught a modern rhetorical theory course with the subtitle (off the record, but on the syllabus) of "Truth versus Truthiness." We discussed, on the first day of class, what truthiness means, and we even watched Stephen Colbert using the term in a video clip. Describing something as "truthy" became a part of our class's lingo and a helpful shorthand for some of the texts we were analyzing. We challenged one another all semester long to look up what seemed true, and we heaped praise upon those who went the extra mile to verify information about anything at all. I modeled this the first few times, but the students took over quickly.

You don't have to make truth and truthiness the theme of your class, but you can foreground the concept and have students complete a reading about, say, the backfire effect, and come to class with examples of how motivated reasoning could be detrimental to the subject area of the class—whether it's a class on Systems Ecology or Recreation Therapy.

Another way to embed inquiry as a habit is to go through a difficult reading ahead of time and select terms, names, locations, dates, etc., that will either challenge your students or that offer contextual information for the reading. Choose terms that are in the reading, but that students are likely to glide right past as they hurry to complete the assignment (significant names, places, dates, new terminology, etc.). Put each term on a slip of paper, numbered, and distribute them to the class the day before the reading is to be discussed. Ask students to find out what their term means and how it relates to the reading. On the day you discuss the reading, give each student one minute (this can be done in pairs or small groups or by lot in a large class) to share his or her findings with the class. Students can share maps on the screen, photos, short videos or sound clips, etc. I call this the "One-Minute Drill." Once every term has been explained by the student or students responsible for it, you might say something like, "Imagine how your reading would change if you were in the habit of completing this exercise for yourself, even sometimes." Discuss how knowing all of these terms changes their understanding of the reading.

Coding expert James Marcus Bach, author of Secrets of a Buccaneer-Scholar, tells teachers to "convey deeper trust in the method of systematic doubting (and in the judgment of the doubters) than in the sanctity of received wisdom." He reports that he is "rather uncritical about my support for critical thinkers as they begin to spread their wings" (Bach, 2013), and we might all gain from his spirited approach to creating a culture of questioning—and investigating.

2) Model inquiry every chance you get.

When students ask a question you can't answer, seize the opportunity. There are so many ways to model great inquiry here: Ask that student (or another, depending upon what's happening in your class) to find out before the next class and report back; offer an incentive to the student who comes back with the best answer in the next class meeting; if it's something fairly straightforward, look it up on the instructor's computer right then and there, or ask students in the class to pull out their smartphones and look it up. It's also helpful to poll the class: What is the popular vote for this one? Then seek out the actual answer, and the class can discuss any discrepancy.

The most important factor here is admitting that you don't know, that you want to know, and that the members of the class are all responsible for finding out. If you can muster genuine enthusiasm for verifying answers, for solving informational mysteries together, you may find that your enthusiasm is infectious.

Critical thinking expert Stephen Brookfield builds upon this approach by encouraging teachers to "explain why we're doing what we're doing" (Brookfield, 2012, p. 61). Brookfield cites thousands of student surveys to support his advice that "when it comes to a threatening activity like being asked to think critically about their long-held assumptions, it inspires confidence when [students] see their teachers clearly have a plan for doing this, a set of reasons informing their actions" (Brookfield, 2012, p. 61). Tell students why you're making the moves you're making to create an atmosphere that encourages critical thinking.

Model the inquiry practices you hope to instill in your students and make "Let's find out!" a refrain.

3) Find out what they're already doing.

Find out what your students believe. Tap the greatest data source about your students: your students. When you want to encourage them to improve their reading strategies, for example, ask them what strategies they are currently using. When you want to convince them that more practice would improve their skills, find out just how much they are already practicing. To convince them to expend more in your class, find out what they expend now.

Once you know, affirm that their choice and its consequences belong to them. They can continue to act in precisely the manner in which they have been acting. They will not necessarily be ready to believe that doing something different will make a difference—or, at least not enough of a difference to justify the extra effort. But you can let them know that they own their performance and their ideas. A little ownership is a powerful thing.

With insight into their study habits and reading practices, you'll be better able to intervene. Now you can show them more effective reading strategies, explain that "critical" reading doesn't mean that we are giving every text a bad review, or offer more targeted ways of researching in your field. By doing so, you'll be offering better access not just to the current research, but to the ways of thinking in the field—and point out the distinctions as you do so.

4) Make it worth their while.

What you want, of course, is for your students to absorb and engage with the material in your course and to take genuine academic interest in it. What they want, alas, quite often boils down to a good grade. None of us has the power to upend that entrenched dynamic. The best we can do is work within it.

When it's time to recommend new strategies, to proffer ideas that might fall victim to the backfire effect or motivated reasoning, find ways to motivate that reasoning in your direction. Clarity works well here: Spell out everything that you would never think should have to be spelled out, and frame behaviors in terms of student-defined success—at the same time that you strategically place reminders about the other benefits of shifting beliefs.

Like anyone else, our students are constantly calculating a cost-benefit ratio regarding their expenditures of time and energy. If you attach consistent and proportionate rewards to the behaviors you want to encourage, you may have better luck at achieving them than by your encouragement alone (see Carol Pilgrim's essay on this topic in this volume for more on this idea). It may seem like splitting hairs to count a specific percentage for fact-seeking behaviors, but your goal is bigger: You want to incentivize the practice until it becomes a habit. Once it becomes a habit, its value sustains itself.

A nice example of this practice occurs in Shirley Mathews' Theory and Practice of Editing class, English 310. She wants to encourage students to pick up the habit of daily newspaper reading and of instinctive copyediting while they're at it. So, in this exceptionally challenging course, she offers a limited number of extra credit points to students over the course of the semester if they bring in errors they've found in the Wilmington Star-News. Students must identify the error and explain what Associated Press rule has been broken in the specific instance in order to gain the points.

I like this version of encouraging fact-checking because it is unrelated to any assignment; it requires students to read the newspaper through their own impetus, and to cite why an error is wrong rather than simply saying, "this is wrong." It's an assignment that encourages two habits of intellectual curiosity—newspaper reading (important for journalists) and AP Stylebook checking (essential for journalists)—while also promoting individual initiative (another journalistic imperative).

5) **Pump up your feedback: If you want critical thinking, prompt and praise critical thinking.**

When you offer feedback to students during class discussions online or face-to-face, consider peppering your phrasing with language that encourages precisely what you want to encourage. If you're just saying, "Good" or "Right" in response to student comments, then you're missing an opportunity to send powerful messages. I hear that kind of feedback a lot when I sit in on classes, and I always encourage instructors to put more information in there. "I like the way you're thinking" sends a very different message than "Good," indicating to the entire class that you are noting the student's thought process, that reasoning is as important to you as simply responding. More possibilities along these lines: "That's true, and how do you know? How did you arrive at that idea?" or "What would you say to someone who wasn't ready to believe you?" or "Can anyone else tell me what she needed to know to figure that out?" As long as your responses extend the reasoning aspects of the student's answer, you're doing more than offering positive reinforcement—you're encouraging clear thinking.

6) Consider adding a <shudder> critical reflection to your course.

I never thought I'd come to this. I never thought I'd be one of those teachers who tout the reflection. Ugh! So touchy-feely! Such busywork! Not for me. I'm hard-core!

Once I got involved in the Applied Learning and Teaching Community, though, I was exposed to more information about the so-called "critical reflection." The word "critical" helped a bit. But I was still not sold. I went to the ETEAL Summer Institute (twice!) and decided to try a version of Sarah Ash and Patti Clayton's DEAL Model of critical reflection (Ash & Clayton, 2009). Clayton was a facilitator at both of the first two Summer Institutes, and she was pretty convincing. Her DEAL Model had more heft than my prejudices. I tried it in English 307: Advanced Composition Studies. This theory-based class was difficult and potentially dry, so I devised a couple of service-learning projects to give the students experiences for discussing the theory.

The DEAL Model offers an extensive list of questions in these categories: "Describe the experience objectively," "Examine the experience: from a personal perspective, from a civic perspective, from an academic perspective," and "Articulate Learning." It was easy to adapt the published model to our class project, and the many questions gave my students plenty of avenues for thought.

I'm now a cautious recommender of critical reflections. I don't recommend them wholesale because if you're going to throw a prompt out and not do anything with it, then no one will benefit much. However, if you start with a good model like Clayton's and customize it to your course, talk with your students about why you're using it, and then make the reflections a part of the course, then you have genuine value added. If you won't have time to read or respond to reflections, then don't assign them.

If you can make them a part of the class with intention, then you may find that students will surprise you. Yes, some students will write what they think you expect them to write. That is why a good model like Clayton's is essential—it asks better questions than just "what did I learn?" (though it does, in fact, ask that very question toward the end). A critical reflection, however, asks students to connect course concepts to their experience and to consider big-picture concerns when assessing their experience. It also asks them to think about their own role in the success or failure of their learning process. All of these questions nudge students toward the habits of mind that are the basis of inquiry.

I'm preparing right now for another semester of bringing out these strategies and a few others. I'm optimistic about that; it's one of my favorite classes, and the clean-slate feeling of a new semester has me ready to give it another go. Students respond well to the notion of intellectual inquiry as pretty much the reason they are here, and if I can summon enthusiasm, they can generally match mine after a while. The strategies here will work for many of them, and I'm always trying new ideas to make inroads with the rest. We can make a significant difference in the tone of the class simply by saying that this is what we're doing: that we value critical inquiry, modeling inquiry for them, asking how they investigate what they don't know, putting value on inquiry in terms they recognize, using feedback that incorporates inquiry, and perhaps even completing critical reflections for some of our assignments. All of these strategies demonstrate for students the ways in which critical thinking operates—in both academic and non-academic settings. Combating the forces of truthiness begins one class, one strategy, one student at a time. Truthiness is powerful stuff, but I think we can make a difference.

At home, though, I'm not so sure. The dog ate another round of bagel crusts this morning, and the outlook is not so good. Milhouse seems chubbier than ever, and Donovan just shrugged and said, "Oops!" when I discovered the cream cheese evidence smeared on the floor. Perhaps it's time for a new plan. Is my son too young to see Stephen Colbert's "Truthiness" video?

Postscript: In the weeks since this essay was drafted, an exciting new development: My son told his father that he knows that bagel crusts are the same as the rest of the bagel, and that avoiding them is "just a habit." Perhaps this metacognition signals the verge of a critical thinking breakthrough . . .

REFERENCES

American Dialect Society (2006, January 6). Truthiness voted 2005 word of the year. Retrieved from http://www.americandialect.org/truthiness_voted_2005_word_of_the_year

Ash, S. L., & Clayton, P. H. (2009). Generating, deepening, and documenting learning: The power of critical reflection in applied learning. *Journal of Applied Learning in Higher Education, 1,* 25-48.

Bach, J. M. (2013, November 29). Teaching critical thinking with dog food. Retrieved from http://www.edutopia.org/blog/teaching-critical-thinking-dog-food-james-bach?page=18

Brookfield, S. (2012). *Teaching for critical thinking: Tools and techniques to help students question their assumptions.* San Francisco, CA: Jossey-Bass.

Colbert, S. (Writer), & Hoskinson, J. (Director). (2005). Stone Phillips [Television series episode]. *The Colbert report.* New York, NY: Comedy Central.

Kuhn, D. (1989). Children and adults as intuitive scientists. *Psychological Review, 96,* 674-689.

Nyhan, B., & Reifler, J. (2010). When corrections fail: The persistence of political misperceptions. *Political Behavior, 32,* 303-330.

Sampson, V., Grooms, J., & Walker, J. P. (2011). Argument-Driven Inquiry as a way to help students learn how to participate in scientific argumentation and craft written arguments: An exploratory study. *Science Education, 95,* 217-257.

LISA POLLARD
DEPARTMENT OF HISTORY

Teaching to Controversy: The Source and the Student

I was not prepared for the quick up-swell of interest in the modern Middle East that resulted from the events of September 11, 2001. While I had long found the topic of my graduate training to be fascinating, I had also grown accustomed to people dismissing it as a peculiar interest. In graduate school I became accustomed to being asked "what are you going to do with a Ph.D. in Middle Eastern history?" Even my parents, both of them educators, fretted that my decision to study modern Middle Eastern history would leave me unemployable. Their concerns were reflected in the small number of jobs posted in my field as I ventured into the market in 1996: that year, only 16 universities in the United States (including UNCW) advertised for historians of the Middle East. As I settled into UNCW in 1997, my courses were certainly well enrolled. But students typically told me that their interest in my classes reflected their desires to study something other than American or European history rather than a burning interest in the Middle East itself. After 9/11, however, both university and student interest in the region burgeoned: the Middle East became one of the fastest-growing subfields in the historical profession, and the number of colleges and universities hiring specialists in Middle Eastern and Islamic history swelled. (Thirty-nine history departments in the United States hired Middle East historians in 2003, for example, representing a growth of over 100% from 1996 (Townsend, 2005). In 2011, the American Historical Association announced that the history of the Middle East was one of the two fastest-growing subfields in the discipline (Townsend, 2011). Student interest grew at a similar pace and students now took my courses out of a genuine interest in the Middle East, and not simply out of a desire to bypass Western Civ.

Increased interest brought a second surprise, one for which I was equally unprepared: controversy. As a graduate student trained in the years following the 1979 publication of Orientalism, in which the Palestinian-American political activist and professor of English Edward Said laid out the various ways in which Western anxieties about the Islamic World over the centuries have resulted in negative stereotyping in popular culture as well as in foreign policy, I was prepared to engage in a certain amount of myth-busting in the classroom (Sain, 1979). As an historian I was trained both in the history of the Middle East and in the history of the West's fascination with that region. So as I started my career at UNCW, I favored an approach to teaching potentially controversial topics like veiling, polygamy and the seclusion of women, for example, that involved two tasks. On the one hand I had to situate those phenomena within the history of the region in which they have been practiced. On the other hand, I had to contextualize our discomfort with them within a larger history of the West's anxieties surrounding what it perceived to be Islamic practices.

But the post-9/11 world brought a new kind of controversy to the classroom. As American citizens sought answers to their questions about the context out of which the attacks of 9/11 arose, American scholars of Middle Eastern and Islamic studies were thrust into the public spotlight as never before, speaking to audiences in university settings as well as religious and civic institutions. Academics' responses to questions such as "why do they hate us," when answered from the perspective of a lengthy and frequently unbalanced set of relations between the West and the Middle East, were a source of comfort to some and of ire to others. While the idea that an historical framework for understanding the grievances of our attackers did not seem to motivate the former group to justify the events of 9/11, it did seem to provide it with a means for understanding the West's sometimes troubled historical legacy in the Middle East. For the latter group, the idea that there was a context in which grievances could be understood was treacherous, and academics who advanced such notions were soon labeled as anti-patriotic. The wife of then Vice President Dick Cheney, for example, teamed with Senator Joe Lieberman to publish a black list of professors whom the pair viewed as "failing America" and as "giving comfort to its adversaries" (Gonzalez, 2001). In a similar vein, web sites such as Campus Watch, the web project of the Philadelphia-based Middle East Forum, encouraged students to report such professors, who were thought to be mixing politics with scholarship. (Members of the Mid East Forum suggest that American Academics typically portray the Middle East falsely, for example, underplaying such phenomena as militant Islam.) "Campus Watch...gathers information on Middle East studies…invites student complaints of abuse… and makes these known" (The Middle East, 2013). American students were not unaware of the politics surrounding the teaching of Middle Eastern and Islamic topics, and the classroom—as well as the topics taught in it—became sites of potential discomfort and distrust.

In order to create a context in which the study of history could go on, and in which students could trust that they would not be subjected to the current politics of teaching Middle Eastern history, I came to rely on two sets of exercises. The first, not of my own design but useful nonetheless, helps students to understand the importance of sources in the making and reaching of conclusions. I designed the second exercise to help students understand their relationship to the sources from which they gather and digest information, and to identify themselves as sources of knowledge. While the 2001 maelstrom surrounding the study of the Middle East and Islam has calmed down somewhat, I continue to use these exercises as a means of creating a classroom in which arguments are grounded in sources, rather than opinions, and in which opinions can easily be traced to their sources.

Primary sources are essential to the study of history. They serve as the material through which historians reach, and illustrate, their conclusions. History undergraduates typically become the most comfortable with primary sources when they begin to write their own research papers. (In UNCW's history department, that adventure begins in HST 290, our gateway seminar for majors. It is in HST 290 that our students produce their first research-driven essays). In lecture courses, however, through which students become familiar with the major events in a region's history and with the approaches and arguments that make up that region's historiography, students can rely on the opinions of others. Professors are usually careful to inform their students about the sources from which they gather their information and make their arguments. But undergraduates in lecture courses in history are typically more concerned with grasping what happened than they are with wrestling with how we know what happened. In addition to lectures, therefore, I have come to rely on exercises in which students start with the sources. Prior to lecturing on the effects of the post-WWI treaties on the modern Middle East (territories previously held by the Ottomans), for example, I ask students to read the treaties and to place them within an historical context. Using the late Ottoman history that they are already familiar with, students discuss the continuity reflected in those treaties, and reflect upon the possibilities for change. Working together, and without the framework of a lecture (in other words, without the potential opinion of the professor), students go straight to the sources and ask what they might make of them and what they might do with them. Once they do hear my lecture on WWI, they are familiar with the evidence through which I (and the other historians whose work I draw upon) have reached my conclusions.

Documents also serve as the starting point for debates, both in and outside of the classroom. I request that students shape their contributions to discussions by revealing the sources through which they reached their conclusions. In web-based conversations, they must cite their sources directly. When in classroom discussions they resort to opinion, which is easy to do when the topic is heated, I ask them to tell me (and their classmates) if they can substantiate that opinion with a source. Potentially controversial conclusions, when grounded in sources, thus appear historically grounded rather than driven by emotions.

I similarly ask students to use documents to challenge my conclusions. I give them one opportunity per semester to get 5 points of extra credit for using a source of their own choosing to contest –something they have heard, disagreed with or disliked in my classroom over the course of the semester.1 The point is not necessarily to prove me "wrong" (although that certainly happens!), but rather to uncover and analyze the kinds of sources that allow for different perspectives and that open new avenues for debate.

My own innovation for teaching to controversy has been the use of an exercise designed to get students to think about themselves in relationship to knowledge about the Middle East. During the first week of class, I give them a questionnaire to fill out. I also provide them with an envelope and ask them to seal the finished questionnaire in it, and to sign their names across the sealed envelope's flap. This way they are assured of my promise to them, that I will not read their answers.

I keep the signed and sealed envelopes in my office until the final weeks of the semester. At that point, I give them a fresh copy of the original questionnaire, and ask them to fill it out again. I then return the original questionnaires to them and ask them to write a short essay (1000 words) about change over time in them. How were their answers different the second time around? Why? What had changed about them or about their relationship to knowledge and to the history of the region? Why might that change be important, both to them and to their understanding of the Middle East?

In my modern Middle Eastern history course (I also use the questionnaire exercise in my classes on early Islamic history and on the history of women and gender) I start with a series of content questions. What, I ask them for example, has been the most significant event to take place in the

---

1 This is a technique I have borrowed from my colleague Sarah Shields at UNC Chapel Hill.

Middle East in the 21st century? The twentieth? The nineteenth? In each case, I ask them to tell me why they chose the event that they did. (The question about the nineteenth century typically remains blank the first time around, as most students have little experience with that period of Middle Eastern history). I ask them about the nature of the struggle between Palestinians and Israelis (in other words: what are they fighting over). I ask them to identify the origins of Islamic extremism. Finally, I ask them to identify the most important catalyst for change in the Middle East over the course of the twentieth century.

Then I ask them to identify the sources that inform their knowledge of the Middle East. Do they get their information from a religious institution? Do they watch television or draw from other media outlets? If so, which ones? Have they taken other university-level courses? Have they read books on the topic? Have they traveled to the region? Have they studied there? Have they served in Iraq or Afghanistan? Do they talk about the Middle East with their families? If so, how do their family members inform themselves about the region? The point of this second batch of questions is to get them to think about their relationship to information, and about the role of that information in shaping their thoughts.

Typically, by the end of the semester, students have forgotten all about their answers to the first questionnaire. They take longer to fill out the second one, have much more to say about the nineteenth century, and giggle at their answers to the first one. They take both questionnaires home in order to answer the following questions: "What did you learn about your relationship to the history of the Middle East? What do you know now that you did not know before? Why might that shift in knowledge be important? Have your sources for the study of the Middle East changed? Do you look at particular events differently?"

The point of the assignment is not to point out students' ignorance (although they pretty typically delight in telling me about how much they have learned over the course of the term), but rather to foster critical thinking about their relationship to what they know. Students' answers to the content questions change, predictably, from the first questionnaire to the second, as do their perceptions of what has caused change in the Middle East over the last several centuries ("religion" is typically the most common response in round one, whereas answers such as "the economy," "oil," "geopolitics" and "war" dominate the second questionnaire). But the greatest change in students is frequently reflected in perceptions about themselves. At the beginning of the semester, they do not often know where they get their information about the Middle East from, suggesting that it is maybe their friends, maybe their parents, maybe their religious leaders who shape their sense of what is happening "over there." Those who watch television suggest that they are devotees of one talking head or another, and that they trust him or her to provide unbiased coverage. By semester's end students suggest that—at least in theory—they should trust no "take" on the modern Middle East without further investigation into the sources through which such a "take" is derived. Similarly, they seem to understand that, in conversation about the Middle East with others, they should reveal their sources and encourage further research from their friends, colleagues and family members.

Taken as a whole, these exercises help students understand that controversy stems less from a differing of opinions than it does from a lack of clarity surrounding the process through which conclusions are reached. At the end of the semester my students are familiar with the narrative of events that have shaped the modern Middle East. They are familiar with the sources through which that narrative has been constructed and through which it can be contested. Finally, they understand their own relationship to sources and to the place of those in scholarly debates over "what happened." At the end of a semester structured around the use of and debates surrounding a common set of sources, students trust that we have left the polemics of politics aside in favor of honest interrogation of the evidence before us. Like my students, I leave the courses in which I use these exercises confident in the sources of my information, knowing that my conclusions are based in evidence, sure that I have kept the classroom free from controversy.

REFERENCES

Gonzalez, R. J. (2001, December 13). Lynne Cheney-Joe Lieberman groups puts out a blacklist. *San Jose Mercury News*. Retrieved from: http://www.commondreams.org/views01/1213-05.htm

Sain, E. (1979). *Orientalism*. New York, NY: Vintage Books.

The Middle East. (2013). *About Campus Watch*. Retrieved from: http://www.campus-watch.org/about.php

Townsend, R. B. (2005, January). Job Market Report 2004. *Perspectives on History*. Retrieved from: http://www.historians.org/perspectives/issues/2005/0501/0501new1.cfm

Townsend, R. B. (2011, March). New History PhD's in 2009 surged to second-highest level in 32 years. *Perspectives on History*. Retrieved from: http://www.historians.org/Perspectives/issues/2011/1103/1103new1.cfm

PATRICIA KELLEY
DEPARTMENT OF GEOGRAPHY AND GEOLOGY

Controversial Topics in the Classroom: (How) Do We Dare Discuss Them?

"I can't believe what my professor told us today!"
"We're getting into all this weird stuff in class that I know can't be right!"
"I'll memorize this stuff for the test, but I'm sure not going to believe any of it!"
"If this topic comes up again, I'm not going to sit there - I'm going to give the professor a hard time."

Sound familiar? No matter what our discipline, many of us will be faced with teaching a controversial topic at some point in our careers. I don't necessarily mean a controversy within our discipline – pondering such controversies, especially with advanced students, makes teaching fun. I refer instead to topics that our students (especially those in our introductory classes) may find threatening – topics that may elicit comments such as those listed above. As a paleontologist, the touchy topic I teach is evolution; faculty in biology, anthropology, psychology, science education, and history of science also teach aspects of this controversial topic. Other disciplines have their own threatening topics. A quick scan through the UNCW undergraduate catalog yields a wide range of courses with topics that some students may find offensive: Rhetoric of Faith Healing; Minorities, Crime and Criminal Justice Policy; Bible as Literature; Topics and Issues in Sustainability; Global Climate Change; Reproduction and Sexuality; Issues in Modern Science: Race, Religion, and Politics; Gerontology/End of Life Care; Bioethics; Atheism and Unbelief; Naked-eye Astronomy and Archaeoastronomy; Religion and Politics in the United States; Human Sexual Behavior; Social Welfare Policies; Sexuality and Gender.

"I can't believe what my professor told us today!"

"We're getting into all this weird stuff in class that I know can't be right!"

"I'll memorize this stuff for the test, but I'm sure not going to believe any of it!"

"If this topic comes up again, I'm not going to sit there - I'm going to give the professor a hard time."

WHY do we dare to teach such controversial subjects? Why invite comments like these? In some cases, the potentially offensive topic is fundamental to the content of our course or field. As evolutionary biologist Theodosius Dobzhansky famously stated (and titled a 1973 essay), "Nothing in Biology Makes Sense Except in the Light of Evolution." The same could be said of my own field; paleontology makes no sense without reference to evolution. Even if a controversial topic is not fundamental to our field, we may choose to teach it in order to help students develop skills such as critical thinking and the ability to articulate a position.

"I can't believe what my professor told us today!"

"We're getting into all this weird stuff in class that I know can't be right!"

"I'll memorize this stuff for the test, but I'm sure not going to believe any of it!"

"If this topic comes up again, I'm not going to sit there - I'm going to give the professor a hard time."

HOW do we dare to teach controversial subjects? How can we avoid student reactions such as these? Should we even care if students react this way? The answer to these questions may not be obvious, as alternative approaches are possible. We may choose to ignore that a controversy exists and plunge into the subject without acknowledging the controversy. After all, we may think, this is college – it's time for students to broaden their perspectives. We need to pose anomalies for them to consider and open their minds to challenging topics. But is ignorance bliss? If our students are upper-level majors or graduate students, they usually have some background in the controversial topic and their learning is less likely to be impeded by this direct approach. However, students in our introductory classes may be enrolled simply to fulfill a requirement without having a genuine interest in the material; they may not have the background to feel comfortable discussing topics they perceive threatening. If such students who find a topic offensive are aggressive in voicing their objections, they may disrupt class and create a hostile learning environment for others. Even if such students are passive, hostility may build and interfere with their learning. Thus I have found that it is more helpful to acknowledge that controversy exists and address it.

But how? In the past nearly 35 years that I have been teaching evolution, my teaching approach itself has evolved. In this essay I describe my pedagogical journey and my current approaches to teaching controversial subjects, focusing on my introductory paleontology course, Prehistoric Life. In so doing, I discuss best practices that I consider helpful in teaching any course, but especially in courses with controversial content.

My pedagogical journey. When I began teaching in 1979, the standard pedagogy (we didn't use that word then) was lecturing. Even in graduate courses, faculty lectured. Courses that were taught as seminars, in which students contributed to the discussion, were rare. Thus my goal as a novice teacher was to become an excellent lecturer. I hoped to emulate my PhD advisor, Stephen Jay Gould, a superb lecturer who captivated his students, inciting them to applaud nearly every lecture. I was certain that if my lectures were clear and well organized and followed the syllabus predictably, I too could be an excellent teacher.

The approach seemed to be working. My student evaluations were strong, I attracted graduate students, and I rose rapidly through the academic ranks at the University of Mississippi to become a full professor 10 years later. Yet I felt myself growing dissatisfied, even bored, with my teaching. Perhaps that's why I welcomed opportunities for challenging administrative positions, first at Ole Miss and then at the National Science Foundation. Administration also gave me an opportunity for mobility, and I accepted department chair positions at the University of North Dakota in 1992 and at UNCW in 1997 (trading in Dakota blizzards and floods for Carolina hurricanes and floods).

During the fifteen years in which administrative duties claimed more of my attention than teaching, the academic world began to change. I don't think I was aware of these changes consciously, but I began to institute new pedagogies (though I still don't think I knew that word). I found myself trying to enliven my courses (and enjoy my teaching more) by making them more interactive. At North Dakota I introduced hands-on research projects, using samples I'd collected in my field work, into my graduate paleoecology course, and I started pausing my paleontology lectures to undergraduate majors to allow them to brainstorm ideas in small groups. And the students seemed to like it! Students reported in focus groups, conducted through UND's "Small Group Instructional Diagnosis" teaching evaluation program, that these activities aided their learning. Still, in larger introductory courses, I forged on in lecture mode. I saw no reason to change my approach; evolution didn't seem to be an issue in North Dakota and I found no need for different teaching techniques when presenting this topic.

Then I moved back to the south! But I was still sheltered from run-ins with students on the topic of evolution because, with my reduced teaching load as department chair, I mostly worked with majors or graduate students. When I finally shed the administrative mantle in 2003 to return to the classroom full time, I began teaching regularly a new (to me) course, GLY 135 Prehistoric Life – a course premised on evolution. Most students in the course, which fulfills University Studies requirements (and now also the Thematic Transdisciplinary Cluster on Evolution), are not science majors. About 80% of them are religious (Kelley, 2012) and some are initially skeptical of evolution. Although few of these students will have careers in science, they may be asked to make public policy decisions related to evolution (e.g., regarding teaching of creationism). I wanted them to be prepared appropriately to make informed decisions. In addition, the course is popular among education majors, who may someday be science teachers. I wanted to reach these students, and I sensed that traditional lecturing would be a poor vehicle for overcoming resistance to learning about evolution, as students could easily "tune out" material perceived as offensive or at best memorize enough to pass a test without internalizing it. Thus I quickly realized it was time for a change in pedagogy (I think by then I had learned that word) if I wanted to reach my students. I needed to make the class more interactive, engaging, and thereby less threatening. But how to do this in a setting that was clearly intended to be a lecture-only course? How could I win these students over?

Winning them over. The cards were stacked against me. To accommodate as many students as possible, the course is taught in the only large (100 seat) classroom in DeLoach Hall. The class size and seating arrangement in DeLoach 114, with fixed, closely spaced rows (not to mention its own microclimate!), makes it challenging to institute pedagogies other than traditional lectures. Nevertheless I have been persistent and, I believe, inventive in overcoming these difficulties. As a model to others teaching controversial topics, I briefly summarize the pedagogical approaches I have developed over the past decade to create a "student-centered classroom" (another term I've learned recently that describes what I do), overcome the difficulties inherent in the traditional lecture format and venue imposed on this course, and engage students who may feel threatened by the course material. Although I developed my ideas independently, I have since discovered that they compare well with strategies now found in the pedagogical literature (see, e.g., Science Education Resource Center at http://serc.carleton.edu/

index.html). These approaches incorporate best practices in teaching any material but I have found them particularly important in engaging students on controversial topics such as evolution. To guide the reader through this essay, I've italicized the general principles that undergird my teaching (so if you don't want to read the details of how evolution relates to Johnny Depp, but are interested in best teaching practices in general, you can skim the highlighted points).

1) I believe that students are more willing to listen to information that challenges their preconceptions if it comes from someone they know and trust. Thus I consider it crucial to get to know my students and to let them know me. I begin this process the first day of class, by asking the students to write down and turn in something special about themselves – their "special thing," using as an example my own special thing ("I am completely obsessed with Johnny Depp"). Each day of class, I find a way to connect the lecture material to several students' special things, and if they are present on their special day they get an extra credit point – and applause from their class-mates! For instance, someone who skydives might have a special day when we study pterodactyl flight; discussing the tsunami that resulted from the (possibly) dinosaur-killing asteroid impact might provide a special day for a surfer. Although I also use the students' photos in the Seaport roster to help me recognize them and learn their names, knowing their special things really makes each student memorable to me. Since inventing my "special thing" technique, class attendance has increased (typically 80 – 90% of the class is present; Kelley, 2012), and students appear to be more engaged in the class and more comfortable interacting with each other and with me. I also make sure they get to know me. As a consequence, quite a few "friend" me on Facebook, or stop by my office to ask about my family (pictures of my kids seem to end up in a lot of my PowerPoints). Former students con-tinue to send me emails about new discoveries, or sometimes about Johnny Depp – or both! (Several former students were very excited to tell me of the recently discovered 500-million-year-old Kootenichela deppi, a scorpion-like creature with claws like Edward Scissorhands, named by another Depp fan!) I find that knowing each student in the class personally makes them more open to listening to me.

2) In order to engage students, I minimize the use of text on PowerPoint slides, primarily showing images of fossils or reconstructions of extinct or-ganisms. (I post PowerPoints on Blackboard Learn prior to each exam, but students cannot do well by skipping class and depending on the PowerPoints instead; active participation in class is required.) My lectures are interactive; the notes I write on the DeLoach 114 blackboard are often built from student

responses to my questions. For instance, students propose hypotheses (e.g., for the function of a particular anatomical structure of an extinct species) and draw predictions from them; I then provide the relevant data and as a class we discuss whether the data uphold the proposed hypotheses. Thus we construct the course content together. In doing so, I use the technique of "bending" their answers (Kenny and Wirth, 2009), building on incorrect or incomplete answers to reach the desired answer. This approach increases students' willingness to speak up in class and creates an atmosphere of mutual respect.

3) I make frequent use of collaborative learning such as "think-pair-share" or "write-pair-share" approaches (more terms I learned only after devising these activities myself), circulating as much as the room configuration will allow to answer any questions. I introduce such activities the first day of class. Rather than simply going over the syllabus, we dive into course content. I liken the course to a trip through time and, using the metaphor of a movie trailer, I show a PowerPoint "preview" featuring reconstructions of extinct organisms we will study. I then ask the class how we know about extinct organisms, and when someone mentions fossils I pass out a set of specimens. Students break into groups, introduce themselves to their neighbors, and try to determine whether their group's specimen is a fossil or not, and if it is not, what characteristics of fossils it displays. Included are actual fossils and an assortment of non-fossils that have some traits of fossils (e.g., modern sea shells, arrowheads, a paperweight containing Guinness beer, a plaster-of-Paris imprint of my son's hand at age 3). I then guide a discussion involving the whole class, in which we construct a definition of fossils. This activity allows us to begin to get to know each other, sets a pedagogical tone for the course, and engages students in the material. What's more, students are introduced to real fossils–tangible evidence of evolution.

4) Some controversial topics such as evolution may seem abstruse to students. Thus, making complex ideas tangible is key. Although the course has no separate laboratory section, I consider it important for students to have hands-on experience with fossils in order to understand life's evolution. At least one class a semester is thus held as a lab, in which students collaborate to examine specimens and answer questions about fossil preservation, classification, and life mode. Additional brief "minilabs" are interspersed throughout the semester, often involving specimens passed around the classroom. A student who has held a long-extinct trilobite in his or her hands has a more difficult time arguing that life hasn't changed through time!

5) In order to make concepts tangible, I also employ a variety of class demonstrations and enactments of concepts, giving student volunteers

extra credit for their participation. This approach maintains interest and helps students better understand and remember what we are studying. For instance, in the "dance of DNA," students pretend to be different nucleotide molecules and team up to build chains of amino acids portrayed by other students. When we study horse evolution, I want students to understand how the change from forest to grasslands produced a natural selective advantage for increased speed and hence evolutionary loss of toes. One student portrays an early horse attempting to escape another student portraying an archaic predator. The "horse" is able to hide when classmates are standing up, pretending to be trees. But when the rest of the class sits down, the victim is exposed and easily caught by the "predator" – especially when I ask the victim to put my husband's wooden shoes on over her own shoes (mimicking the unwieldy foot construction of early multi-toed horses). In addition, I am not averse to performing my own demonstrations. (All that laughter coming from my classroom? I may be lying on a table, pretending to be an osteolepiform fish evolving into a tetrapod, or running across the room portraying a primordial bird taking to the air.) Students seem to enjoy having an atmosphere of play in the classroom, which enhances their willingness to invest in the course content – even for a controversial topic. I enjoy it too!

Handling the controversy. All these approaches tend to produce a more receptive audience and an improved climate for teaching a controversial subject. However, careful handling of a topic that may be perceived as controversial is equally important. In teaching evolution, my goal is to proceed with sensitivity and integrity.

To teach a controversial topic with both sensitivity and integrity, a firm conceptual foundation must be prepared. In teaching evolution, I find it important to lay the foundation of what fossils are and how they are preserved. Students thus learn that fossils provide an incomplete picture of past life (and thus cannot be expected to show infinitely graded sequences of transitional forms between groups), yet one that is rich enough to document evolution. Also essential is familiarity with how geologists "tell time" and in particular are able to place fossils and geological events in chronological order. (I indulge my Johnny Depp fetish here, as we model geologic time-telling by putting his films in chronological order.)

Given this foundation, which typically is not perceived as threatening (yet!), I then proceed to introduce the topic of evolution. My initial step is to acknowledge that controversy exists and to define what is controversial. I state that evolution is not scientifically controversial, but that it is perceived by some as conflicting with their faith. Thus the controversy is societal rather than scientific. I also stress the point that evolution and religion need not conflict (although admittedly evolution and certain religious beliefs do conflict) by sharing my personal perspective. I state that I am the wife of a Presbyterian minister; for more than 35 years I have taught Bible study on Sunday and evolution during the week and find no conflict (Kelley, 2000, 2009). This one-sentence statement defuses hostility and creates an atmosphere of tolerance that gets students to listen to what I have to say about evolution. (Although my perspective is unusual, it is not unique; many scientists have written about their faith and could be cited, along with pro-evolution statements from religious denominations, to make the same point.) In general, students seem relieved to hear I am not expecting them to renounce their faith by taking this course! (see also Antolin & Herbers, 2001; Wise, 2001). They appear comfortable with the course boundaries I then set: this is a science class in which we will restrict our discussions to scientific explanations.

To reinforce the idea that science and religion need not conflict, we then undertake a "think-pair-share" exercise in which students consider whether a set of statements I provide represent science or not, and further whether they represent fact, theory, or "something else" (e.g., as The Dude says in The Big Lebowski, "well, that's just, like, your opinion, man"). As in discussing any controversial topic, I consider it important to clear up any misconceptions regarding terminology; in this case, the terms "fact," "hypothesis," "theory," and "science" in particular are frequently misunderstood. Our discussion leads to a concept of science as a distinct way of understanding the natural world by testing hypotheses (and thus is restricted to natural explanations, as only they are testable). Unlike religion, it is incapable of addressing questions about the supernatural; scientific ideas must always be open to testing.

We then go on to discuss the meanings of "evolution" and whether they are fact or theory (with new understanding of what is meant by those terms). Change in life through time is a fact, observable around us today and in historic time as well as in the fossil record; we review this evidence. Descent with modification is an explanation for change in life through time and thus a theory (an explanation that has been tested repeatedly and confirmed). I ask students to "think-pair-share" predictions based on this theory (e.g., relating to similarities among living organisms or to transitional fossils). I anticipate and confirm their predictions with examples presented by PowerPoint, thus enabling them to "buy into" this theory. Finally, we discuss yet another meaning of evolution – mechanisms for descent with modification. We review the process of inheritance and development (hence the "dance of DNA"), sources of variation, and how natural selection occurs.

Throughout this discussion I maintain a sense of humor and playfulness, using photos of my daughter (pretty much my clone) to demonstrate inheritance and of my 6'6" son, towering over pedestrians on a crowded street in China, to demonstrate genetic variation. Appropriate use of humor also aids in defusing hostility.

At the conclusion of this evolution unit, I give students a chance to express their views about evolution in writing. I ask them to write a reflection paper in response to the Geological Society of America's position statement, "Teaching Evolution" (which I helped draft a decade ago). Students are informed in advance that they will receive full credit, regardless of the opinions expressed, if they write a thoughtful essay. Most students take the assignment seriously and turn in a few pages of candid reflection. (I think they are encouraged by our discussion delineating the boundaries of science and religion and the fact that I am forthright in stating my personal perspective.) The process of writing helps students consider seriously the material we have just discussed and formulate their own views. Although some students only consider the scientific, educational, and/or political aspects of teaching evolution, most make some comments about their religious perspectives. Over the years, about 80% of students have indicated they are religious but find evolution compatible with their faith. The other 20% are usually equally divided between those who lack a religious background and/ or consider themselves atheists or agnostics, and those who reject some aspect of evolution for religious reasons. This assignment assures such students that their religious beliefs are respected. It also fends off potential hostility during class; students have a more reasoned view after reflection and recognize that conflict is not inherent. I grade each essay and return comments, correcting any misconceptions about science or religion (e.g., "I'm a Catholic, so I can't believe in evolution"). However, I do not criticize their personal views. I also invite students to meet with me individually if they wish to discuss any topics beyond the scope of the course. One or more students take advantage of the offer each semester, and sometimes the dialog continues beyond semester's end.

We spend the remainder of the course tracing the history of life through the past 3.5 billion years. Evolutionary thought is thus reinforced on a daily basis, as we examine the rich evolutionary sequences represented by the fossil record of early limbed animals, dinosaurs and birds, primitive mammals, whales, horses, and humans, among others, as well as the processes that shaped these transitions.

I take heart in the fact that my approach to teaching evolution has never been met with confrontation inside or outside of class. Although some students still may not accept evolution as the scientific explanation for the history of life, they come to recognize that evolution is not a synonym for atheism and that science and religion provide valid and complementary ways of knowing. They no longer feel threatened by the findings of science.

So, YES, it is possible to teach a controversial topic in a way that edifies rather than alienates students. The task may seem a bit intimidating at first but, armed with the proper pedagogies in addition to the correct information, you too can teach your controversial topic with sensitivity and integrity. After all, UNCW faculty are Seahawks and our motto is "Darc to Soar." The sky's the limit!

ACKNOWLEDGMENTS

Caroline Clements first spurred my thinking about this topic in 2005 when she asked me give a Center for Teaching Excellence presentation on teaching controversial issues. The ideas presented here were further developed during my service as a National Association of Geoscience Teachers Distinguished Speaker and as the Paleontological Society's Distinguished Lecturer on Evolution and Society. My exploration of the pedagogical literature was fostered by participating in the Paleontological Society's topical session and resultant volume on Teaching Paleontology in the 21st Century, edited by Peg Yacobucci and Rowan Lockwood. Two anonymous reviewers provided comments that helped fine-tune the manuscript. I thank Diana Ashe for inviting me to contribute to Best Practices in University Teaching and for guiding my manuscript into print.

REFERENCES

Antolin, M. F., & Herbers, J. M. (2001). Perspective: Evolution's struggle for existence in American's public schools. *Evolution, 55,* 2379-2388.

Dobzhansky, T. (1973). Nothing in biology makes any sense except in the light of evolution. *American Biology Teacher, 35,* 125-29.

Kelley, P.H. (2000). Studying evolution and keeping the faith. *Geotimes, 45,* 22-25.

Kelley, P.H. (2009). Teaching evolution during the week and bible study on Sunday: Perspectives on science, religion, and intelligent design. In J. S. Schneiderman & W. D. Allmon (Eds.), *For the Rock Record: Geologists On Intelligent Design Creationism* (pp. 163-179). Berkeley, CA: University of California Press.

Kelley, P.H. (2012). Strategies for teaching evolution in a high-enrollment introductory paleontology course for non-science majors. In M. M. Yacobucci & R. Lockwood (Eds.), *Teaching Paleontology in the 21st Century* (pp. 77-92). Paleontological Society.

Kenny, R. F., & Wirth, J. (2009). Implementing participatory, constructivist learning experiences through best practices in live interactive performance. *The Journal of Effective Teaching 9,* 34-47.

Wise, D.U. (2001). Creationism's propaganda assault on deep time and evolution. *Journal of Geoscience Education, 49,* 30-35.

HERBERT BERG
DEPARTMENT OF PHILOSOPHY AND RELIGION
INTERNATIONAL STUDIES

Atheism as a Foundation for Effective Pedagogy in Religious Studies

> "I contend that we are both atheists. I just believe
> in one fewer god than you do."
> —Stephen F. Roberts

For many scholars and students of religion it seems odd, misguided, perhaps even misanthropic to suggest that one would teach religion from the perspective of an atheist. After all, is not the presence of sacred or transcendent realities the *raison d'être* of Religious Studies as a discipline? They might advocate, therefore, that it would be better either to treat all such "sacred" things as equally true, or at least to remain neutral on the question of the existence of the various gods and other transcendent realities. By looking at these three approaches, I will show that atheism is no more problematic as a foundation for an Introduction to Religion or a tradition-based course than the other two are. Furthermore, by drawing a distinction between theoretical and practical atheism, I will argue that, even if one is not an atheist, one should, nevertheless, employ an *atheistic* approach when teaching *about* religion in a secular institution—that is, one should teach as though one were an atheist.

Before proceeding, several preliminaries need to be discussed. First, in emphasizing "teaching *about* religion" as against "teaching religion," I am assuming that whatever else the study of religion is, it is decidedly not an explicitly theological activity. Furthermore, I maintain that the purpose of a university course on religion is not simply to report what a particular group of people say, do, and believe. This reporting is necessary, for it is the data we use for the primary purpose: to engage in critical analysis. Critical analysis is central to all scholarly activities, including religious studies, and, at the very least, it requires us to evaluate and attempt to *explain* our data. Without this component, religious studies courses are little more than religion appreciation courses. Second, my goal here is not to argue whether or not God (or other gods and realities) exist. Such a task is irrelevant and perhaps even impossible. Rather, I am arguing that an atheistic approach is more appropriate and less problematic in the classroom than other approaches. Third, I am using the broadest definition of atheism: it is not simply a belief in the non-existence of God (the one(s) associated with Judaism, Christianity, Islam, Bahá'í Faith, and so forth). It also assumes not only the non-existence of all other gods, goddesses, and spirits (for example, Manitou, Shiva, Aphrodite, Satan, and even the New Age-y "Spirit"), but also the non-existence of the various ultimate realities (for example, Brahman, Nirvana, Buddha Consciousness, Tao, and even the various forms of Fate). Thus, "god" is just a convenient, albeit ethnocentric, label for all of those things—beings, entities, principles, consciousnesses, and "non-realities" that common sense (but little else) suggests are "religious." Fourth, I assume that religion is not *sui generis*. At a theoretical level, this is an important assumption, for one could argue that it biases me in favor of the atheistic approach. However, at a practical level even those who believe religion is *sui generis* will have no choice but *teach* religion as non-*sui generis*. And so, it is for primarily practical considerations, not theoretical ones, that I support the use of an atheistic approach in teaching religious studies.

The Alternatives

There are three main stances teachers can adopt when teaching a course about religion. (1) Some teachers prefer not to say if gods exist. That is, they remain neutral about the truth claims of religions. (2) Some teachers similarly, but more generously, speak of all religions as equally true. A less generous version maintains that only one particular religion is true. And (3), some teachers hold that they are all equally false—the atheist position. Each of these approaches has some merit in a university setting. However, each is also problematic in theory and pedagogically dangerous in practice. An examination of these merits, problems, and dangers of each shows that the atheistic approach is the best option.

Remaining neutral is the natural instinct for many scholars of religion, especially in the United States where teachers as members of state (or state-funded) institutions are bound by the First Amendment's "Congress shall make no law respecting an establishment of religion, or prohibiting the free exercise thereof." Moreover, it seems in line with traditional academic virtue of being objective, or the more recent virtues of being liberal and pluralistic. At a purely practical level, the danger of trying to remain neutral is its inherent dishonesty, except, perhaps, for agnostics. However, rare indeed is the scholar of religion (or any other person for that matter) who is completely devoid of conviction on a particular religious tradition or religion in general. And students are surprisingly adroit at spotting when we are advocating positions that we ourselves do not hold. More importantly, there are several theoretical problems with this approach, some of which touch on important debates within the study of religion. Scholars of religion normally have a working definition of religion; these definitions explicitly or implicitly make some claim about the nature of religion. William E. Arnal argues, "no statement about what religion *is* can avoid at least partially *explaining* what religion *does*, where it comes from, and how it works" (Arnal, 2000, p.22). Thus, maintaining absolute neutrality is impossible. However, one might argue that absolute neutrality is not necessary—just neutrality with regard to the truth claims made by people regarding experiences, concepts, activities, social structures, etc., that they deem to be "religious." Such a neutrality is feasible, perhaps even desirable, but only if one restricts oneself to description. Any (reductionist) explanation makes neutrality about such claims impossible. Perhaps several mutually contradictory definitions of religion can be employed—or ones so vague and inclusive so as to be utterly devoid of pedagogical value. Consequently, neutrality about religious truth claims is tantamount to restricting oneself to description or to treating all religions as equally true. Therefore, this neutrality, whether based on a fear of offending students or of violating some liberal agenda, tends to lead to a course devoid of critical approach.

The second approach maintains that all religions are true. It does not privilege one religion over the others, nor does it feign neutrality; many scholars of religion believe that all religions do, in fact, express the same ultimate truth, or, in more relativist terms, that everyone's truth claims are equally valid. Either way, the different religions are simply different paths up the same mountain. Or expressed differently, all religions are based on the human reaction to, or interaction with, the sacred or holy—something understood to be ultimate, mysterious, and awesome (Otto, 1928). This approach also has the advantage of fitting well with our pluralistic, cosmopolitan values, but it suffers from more serious problems. First, it is either overtly or covertly theological through its use of "sacred" or "holy" as a *sui generis* category. To believe that Yahweh is Allah, is Marduk, is Buddha Consciousness, etc. or to assume that each is a different cultural expression

BEST PRACTICES IN UNIVERSITY TEACHING

of "the Sacred" is really just a modern variation of pantheistic or monistic (mono)theism. Thus, to say that all religions are true is no less theological than to say that only one is true. (At least on this one point, the atheist and the fundamentalist find some common ground.)[1] This type of missionary or theological activity is harmful to the academic study of religion and hardly justifies its advantage of being politically correct. Furthermore, the approach is dangerously naïve. Only by being incredibly inclusive and uncritical can the diverse practices, beliefs, social structures, etc. of different cultures be conflated into this one category. Gullibility is certainly not something we should be inculcating in our students. In other words, it is naïve because we must assume what we are trying to prove: We can only see the same "sacred" behind all these "religious" things by assuming it is there. Finally, this approach inhibits analysis as all theological positions do. There is still one area that cannot be analyzed: "the Sacred," which is defined as ultimately mysterious and unknowable.

As for the equally popular variation of advocating one particular religion such as Christianity, Western Buddhism, or New Age-y spiritualism (to name those that seem to me the most prevalent within the discipline), it has the lone advantage of at least being honest and clear about its assumptions and biases and so might be appropriate in a university or college that has a specific religious or denominational allegiance. Obviously, the greatest problem is that a course with this approach will be overtly theological. The definition of religion may be reduced to Christianity (for example); the study of religion is then merely the study of *a* religion and (at best) the activities of a lot of misguided people. Such an apologetic approach is, therefore, also dishonest in that it privileges one religious tradition while subjecting all others to criticism. In addition to this inconsistency, there exists a danger that any student who examines that privileged religion too critically might be discouraged from so doing or even be accused of blasphemy. Also, the study of religion will come far too close to some sort of missionary or, at least, apologetic activity. In so doing, it weakens the credibility of the academic study of religion. Many colleagues outside of the study of religion still do not see the distinction between theology and the study of religion (or, "teaching religion" versus "teaching *about* religion"). This approach, therefore, is a giant step backwards.

---

1 See, for example, John Hick who uses "… our Christian term, God, to refer to the ultimate Reality to which, as I conceive, the great religious traditions constitute different human responses." Hick, "The Non-Absoluteness of Christianity," in *The Myth of Christian Uniqueness*, edited by John Hick and Paul F. Knitter (Maryknoll: Orbis Books, 1987), p. 34

The Atheistic Approach

This then leaves the atheistic approach. Like the other approaches, it is problematic theoretically. However, more practical considerations, such as the nature of academia and the nature of things "religious," make it the only viable and effective approach.

Theoretically, the atheistic approach to the study of religion has an inherent contradiction. As Arnal points out, "any effort to define religion … as a human entity … that is meaningfully distinct from other types of human cultural production, entails an implication or assumption that religion is, in fact, *sui generis*" (Arnal, 2000, p.30). Therefore, to teach a course about *religion* is to invoke "specific and specifically *theological* assumptions" (Arnal, 2000, p.30). To approach such an implicitly theological endeavor atheistically, is oxymoronic. Therefore, if even teaching *about* religion is a theological enterprise, then in a secular institution, religion should not be taught (regardless of the approach used). Be that as it may, Departments of Religious Studies and Religion courses are institutional realities, and, as such, this theoretical critique, though valid, is moot. Courses on religion are and will continue to be taught. The only practical question which remains is, "What approach is to be used?"

Also, many scholars of religion see the atheistic approach as reductionist. In the broad sense of the term, yes, many atheistic theories of religion are reductionist. E.B. Tylor's theory reduces religion to simple mental assent (to a belief in spiritual beings). Emile Durkheim reduces religion to its social functions. Michael Persinger reduces religion to its biological functions. And, Sigmund Freud reduces religion to its psychological functions. One need not dwell on this form of the critique since one could simply argue that each perspective addresses some aspect of the phenomena we describe as "religious." The sharper critique is that the atheistic approach is reductionist in a more narrow sense: The atheist leaves out the "sacred" (or, "God")—the key element that makes something "religious." Of course, it is only reductionism if the atheist is wrong (a notion which most atheists probably do not seriously consider). However, to take this critique more seriously, one might liken an atheist teaching religion to a deaf person teaching music or a blind person teaching art appreciation. But this analogy is misleading. Music and art can be reproduced in the classroom through recordings and images. God and/or the Sacred cannot. The one thing we cannot bring into the classroom is the eternal, the transcendent, the ineffable, the absolute. We cannot bring in a bucket of the Sacred, give the Olympians a survey, make Thor run through a maze, give God an MRI, etc. That is, if one describes something as transcendent, then, by definition, there is no way to measure or examine it the way we would "ordinary" human activities. As A.J. Ayer has argued, "no sentence which purports to describe the nature of a transcendent god can possess any literal significance" (Ayer, 1946, p. 114-118). What we can study, however, are the activities (whether mental, verbal, physical, or social) of humans, which they ascribe to something to which we have no objective access. Therefore, if we are to be intellectually honest, we must at the very least, be practical atheists. That is to say, we are "without god" in the classroom because the gods are not (and cannot be) with us in the classroom. The atheistic approach, therefore, is unavoidable—even were we to think of religion as *sui generis*. The only question is whether one is willing to obscure the facts by employing terminology such as "Sacred" and accusations such as "reductionist."

There are a few dangers associated with the atheistic approach, as well. Atheists can also be missionaries, that is, advocating a particular belief. This danger can be obviated by presenting other perspectives and by making a clear distinction between teaching from an "atheistic approach" and "teaching atheism." A second danger is that of alienating religious students (both those who belong to one of the more traditional religions and those who attempt to distance themselves from institutional religion and term themselves as "spiritual"). Yet, all approaches risk alienating some students. Unless teaching has been reduced to a popularity contest, this hardly constitutes a major concern. The only remaining practical reason not to use an atheistic approach is fear. This fear might be of one's place in the afterlife, but I suspect it has more to do with that caused by colleagues, students, and even the community. Anyone who has even a modicum of critical analysis in their religion courses has probably been labeled an atheist or unbeliever. This labeling is not uncommon from students, but even colleagues and the community around the university can express concern about "atheists teaching religion." If this hostility is not life-threatening or career-hampering, then it should not be used as an excuse to shy away from the atheistic approach.

These dangers are counterbalanced by several advantages of atheistic approach. If asked, "Why are people religious?" a non-atheist might say because we have an innate longing for or connection to God, the sacred, etc. However, the atheist is confronted by the fact that most of humanity, all around the world and for all of its recorded history, has been "religious." Thus, the teacher who uses an atheistic approach must be able to explain why so many people orient their lives around nonexistent things (though "religion" hardly has a monopoly on such entities). The approach, therefore, requires the teacher to have a greater sophistication in theories of religion; s/he must know the theories and must be able to teach them. While this requirement is a burden, I doubt very many people would want to advocate a different approach simply because it requires less intelligence and less effort. In fact, the requirement turns out to be pedagogically advantageous. Even most religious students can be drawn into an atheistic approach by pointing out that they are "atheists" with regard to all of the religions to which they do not belong. Even fundamentalist Christian students want to be able to explain why Muslims and Buddhists believe what they do. This, I tell them, is where theories of religion might prove useful. The atheistic approach also has the merits of being in agreement with the worldview of a secular institution. A "secular education" means an education free from the domination or influence of (a) religion. Right or wrong, a secular university course (even in religion) is the same as "a-theism," (i.e. "without god"). Thus, even if one could convincingly argue that the approach that assumes the truth claims of one or all religions is better, ultimately it is irrelevant at a secular university. That is not to say that the atheistic approach is somehow unbiased; that would be far too naïve. But the atheist agenda has the virtue of being aligned most closely with what we do in the classroom of a secular university. Should the mission statements of universities and colleges change to include inculcating spirituality, Christianity, the Zulu religion, etc. into our students, then, indeed, the other approaches might be better suited. Until that happens we must—if not at a theoretical level, then at a practical level—be atheists (or atheistic) in the classroom.

Conclusion

Speaking of "practical," how does this atheistic approach play out in the classroom of my PAR 230: Judaism, Christianity, and Islam course? The following three examples show how "atheistic" explanation follows description. That is to say, religious beliefs, practices, institutions, and so forth are first accurately described in a way that believers would recognize, but then they are critically analyzed. (1) I demonstrate using primary sources that most Muslims believe that the deity that they worship, Allah, is the same as the deity worshipped by Christians and the deity worshipped by Jews.[2] For

2 Although both Christians and Jews generally assume they worship the same God, this is merely a narrower version of the approach that assumes all religions are true. This theological assumption need not be addressed directly with students. Consistently using phrases such as "the Jewish God" and "the Christian God" in place of "God" whenever the traditions are being compared is usually enough for students to recognize that the conceptions of these entities differ. Not surprisingly, most of my non-Muslim undergraduate students already distinguish "the Muslim God" from their "Lord." If the issue arises, all I need do is highlight that the Jewish monotheism differs far more from Christian Trinitarian monotheism than it does

Muslims, the Qur'an's references to many biblical characters including Adam, Abraham, Moses, David, and Jesus are present because they all interacted with the same deity. In fact, they are all considered prophets of Islam. This belief is data to be analyzed, but it is not an explanation for their presence in the Qur'an. The explanation is far more mundane and ordinary; Islam was born in a Judeo-Christian (probably sectarian) milieu, evidence for which comes from Islamic texts themselves. (2) For Christians, the gospels are usually seen as four independent and corroborating historical accounts of the life of Jesus. But the similarities indicate textual dependence, not independent accounts. Moreover, those accounts are not historical texts, but mythic ones, as noted in Arnal (2005):

> The Gospel of Mark, for example, is a narrative that includes a cast of characters comprising, inter alia, God, a son of God, angels, the devil, demons, holy spirits, evil spirits, and what seem to be the ghosts of Moses and Elijah. It is a story that features miraculous healings and exorcisms, as well as walking on water, feeding thousands of people with a handful of loaves and fishes (twice!), face-to-face conversations between people who lived centuries apart, spooky prognostications, trees withering at Jesus' simple command, a sun darkening in the middle of the day, and a temple curtain miraculously tearing itself in half. (p. 75-76)

The texts are a historical source for what early Christians believed, but to view the texts as sources for the historical Jesus is to quest after a figure in whom the texts have no interest. (3) For Jews, the biblical account of their descent from Noah and his son Shem to Abraham, Isaac, Jacob (or Israel) is an example of the Jewish God's providence and an explanation for their divine election as the Chosen People. Without any corroborating textual, archeological, or genetic evidence, the historicity of the genealogy or the figures mentioned within it cannot be determined. That Noah cursed his grandson Canaan (and his descendants) to perpetual slavery,[3] that Abraham disinherited his son Ishmael whose descendants lived in the Desert of Paran

---

from Muslim monotheism, at which point they usually recognize the conceptual differences between these deities.

3 The Curse of Ham (a misnomer since it was his son Canaan who was cursed) can be used to show how stories serve ideological purposes. During the 18th and 19th centuries, black Africans were identified as the "sons of Ham," thus justifying the slave trade. When I ask students what they think of this use of the story, they are rightly disgusted and quickly suggested it was misused for ideological purposes—though not in those words. It is then that I point out that the original story was most likely first circulated just when the Israelites were in political competition with the Canaanites.

(often identified as Sinai), that Abraham's nephew Lot's sons (or grandsons) Ammon and Moab were the product of incest, that Isaac gave his birthright to the younger son Jacob instead of Esau, the progenitor of the Edom make it very clear that the genealogy reflects the political situation roughly a millennium and half later when the Israelite kingdom found itself surrounded by fellow Semitic Canaanites, Ammonites, Moabites, and Edomites. The ideology is fairly obvious: They might be similar peoples, but the sins of their fathers ensured that the Israelites could claim superiority. For a religious studies instructor to avoid or even downplay these reductionist or "atheistic" explanations for the sake of reverence would be simply to reproduce theology in the guise of scholarship. It would exempt one of the most unique and influential important aspects of the human experience from critical thought.

Ultimately, atheism, like theism, is a belief. Since it is impossible to teach about religion from a completely neutral point of view, teachers are forced to privilege a view that would be seen by those who do not share that view as advocating a particular belief. The issue is, therefore, reduced to selecting the approach which is best suited to teaching about religion in the university setting. I have argued that *all* approaches are *theoretically* problematic: those that assume the truth of one or all religions, those that assume their falsity, and those that attempt to remain neutral. However, it is the *practical* reasons (that is, the purpose of the academic enterprise, the very definition of the word "religion," the definition of "transcendence," and the nature of what we do within secular universities) that make the atheistic approach the most academically appropriate and pedagogically effective approach when teaching about religion. As long as critical thought remains more important than reverence,[4] even the agnostic and theist (whether a monotheist or pantheist) should take the stance of an atheist in the classroom.

---

4 "Reverence is a religious, and not a scholarly virtue. When good manners and good conscience cannot be reconciled, the demands of the latter ought to prevail." Bruce Lincoln, "Theses on Method," *Method & Theory in the Study of Religion* 8.3 (1996): 225-227.

REFERENCES

Arnal, W. E. (2000). Definition. In W. Braun & R. McCutcheon (Eds.), *Guide to the study of religion* (pp. 21-34). New York: Cassell.

Otto, R. (1928). *The idea of the holy: An inquiry into the non-rational Factor in the idea of the divine and its relation to the rational* (J. W. Harvey, Trans.). London: Oxford University Press. (Original work published, 1923).

Ayer, A. (1946). *Language truth and logic.* New York: Dover Publications.

Arnal, W. E. (2005). *The symbolic Jesus: Historical scholarship, Judaism and the construction of contemporary identity.* London: Equinox.

Lincoln, B. (1996). Theses on method. *Method & Theory in the Study of Religion*, 8(3), 225-227.

Hick, J. (1987). The non-absoluteness of Christianity. In J. Hick & P. F. Knitter (Eds.), *The myth of Christian uniqueness* (pp. 16 -36). Maryknoll: Orbis Books.

CAROL PILGRIM
DEPARTMENT OF PSYCHOLOGY

On Shaping Student Behavior...and Being Shaped by Student Behavior

A typical three-credit university course meets for a total time of approximately forty hours. Formally then, the instructor has a basic "work week" (don't we wish!) in which to have some lasting impact on her or his students. That's not much time. Teaching can be a tremendously exacting responsibility.

And the challenge is not eased by the seemingly elusive nature of our enterprise. By many accounts, teaching would appear to be one of those "we-know-it-when-we-see-it" sorts of phenomena – a view of precious little solace to a novice instructor, faced with a full teaching load for the first time, or even a veteran instructor, faced with a full teaching load for the umpteenth time. Consider the helpful guidance provided by these "job descriptions," taken from The American Heritage Dictionary, as one convenient reference. (It is hardly unique.) To teach is defined as follows: to impart knowledge or give instruction to, to advocate or preach. And a teacher is one who does these things. Not much help there as to what or how. To educate is defined similarly: to provide with information; to provide with knowledge. And an educator is one trained to do so. It gets worse from there. A listed synonym is pedagogue, defined as: [an] educator; one who instructs in a pedantic or dogmatic manner, with pedantic defined in turn as: characterized by a narrow, often ostentatious, concern for book learning and formal rules. And pedant as: one who pays undue attention to book learning and formal rules without having an understanding or experience of practical affairs. I felt it best to stop the exercise at this point.

Aside from their less-than-flattering connotations about our chosen profession, what is striking about these definitions of teaching (and the many others like them) is the near-universal omission of any mention of students. An alternative view, however, and the crux of this essay, involves a definition of teaching explicitly in terms of student behavior. (For further introduction to this view, see Skinner's Technology of Teaching, 1968, or Keller's Pedagogue's Progress, 1982.) By this view, teaching includes, and is limited to, any activity that facilitates improvements in what a student says or does. While simple on the surface, this basic functional definition can have tremendous implications for an approach to teaching. Certainly it has for my own practices.

At the most general level, one could argue that there are two basic approaches to teaching. (Most of us likely employ some of each, whether by accident or design.) One strategy could be described as the "learn or else" approach, in which the teacher presents material and then holds the student responsible for its mastery. This approach has considerable history on its side, but has been known to result in unfortunate side effects, as a number of students do, indeed, encounter the "or else." The alternative strategy, possibly less often considered at a formal level, places more responsibility on the teacher in providing for the student to achieve mastery. Rather than function simply as a presenter of information (although that's required, too), the teacher is responsible for the architecture of the learning experience. Known technically as "shaping," this approach represents a method by which behavior is changed in a series of steps from an initial, often relatively crude or unsophisticated performance, toward a specified target performance. At each step, those behaviors that most closely approximate the target (i.e., the best of the current lot) are reinforced, and each successive step involves a slightly more stringent criterion for reinforcement, based on the best approximations from the previous step. In this manner, increasingly sophisticated performances can be gradually molded with the learner's successful advances.

Shaping has proven tremendously effective in promoting behavior change in a wide array of circumstances, including the college classroom. Indeed, empirical analysis, assessment, and application of shaping procedures have been ongoing for more than sixty years now in behavioral psychology, in studies ranging from carefully controlled laboratory experiments (e.g., Bernstein & Wolff, 1964; Eckerman, Hienz, Stern, & Kowlowitz, 1980; Galbica, 1994; Levin & Shapiro, 1962; Pear & Legris, 1987; Platt, 1979; Stokes & Balsam, 1991) to evaluations involving socially significant settings and targets (e.g., Agras, Leitenberg, & Barlow, 1968; Athens, Vollmer, &

St. Peter Pipkin, 2007; Budzynski & Stoyva, 1969; Horncr, 1971; Howie & Woods, 1982; Scott, Scot, & Goldwater, 1997; Sepler & Myers, 1978; Smeets, Lancioni, Ball, & Oliva, 1985). At a more casual level of implementation, shaping approaches are in some ways ubiquitous, if often poorly applied. Common aphorisms such as "One step at a time," "Rome wasn't built in a day," and "You have to learn to walk before you can run" capture the spirit, if not the science, behind the shaping strategy. Despite its common-sense appeal, however, several critical dimensions of a good shaping program must be carefully executed in order to be successful. In what follows, these dimensions will be described in the context of a university course.

Finding a starting point. A key element of shaping is that it builds on a student's current skill level. This implies that teaching any new concept or line of inquiry must necessarily begin with something the learner already understands. In a classroom setting, where beginning levels can be wildly disparate, there may be no such thing as starting too simply when introducing a new topic. By way of example, I have often taught a senior-level capstone course in the undergraduate psychology curriculum, on learning and behavior analysis. My first lecture deals with unadorned definition of the basic terms stimulus and response. Every one of my students will have heard and used these terms hundreds of times in prerequisite courses. Many will still be confused about them. It is essential to establish some common ground to build on before proceeding.

In most cases, it's not necessary to dwell on preliminaries for long, but neglecting careful consideration of an appropriate starting point can undermine even the most erudite of lecturers. Student commentary on instructors and their teaching style can be enlightening on this point. On more than one occasion, I've been offered the following observation: "Professor X is so brilliant." The evidence? "I don't understand a single word he says!" Professor X may well be remarkable, and along many dimensions, but, by this view, teaching isn't one of them. Effective teachers make contact with their student's current repertoire, or little behavior change can follow.

This basic premise provides an underlying structure in designing each step of my course presentation. For example, I find it useful to begin every lecture by reminding my students of what they already know about the topic at hand. Even a brief review can serve multiple purposes, reinforcing the student's developing understanding and reestablishing a foundation and a framework for the new material to be presented. It might be nice to assume that students come to each class prepared to move forward from exactly the point where we left off in the previous lecture, but ... alas. And while review of relevant background is hardly a novel suggestion for a university course, considering the review as a mechanism for guiding students to an effective starting point on which to build may allow refinements that can contribute to particular course goals.

Generating student behavior. This consideration deserves two stars. It's doubly important in the context of college teaching for reasons described below, but a second key principle of the present approach is that behavior must occur before it can be shaped. As a corollary of this principle, the more behavior, the more opportunity for the sorts of feedback necessary to strengthen and refine the student's progress. Thus, a critical skill for effective teaching involves getting students to do something more than simply sit and attempt to "soak it up." (The sponge technique has never been a very good model of learning.) For a perspective that views learning as demonstrable student behavior change, the importance of active participation by students cannot be overemphasized. This implies that student involvement deserves careful consideration in all phases of course design.

Fortunately, student involvement can be scheduled into a course in a myriad of meaningful ways. Labs, writing assignments, and structured discussions are clear examples. In the senior capstone course described earlier, I've had good luck with the following arrangement. On the day of each scheduled quiz (of which there are many – more behavior), students are required to turn in questions reflecting any uncertainties about the as-signed material. These questions are graded for quality and thoughtfulness and are used as the basis for a class review. The class is organized into small groups, each of which is responsible for formulating answers to a subset of their classmates' questions. Following the small group discussions, the students present their answers to the class as a whole. Each student in the class takes part in these presentations, and any unclear points are discussed further by the class, with a liberal dose of commentary from the instructor. This review requires students to deal substantively with the course content, going beyond reading and listening to discussing and producing their own mini-lessons, intended not simply to repeat but rather to clarify an issue. Effective peer modeling and feedback are provided throughout the exchange, and I have the opportunity with each individual student to emphasize points made well (i.e., to reinforce), to ask for more (i.e., to raise the criteria), and to clarify as needed. Finally, by timing the quiz to immediately follow the presentations, close attention to the discussion is ensured throughout the several steps of the process.

Even in large lecture courses, opportunities for active participation can be programmed effectively and needn't take time away from the lesson. A lecture laced with well-timed closed-end questions (e.g.," Do these data support theory X?") can keep students responding and progressing as the lesson does. My students are asked to give "thumbs-up/thumbs-down" votes at strategic points throughout the lecture. The flow of the lecture is not disrupted, each student must respond, and I get a clear indication of whether to expand on a point or proceed to the next one. In a somewhat more elaborate version of this strategy, a colleague at another university equips his students with a fan of five colored paper strips, one color for each answer, A through E, in a multiple-choice format. He presents multiple-choice questions throughout his lectures, and asks for an immediate response from each student. Of course, higher tech versions of this technique are now available in the form of handheld clickers, available through many textbook companies. These systems provide for some "gadget appeal" and for the ability to present data on responses from the class as a whole (which may or may not be useful), but they lose the possibly critical accountability that comes with the instructor having direct access to each individual's response.

Of course, frequent quizzes or tests will also generate a good deal of behavior, if they figure in to the student's course grade. Although it might sound like more "or else," students tend to respond favorably because small units of material are manageable and can leave them prepared for the next unit to come. Even requiring that students distill key points from a lecture on their own, rather than providing handouts of PowerPoint presentations, demands some level of involvement. Having students turn in class notes or outlines for evaluation can provide an additional motivation for careful responding to lecture content and may be especially useful for individuals having difficulty in a course. The options for incorporating student participation are probably limitless – the key to the effectiveness of each option can depend heavily on the next topic.

Reinforcing immediately. The old adage that "practice makes perfect" is, unfortunately, an incomplete description of the conditions necessary for learning. In fact, practice alone does little in the absence of some form of feedback about quality. Further, the emphasis in a shaping approach is on what's done well (or at least better than the rest). The idea is to strengthen and enhance those behaviors that indicate increasing facility with respect to the course content. An exclusive focus on errors, common to many grading schemes, may help a student learn what not to do, but fails to supply the alternative, which is our true target. Thus, once behavior has been generated, and closer approximations to the course objectives are observed, reinforcers are needed and the quicker, the better.

An instructor's thoughts about reinforcers are likely to turn first to grades for exams and papers, and of course, these are important. However, relying solely on grades for major assignments is risky. For most courses, the number of such assignments for the semester is small, and even with rapid turnaround, the grades follow the work that was done after considerable delay. These are nonoptimal conditions for maximal behavior change; they may also fail to take full advantage of another, often underappreciated, source of reinforcement inherent in a college course. Signs of progress in mastering new material or understanding new ideas can be tremendously powerful. When students discover that they can deal effectively with a new subject matter in new ways, they make direct contact with the goals of education. The challenge is to make signs of progress obvious to each student, as they go.

This brings us once again to the importance of frequent opportunities for active responding on the student's part. Students' responses during a discussion or lecture produce immediate reinforcers when their answers match the ones that you provide. Frequently scheduled quizzes or writing assignments on small units of material allow reasonable hope for success by the majority, if not all, of the students in a class, and reinforcing mastery of one unit not only establishes the foundations for the next, but also increases the likelihood of more studying. New material can be followed more easily when studying previous material cannot be put off.

Even with small units of material, some students will struggle, but quizzes or other forms of evaluation can be designed so as to be sensitive to improvements that fall short of full mastery. (Indeed, these may be the most important improvements to act on.) Essays or other writing assignments are well-suited here because partial credit can be allocated. When poor writing skills prevent high marks despite improvements specific to course content, progress can be highlighted by providing separate scores for content points and for stylistic issues (e.g., grammar, spelling, organization). Objective evaluation formats can also be designed to be sensitive to improvements at various levels. In writing quizzes for my classes, I aim for a composition in which approximately 70% of the questions are at a basic level (e.g., those that require an understanding of definitions, procedures, and findings). To earn an A or B on the quiz, questions that require some integration, synthesis, or additional reasoning must be answered correctly. Weaker students in the class may not earn an A, but they have the opportunity to earn a satisfactory grade even while stronger students continue to be challenged. Of course, when students have difficulties, individual meetings provide a host of opportunities for reinforcing the progress in understanding that accrues in small steps, especially when the meetings focus on the student's discussion of the material, rather than the instructor's presentation of it.

As with the other elements of shaping, creative instructors will find a rich variety of ways in which to provide reinforcers for student efforts. Not to be underestimated in this regard is the potency of personal recognition. Knowing each student by name and showing familiarity with her or his progress adds important social contingencies to the mix. Even our "coolest" students care about instructors' opinions of them and their work. As just one example, I write brief, individualized comments on each quiz or paper, noting improvements – or lack thereof – relative to previous work in the course. It may sound corny, but students can usually tell when a teacher cares whether they're learning or not, and that judgment carries some weight.

Judging step size. The final key to successful shaping is gradual progression. Optimally, the learning at each step should leave a student completely prepared for the next. When the requirements for a new step are based on the best approximations that have come before, we avoid asking more of a student than they are capable of providing, and success (i.e., more reinforcers) can be achieved at each stage. Omitting necessary prerequisites (i.e., programming too large a step) can easily lead to failure. In fact, setting the bar too high too soon can even result in loss of progress made prior to that point, as reinforcers for previously mastered steps are no longer forthcoming. Conversely, when shaping programs proceed too slowly (i.e., the programmed step changes are too small), the process becomes tedious, there are fewer signs of progress (i.e., fewer reinforcers), and students are prevented from advancing to the fullest extent possible. In short, valuable opportunities for teaching more are lost.

Finding the proper balance in adjusting the level of each new learning step is a critical component of effective shaping; it may also be one of the more difficult dimensions of applying shaping procedures to classroom teaching. The optimal step size will often vary widely across students, as will the optimal pacing of step presentation. Extremes of these individual differences can probably be accommodated most fully in more personalized teaching interactions (e.g., help sessions, opportunities for directed individual study), but careful attention to appropriate step size is still required for effective design of lectures and course materials. The basic issue is one of determining how much is needed to take a student from point A to point B, where making sound decisions requires knowing both the subject matter and the particular audience.

To use a shaping approach effectively in teaching new material, the instructor needs first to have done her or his own analysis of the essential content issues, with a careful eye toward the basics necessary to understand them. These considerations should determine the order in which concepts are introduced, and the organization of points used to help a student appreciate an argument. This is not an easy assignment. Despite best attempts, I am frequently reminded that some bit of reasoning I had assumed to be so obviously implied failed to come across. For me it has helped to teach the same course on multiple occasions. Much of my progress as a teacher has come in the form of learning which conclusions most students can reach on their own and which I need to provide or cajole more directly. A good shaping program, then, includes all prerequisites for understanding, introduced in the proper sequence, and at an appropriate pace. The remaining question is how to tell whether these goals have been accomplished.

Return to Student Behavior. At this point, we've come full circle. The efficacy of a shaping procedure can be evaluated only in terms of the behavior change that results at each step. In the absence of students' responding, there is simply no way to determine whether teaching has occurred. Generating student behavior thus serves at least two essential functions for the teaching enterprise. First, student behavior provides the basis for reinforcement and, thus, improvements in learning. Second, student behavior is the most sensitive measure we have of our own impact. In short, our behavior as teachers can, and should, be shaped in important ways by the behavior change that we see (or don't see) in our students. Within a lecture, presentation and discussion can be tailored as students respond correctly, or not, to planned probes for understanding. Across units of material, patterns of errors on quizzes or omissions in writing assignments can reveal when I've taken too large a step, or missed a foundational one, and class coverage can be redistributed accordingly. Across semesters, term paper and lab report assignments become more fully and functionally defined, and students do a better job, as dimensions in need of prompting are identified.

It might be noted that this same "closing of the loop" is the very crux of recent emphases on assessment in higher education. Indeed, good assessment practices utilize some important features of shaping (i.e., specification of behavioral targets/student learning outcomes, requirements for responding/student work products, etc.), but at a more molar level. Where shaping involves a nearly continuous feedback loop between teacher and student behavior at each step of the learning process, assessment, at least to date, has focused primarily on course outcomes at the term's end. Thus, assessment is valuable as delayed feedback to the instructor and perhaps then to later students, if the instructor's practices are impacted positively. Shaping, in contrast, takes its power from emphasis on ongoing changes in the behavior of students learning right now.

In pedagogical analysis, effective instruction often comes across as static and dry, rather than as the rich, dynamic, and creative interchange that is the reality of teaching. For a shaping approach, the focus is that interchange. To the extent that our practices are sensitive to the successes of students, we can continue to become more effective teachers.

In sum, as a psychologist who studies basic processes of learning and behavior, I view teaching as a direct application of my science. While it may be practiced with considerable artistic flair, successful teaching is not an art, but the effective utilization of fundamental principles of behavior. When my students acquire new skills or understanding, I see demonstrations of the importance of the very principles I set out to teach. There are reinforcers here aplenty, and for all involved.

REFERENCES

Agras, S., Leitenberg, H., & Barlow, D. H. (1968). Social reinforcement in the modification of agoraphobia. *Archives of General Psychiatry*, 19, 423-427. doi: 10.1001/ archpsyc.1968.01740100039006

Athens, E. S., Vollmer, T. R., & St. Peter Pipkin, C. C. (2007). Shaping academic task engagement with percentile schedules. *Journal of Applied Behavior Analysis*, 40, 475-488. Retrieved from: http://www.ncbi.nlm.nih.gov/pubmed/17970261

Berstenin, D. D., & Wolfe. P. C. (1964). Shaping of three-man teams on a multiple DRL-DRH schedule of using collective reinforcement. *Journal of the Experimental Analysis of Behavior*, 7, 191-197. doi: 10.1901/jeab.1964.7-191

Budzynski, T. H., & Stoyva, J. M. (1969). An instrument for producing deep muscle relaxation by means of analog information feedback. *Journal of Applied Behavior Analysis*, 2, 231-237. doi: 10.1901/ jaba.1969.2-231

Eckerman, D. A., Hienz, R. D., Stern, S., & Kowlowitz, V. (1980). Shaping the location of pigeons' pecks: Effect of rate and size of shaping steps. *Journal of the Experimental Analysis of Behavior*, 34, 299-310. doi: 10.1901/jeab.1980.33-299

Galbicka, G. (1994). Shaping in the 21st century: Moving percentile schedules into applied settings. *Journal of Applied Behavior Analysis*, 27, 739-760. doi: 10.1901/jaba.1994.27- 739

Keller, F. S. (1982). *Pedagogues' Progress*. Lawrence, KS: TRI Publications.

Horner, R. D. (1971). Establishing use of crutches by a mentally retarded spina bifida child. *Journal of Applied Behavior Analysis*, 4, 183-189. doi: 10.1901/jaba.1971.4-183

Howie, P. M., & Woods, C. L. (1982). Token reinforcement during the instatement and shaping of fluency in the treatment of stuttering. *Journal of Applied Behavior Analysis*, 15, 55-64. doi: 10.1901/ jaba.1982.15-55

Levin, G., & Shapiro, D. (1962). The operant conditioning of conversation. *Journal of the Experimental Analysis of Behavior*, 5, 309-316. doi: 10.1901/jeab.1962.5-309

Pear, J. J., & Legris, J. A. (1987). Shaping by automated tracking of an arbitrary operant response. *Journal of the Experimental Analysis of Behavior*, 47, 241-248. doi: 10.1901/jeab.1987.47-241

Peterson, R. F. (1997). A text that teaches: Review of principles of everyday behavior analysis by L. Keith Miller. *Journal of Applied Behavior Analysis*, 30, 383-384. doi: 10.1901/jaba.1997.30-383

Platt, J. R. (1979). Interresponse-time shaping by variable-interval-like interresponse-time reinforcement contingencies. *Journal of the Experimental Analysis of Behavior*, 3, 3-14. doi: 10.1901/jeab.1979.31-3

Scott, D., Scott, L. M., & Goldwater, B. (1977). A performance improvement program for an international-level track and field athlete. *Journal of Applied Behavior Analysis*, 30, 573-575. doi: 10.1901/jaba.1997.30-573

Sepler, H. J., & Myers, S. L. (1978). The effectiveness of verbal instruction on teaching behavior-modification skills to nonprofessionals. *Journal of Applied Behavior Analysis*, 11, 198. doi: 10.1901/jaba.1978.11-198

Skinner, B. F. (1968). *The Technology of Teaching*. Englewood Cliffs, NJ: Prentice-Hall, Inc.

Stokes, P. D., & Balsam, P. D. (1991). Effects of reinforcing pre-selected approximations on the topography of the rat's bar press. *Journal of the Experimental Analysis of Behavior*, 55, 213-232. doi: 10.1901/jeab.1991.55-213

Smeets, P. M., Lancioni, G. E., Ball, T. S., & Oliva, D. S. (1985). Shaping self-initiated toileting in infants. *Journal of Applied Behavior Analysis*, 18, 303-308. doi: 10.1901/jaba.1985.18-303

LAWRENCE B. CAHOON

DEPARTMENT OF BIOLOGY AND MARINE BIOLOGY

Socratic Oceanography

I gave up using textbooks to teach oceanography at the graduate level a long time ago. There are such texts, and they often do a decent job of presenting the facts and concepts. Some of them even take things to a next level and press close to the edge of what we know – useful for students about to embark on a research career. Students tend to cling to textbooks and other such material, which is not all bad, even with the serious limitations of such hand-feeding approaches. One general criticism I have about oceanography texts is that many tend to describe the oceans without much explanation of how the oceans function. Why should the North Pacific have fresher surface waters than the North Atlantic? Why is the deep ocean so well-oxygenated? Why are continental shelves so productive? But all of them (and I have tried several texts over the years) left out something else important – the messy, back-and-forth nature of science as it's really practiced. So I decided to cut the cord and go with a different strategy altogether, based on readings in the primary literature and intense questioning of the class about that material. I call that a Socratic approach – you ask questions and get the students to answer, driving them toward a larger understanding of the major points you wish to get across. A key reason this works is "brain engagement" – making them think in real time.

This way is not for everyone. If you're a novice teacher with little classroom management experience, you can get into trouble. If you're teaching a subject with which you are not terribly familiar, perhaps you're better off mastering the material before you venture away from the textbooks. Freshmen are a challenge of a different sort, as are large classes – it can be done, but you need certain skills to make this work in those situations.

On the other hand, the Socratic approach I describe here can work very well in a lot of situations. It's adaptable and flexible; you are in total control of each class period. I have found that it is also an excellent remedy for the mid-career threats of boredom and burnout. Thirty-one years into my career at UNCW, I thrive on my time in the classroom. The more interactive each class session gets, the more I enjoy it. Judging from the feedback I get from my students, even years later, they are getting a lot out of it, as well. Most important, I know right away how well they grasp the material without getting big surprises on midterms or final exams.

I consider teaching to be a form of manipulation that must fully engage students' minds to be most effective. All of us who teach professionally have been taught professionally for much of our lives. We can't help but have a sense of what "worked" for us and what didn't. The poor sods who merely read from textbooks or simply recited a written lecture generally lost me (and probably most of us) fairly quickly. Our minds were ready to engage more fully, but the stimulation our brains were getting was not enough, so other thoughts came crowding in. After a while, most of us could take notes with only a portion of our brains engaged. Does that sound familiar? That's not great teaching, and it does not require or instill a more sophisticated understanding of the "big picture," the how and why of doing science (or anything else!). Somehow, we have to be engaged and fixated on the subject before we really internalize it and understand it. That's why the old saw has it that the best way to learn something is to teach it.

I've been doing oceanography as a seagoing scientist since my first year in graduate school, running my own research cruises as Chief Scientist since my third year as a graduate student, and using SCUBA to do research out on the continental shelf since my first year at UNCW. I can't dive anymore, but the lessons I gained from doing my own oceanographic research yielded an important insight: Field oceanography is a messy process. The physical doing of it is a challenge, but, even more, so is the fundamental doing of the science itself in that environment. The ocean is big, deep, opaque, rough, and complex. We wrestle our understandings from it with difficulty. I came to see that our students must have more than a sense of what we think we know from textbooks; they had to have a much clearer understanding of how we approach oceanographic science, so that our findings and understandings make sense. It also helps to comprehend how much we have left to learn and why. Science is a process of continually pushing back boundaries. Students must get a sense of the excitement and difficulty of doing that, as well as the interplay of methodology and paradigms.

There is a larger challenge here. Graduate students in my oceanography classes, who almost invariably have an undergraduate science degree, are still apprentices in the doing of science. They may know the general rubric of observation-hypothesis-experiment, but the practical nature of science is much more complex and is best understood when placed in some context. Oceanography is as good a vehicle for teaching the scientific way of knowing as any other subject, so I use the subject I know to illustrate that way of knowing.

I learned to use the so-called Socratic method in graduate school although I had had it used on me well before then. While serving as a teaching assistant in an animal diversity course, I found that I did not always know the details of every specimen and lab prep. Students frequently asked me about those details, and I found that, if I questioned them about what they had in front of them and ruled out possible explanations until we arrived at the answer (often, but not always, I got there first), they learned the material so much more effectively than if I had just known and told them the answer. I suppose now we call that a form of "inquiry-based" teaching; it works by engaging curiosity – one of the more powerful ways to stimulate learning, and something that has been known and practiced for millennia. The key is to ask questions, consider the answers, and close in on the larger ideas.

The Socratic approach to teaching imposes some special requirements on an instructor. Knowing the answer to every question you ask is not one of them; asking questions in the right way is certainly one of them. The method has its challenges. This is an interactive process, and its path in real time depends on the questions you ask and, equally important, the answers you get back. You may find unexpected detours into areas where the students turn out to be ignorant or misinformed. You have to keep your balance while pursuing a larger goal for the class, so you have to do a lot of real-time juggling. This will test your poise and classroom management skills, so you must also be very nimble. If teaching makes you nervous, if you need a lot of structure in your delivery, or if you have trouble handling a class for any reason, this approach can easily get you into trouble. Students sense weakness and pounce on it.

I use a term for the key quality a Socratic instructor must possess beyond mastery of the subject matter and self-confidence: moral authority. I do not mean that you must be somehow morally superior to your students or some kind of control freak or master manipulator. Rather, you must have some relaxed, distilled essence of these qualities, as well as a clearly discernible level of passion for the business in which you are engaged. Students are very sensitive to the moral authority that an instructor carries in the door. If you think back on your many experiences as a student, you can easily differentiate the teachers who had moral authority and those who didn't.

There are certainly mechanical considerations in using this approach. You must know the material well enough to ask questions about it and move the class toward the major points you wish to make. The students must be prepared for the give and take of a Socratic classroom experience, so I make it clear that they must read the assigned paper(s) before class, and I back that up by having them write one-page summaries of a sub-set of these papers (their choice) that are due by the time class starts. I can tell quickly if they have not read or understood the papers – a few questions suffice, and a little embarrassment goes a long way. I make it clear by example that I expect their participation, that it is safe to be wrong, that it is safe to challenge the instructor (and actually praiseworthy – I make a point of telling them I like to learn new stuff). I ask questions, give them time to muster the courage to answer, make it clear that this is a kind of conversation, and that it is not hotdogging or showing off to answer. Never make someone feel bad about a wrong answer – use such events to pivot and ask the question differently, as if you had not phrased the question correctly at first – often you have not. If you can get the students talking to each other (on topic, of course), you have a home run, but keep them on point.

There are concessions the Socratic method requires in comparison to the standard lecture style. If you think that "covering material" (getting through an extensive outline of subject matter – facts, concepts, illustrations) is critical, you will find it too time-consuming to use a question-answer approach. I find that there are times when I simply must tell them things, from terminology to methodology to quantitative concepts, so I can get at the material that needs more critical thought. But you can pepper even the driest set of "facts" with questions to keep the class thinking while they are taking notes. If you don't have a major concept toward which to drive the class by the Socratic approach, it can fall flat. It really helps to lead them toward a major new understanding that penetrates at the end of your class time by asking questions. Some topics may not lend themselves to that – it's up to you to know those big ideas and to drive the discussion effectively toward that goal or to know when it won't work. This is one critical juncture between scholarship and teaching. "Scholars" can use the Socratic approach, but it's more of a challenge for folks without regular engagement with the cutting edge.

Primary literature – original research publications – makes an excellent platform for teaching oceanography by the Socratic method. One must choose publications carefully, and one must seek to build a larger coherence among those papers, or students cannot see the larger ideas develop. Obviously, if you're going to "teach" a paper, you'd better understand it pretty well. But a strange thing I've noticed in doing this is that, even with papers I've taught for a decade, I still pick up new insights for myself, which helps keep them fresh for me (and empathize with the students who are reading them for the first time!). I have also found that what we (and I) now know helps me comprehend better what was written years ago. Some of that, I'm sure, derives from the conservative nature of scientific writing. We who write those papers often know more than we can claim outright and get past reviewers, but we can certainly drop hints for those who follow.

My graduate biological oceanography course is built around a set of primary papers that I revise every year although I keep some classics that are "must reads." I have several favorites that brilliantly present the scientific method and that pushed oceanography ahead in major ways. I try to choose papers that collectively present what we think about how the oceans work, which is certainly a work in progress. There is a historical aspect to the set – our progress often came at the expense of old ideas that were wrong or at least ignorant of what we now see as huge paradigm shifts. Who knew 30 years ago that iron was an important nutrient in the world ocean? Who imagined back then that the oceans are as much a microbial soup as a mega-fauna zoo? Who could comprehend just three decades ago the pervasive and long-standing impacts of humans on the oceans' biota? And who can thoughtfully forecast what new paradigms will be in place 30 years hence?

I will provide a specific example here to illustrate how I employ this method. If some technical aspects are beyond you, don't sweat it – I want to convey the level of detail with which I engage the students in this grad-uate course, but I'll try to focus this discussion on the main ideas I elicit by Socratic methods. I teach a paper published in 1994 by John Martin and 43 others (Martin et al., 1994) that describes the very first large-scale ma-nipulation of an open ocean ecosystem to test the "iron hypothesis" – the idea that certain portions of the ocean had insufficient bio-available iron to support their full potential primary production (growth of phytoplankton). The "iron hypothesis" presented the possibility that addition of relatively small quantities of iron, a micro-nutrient, could stimulate the growth of phytoplankton, which would draw more of the greenhouse gas, carbon dioxide, out of the atmosphere and transfer it ultimately into the deep sea by the formation and sinking of organic matter. In simpler terms, adding iron to the ocean could fix the greenhouse effect – maybe. Clearly, it was an idea worth testing. As an aside, John Martin proposed the idea, but passed away before the field study to test it on a large scale could be done. He was named senior author of the resulting publication as an honor.

Martin et al. (1994) describe the approach to and results of a massive, ambitious open-ocean experiment. It's a brilliantly designed and executed piece of work – science at its most formidable. Briefly, the team added iron to a patch of ocean they had just sampled, then tracked the fertilized patch by several methods while also sampling a control, unfertilized patch. They sampled a variety of responses by the respective oceanic ecosystems, measuring a large set of parameters. Thus, the design was what we call a Before-After/Control-Impact (or BACI) design. The multiplicity of methods used to verify the manipulation, track the patches, and measure the responses made this a relatively robust experiment. What really adds to it, though, is that the team also sampled a naturally iron-fertilized portion of the ocean (downstream of the volcanic, iron-rich Galapagos Islands) and the iron-poor waters upstream, taking the same set of measurements, allowing for the artificial manipulation to be compared to a natural manipulation by the ocean itself. Altogether, it's a brilliant piece of science. And in case you are wondering, yes, added iron stimulated primary production, but not as much as was expected – so, no, we may not fix the greenhouse problem by dumping iron in the oceans. More research was needed, and more of these experiments have since been done to pursue these issues further. The big punch lines for this exercise are the robustness of the experimental and sampling design, which makes the results more believable, and the fact that the expected massive response did not fully materialize. One take-home point is that really neat ideas, like fertilizing the ocean with iron to fix the greenhouse effect, don't always stand up to actual data.

Martin et al. (1994) is a rich source of prompts for the Socratic approach. I bore in on various technical aspects, such as the use of inert sulfur hexafluoride as a tracer for the iron added to seawater; Fast Repetition Rate Fluorometry, a novel technique at the time, as an indicator of the physiological state of phytoplankton; and remote ocean sensing by satellites to complement shipboard sampling, to reinforce the importance of scientific techniques. But the discussion has to be dominated by the bigger questions: What was the key hypothesis here? What were the predicted outcomes – very specifically? In what ways (I emphasize the plural) was that hypothesis tested? Why measure so many responses? How do we know the sampling program actually tracked and sampled the fertilized patch of ocean? Are the results of the manipulation and the natural experiment congruent? This sounds straightforward enough, but there are numerous other questions embedded in the process – some to see how well the students read the paper, some to see how well they comprehended what they read, some to see how well the major points came across. Nothing is off-limits. I often ask, "So, now that we have done this work, what's the next thing to do?"

The journey is an important part of the story in oceanography as in other subjects. In this case the journey illustrates how science poses questions, suggests explanations, tests them, and discards them when they fail or become inadequate. Students must understand that process, see it work, and appreciate how often our most cherished and passionately defended hypotheses must be tossed out when new methods, new data, and new understandings arise. Students can empathize with the authors of papers whose ideas have now been modified or rejected. The Socratic approach helps them learn that being wrong is part of the process – don't whine, get past your pride, focus on the ideas, and move on. I try to end every class with the thought that we have learned something new today.

REFERENCES

Martin, J. H., Coale, K. H., Johnson, K. S., Fitzwater, S. E., Gordon, R. M., Tanner, S. J.,...Tindale, N. W. (1994). Testing the iron hypothesis in ecosystems of the equatorial Pacific Ocean. *Nature: 371*, 123-129. doi:10.1038/371123a0

JESSICA R. MESMER-MAGNUS
DEPARTMENT OF MANAGEMENT

'Flipping' the College Classroom

"Knowledge is of no value unless you put it into practice."
– Anton Pavlovich Chekhov
"Teaching isn't one-tenth as effective as training."
– Horace Mann
"The art of teaching is the art of assisting discovery."
– Mark van Doren

Research seems to reinforce what Chekhov, Mann, and van Doren have said about the importance of an instructor's role in student learning and practice; students learn more when they have (1) an opportunity to practice what they are taught (Cannon-Bowers, Rhodenizer, Salas, & Bowers, 1998; Mesmer-Magnus & Viswesvaran, 2007), and (2) an instructor who is along as a guide to ensure their practice is effective (Wilson, Majsterek, & Simmons, 1996). Sadly, we often forget the importance of guided practice in the design of the traditional classroom. In traditional classrooms, instructors spend much of class time lecturing to students and then send them home, so they can practice what they learned for homework. Though often students get home and don't know where to begin on their homework assignment because they failed to take good notes during lecture, or they didn't fully grasp the concepts. Then, they spend time "spinning their wheels" to complete a homework assignment they don't fully understand, so they can hand in the assignment during the next class session and get their grade. Even though homework assignments are rarely perfect, instructors typically don't have enough time to work on remediation for poorly understood concepts because they risk falling further behind if they don't quickly move on to the next concept. And, so the cycle continues … .

In this essay, I will outline an alternative to the traditional classroom model ("the flipped classroom"; Ash, 2012; King, 1993) that is meant to address these shortcomings and discuss ways I've found it can successfully be implemented in the college classroom.

The 'Flipped' Classroom

The concept of "flipping the classroom" began as a movement in the K-12 schools as a means of making time spent in class and on homework more efficient and effective. Professors at top universities around the country are now beginning to see the wisdom in implementing this approach in college classrooms, as well (Foertsch, Moses, Strikwerda, & Litzkow, 2002; King, 1993). There are variations on the concept, but essentially a flipped classroom switches (or "flips") what was traditionally done in class with what was traditionally done as homework (cf. Lage, Platt, & Treglea, 2000; Strayer, 2007). In a flipped classroom, the instructor prepares lecture materials for viewing out of class and spends class time on guided practice, application, discussion, and integration. With this approach, students view lectures before class, in addition to completing any required reading or pre-work, so everyone comes to class with an understanding of the basics. The instructor begins class meetings by addressing student areas of confusion, and then moves on to guided practice in the form of class discussion, application assignments, experiential exercises, opportunities for implementation, etc. The essence of this model is depicted in Figure 1.

Benefits of a "Flipped" Classroom

Malcolm Gladwell (author of 2008 book, Outliers: The Story of Success) was once quoted, "Practice isn't the thing you do when you're good. It's the thing you do that makes you good." This statement, backed by scientific research (Mesmer-Magnus & Viswesvaran, 2007), reinforces the importance of students practicing what they are learning in their coursework. Practice has consistently been shown to be the crucial determinant of mastery and long-term retention. But, simply practicing does not guarantee mastery; rather, mastery requires students be practicing "correctly."[1] As most instructors in traditional classrooms can attest, when students fail to accurately understand lecture concepts, time spent on homework is not only fruitless, it is counterproductive to learning and mastery. However, in a flipped classroom model, the instructor can be available to students during their practice period. By being present during practice, the instructor can (1) quickly identify and address areas of misunderstanding, (2) ensure that students grasp and retain the most important concepts, (3) determine the extent to which more practice is necessary (as well as the type of practice

[1] Vince Lombardi echoed this sentiment when he was quoted, *Practice does not make perfect. Only perfect practice makes perfect.*

needed), and (4) shape future materials to the strengths/weaknesses of the class (e.g., Educause, 2012; Gobry, 2012).

Recorded lectures also have several big advantages in the flipped classroom (Gobry, 2012). First, instructors can ensure that all students get the "perfect" lecture every time as recorded lectures permit the instructor to deliver a lecture free from typical classroom distractions. Second, all students see the same material, eliminating concerns about whether the instructor remembered to discuss the same theories, examples, etc., for all class sections. Third, recorded lectures are vastly more time-efficient than in-person lectures as most instructors will find that they can cover the same material in less than half the time. Fourth, students can view lectures as many times as they need in order to fully grasp the material without frustrating students who grasped the material quickly (as is typical in the traditional classroom). Fifth, students can revisit recorded lectures throughout the course to refresh their understanding and prepare for future assignments and assessments. Sixth, once the instructor creates these lectures, they can be used for several semesters, freeing up instructor time to (1) work with students, (2) prepare new and varied practice opportunities, (3) conduct research that will add value to coursework, etc.

Another important benefit of the flipped classroom model is that assessments of student learning can go beyond the typical declarative knowledge assessment to an enhanced focus on the student's ability to unpack and apply that knowledge. Arguably, this level of learning is comparatively more highly valued by employers (e.g., Krathwohl, 2002). With more class time devoted to discussion, experiential learning, and knowledge application, the nature of course assessments should change, too.

The key benefit of a flipped classroom, though, is that class time is used in a way that more efficiently and effectively yields true learning, mastery, and retention of course concepts (Foertsch et al., 2002; King, 1993). Instructors who've "flipped" their classes have found they have significantly more time available over the course of a semester to address new topics and to dive deeper into concepts they'd never had time to get to when their class was structured more traditionally.2 Further, instructors can more efficiently cope with varied knowledge and skill levels of their students. As knowledge-delivery occurs out of class on the students' timeframe, students who need more

2 Indeed, in my personal experience, I've found I can cover up to 30% more material in semesters where I've flipped my class, and that students are more fluent in the material we've covered. What's more? Students don't even realize we're covering the additional material since they don't feel rushed during class time (since the online lectures more efficiently cover factual and theoretical material, and we work together in class to dive deeper into application and implementation).

time to grasp a concept can move at a slower pace (reviewing tricky topics, as necessary) than students who are quicker to understand the concept. Then, all students come to class on a more "level playing field," so the instructor can focus on helping students to take their declarative knowledge to the next level via practice, application, and discussion.

Best Practices for Flipping Your College Course

Over the past few years, I've dabbled in flipping several of my classes, courses that vary in terms of theoretical, applied, quantitative, and qualitative content/foci. From these experiences, I've gleaned a few best practices for "flipping":

1. Carefully consider what material you cover in the course of your semester. Is there any material that is fairly straightforward, factual, or doesn't require a lot of discussion to effectively relay? If so, that material is ideal for being flipped. Similarly, carefully consider what is the best use of class time during the course of the semester. Are there specific projects, discussion topics, experiential exercises, etc., that would add value to the class and be best done with you there? Ask yourself, why should your students come to class? What value does your class time bring them?[3] Then, structure your class sessions around your answers.

2. You will find that recorded lectures free up a lot of class time, so you have the opportunity to add more application-oriented materials to class sessions. However, don't forget that recorded lectures don't replace discussion, clarification, and Q & A. It is easy to forget to review complex topics or hold the same sorts of "random" discussions you used to have when you were lecturing the majority of your class sessions. On the other hand, you should not re-lecture on the same material you covered in your recorded lectures, or

_____

3 I recently attended a conference on the Flipped Classroom concept (FlipCon13). During a social hour, one professor told me that he worked for a university in northern Washington State. Many of his students drove from considerable distances to attend class. During the winter months, transit to class could be quite dangerous with snow- and ice-covered roads. This professor said that he now asks himself when designing every in-person class, "Is what I'm going to cover in class today worth my students risking their lives to attend?" Maybe this seems a little extreme, but auto travel is dangerous even in the best of weather conditions (Cerrelli, 1997), and his comment reminded me of the importance of carefully considering how best to use my in-class time.

you undermine the value of watching the recorded lecture.[4]

3. Consider administering a short quiz on the recorded lecture material either online or at the beginning of class, so you can ensure everyone is on same page for class sessions. When the quizzes are done before class, you can also use the results to quickly identify areas of confusion for in-class discussion/clarification.[5]

4. Have an organized, sequential, and consistent way of delivering out-of-class material, whether your own Web page or a learning management system like Blackboard. Students become frustrated when the online material is not organized in an intuitive way.

5. Be sure to orient your students to your course design. Explain why watching the recorded lectures and doing other pre-work is crucial to effective class time.

6. Don't try to flip your entire course at once. This is an overwhelming amount of work to do at one time, and, based on your experiences and student feedback, you may need to revise it for the next semester anyway. Go slowly, pick a few topics that are easily "flip-able," and start there. Some instructors say that they like to record lectures for future semesters immediately after they've delivered it for a current class since the material, examples, and essence of class discussion is fresh in their minds.

7. When preparing to record lectures, carefully consider how best to chunk the information. Student attention spans tend to decrease

---

4 Student feedback from my first flipping attempt revealed that there would still be value of having class discussion on some of the "trickier" concepts (as determined by the students) presented in lecture. In subsequent semesters, I asked students to jot down questions they had while watching the online lectures and bring them to class or email them to me in advance of class. This approach seemed to allay the fear that they were missing something important by not having in-person lectures. Another approach, which also worked well, was to have an online discussion forum for the class (e.g., on Blackboard or even Facebook) where students could post questions from lectures/assignments and they could interact with each other to clear up confusions. As the instructor, I also contribute to these online discussions, but I've been very impressed with how students embrace these online discussions to teach each other (e.g., Gobry, 2012).

5 In my first attempt at flipping, I failed to test students on the material they were supposed to cover outside of class, and found that some students were not able to participate in class sessions in a meaningful way. In subsequent semesters, I found quizzing the students on the online material before class eliminated this problem.

dramatically over time (e.g., Oken, Salinsky, & Elsas, 2006), so make every effort to keep your recorded videos to 5-10 minutes in length. Chunk information into manageable and meaningful pieces. Students much prefer a greater number of shorter lectures compared with one very long lecture.[6] I also recommend including the video length in the file name for the video, so students will know how long they need to budget in order to view that lecture component.

8. Try to make your online material provocative enough to get your students thinking about course concepts outside of class. Consider having a "thought exercise" required after each recorded lecture that will feed into the next synchronous class meeting.

9. Don't be afraid to use relevant academic online content to supplement your course. If you look carefully, you may find that YouTube, Wikipedia, and news Web sites actually host some quite valuable, easily accessible, (and free!) information that can add value to your course and save you considerable recording time. You don't have to reinvent the wheel. Remember, you bring value by helping students unpack the information and apply it to solve new problems. Use freely available, academically relevant online material and then spend your time devising ways to take it further.

Conclusion

Although there has been some resistance to the flipped classroom model, it seems to come mostly from the more seasoned instructors who have spent their career comfortable with their role as "sage on the stage" (King, 1993). For these instructors, it seems to be a harder transition to move from this role to one as a "guide on the side." However, times have changed; technology has made information much more easily accessible than in years past. Before easy access to information (via the Internet), students had to come to class, so they could gather information they could not easily access otherwise (hence, the former importance of the college professor as a "sage on the stage"). Now, however, professors need to consider what they bring to class that could not be found in a Google search. Although clearly professors bring great value to the college classroom, increasingly we need to remember that our value as a professor lies comparatively less in the knowledge we communicate via lectures and more in our skill in guiding students in dissecting, integrating, and applying knowledge to solve real-world problems. Class time should, therefore, be spent on helping students move from declarative knowledge

---

6 Another benefit of recording shorter lectures is that when/if something changes prompting you to re-record certain material, you don't have to re-record everything.

acquisition (which can more easily and efficiently be done out of class via recorded lectures, assigned reading, and – let's face it – Google searches) to application, integration, and the development of procedural and strategic knowledge. The flipped classroom model moves us in this direction, as is illuminated in a blog by Stubbs (2013) by the following quote from Dr. Eric Mazor, Professor of Physics at Harvard, and a pioneering advocate of the flipped classroom in higher education:

Information comes from everywhere now: the university is no longer the gatekeeper of information, as it has been since the Renaissance. And if it were, the only thing we would need to do is videotape the best lectures and put them online ... But ultimately, learning is a social experience. Harvard is Harvard not because of the buildings, not because of the professors, but because of the students interacting with one another.

REFERENCES

Ash, K. (2012). Educators evaluate 'flipped classrooms'. *Education Week, 32,* 6-8. Retrieved from: http://www.edweek.org/ew/index.html

Cannon-Bowers, J. A., Rhodenizer, L., Salas, E., & Bowers, C. A. (1998). A framework for understanding pre-practice conditions and their impact on learning. *Personnel Psychology, 51,* 291-320. doi: 10.1111/j.1744-6570.1998.tb00727.x

Cerrelli, E. (1997). *Fatal crash involvements – What are the odds?* Research Note for the National Center for Statistics & Analysis, National Highway Traffic Safety Administration, U.S. Department of Transportation. Retrieved from: http://www-nrd.nhtsa.dot.gov/Pubs/97.835.PDF

Educause. (February, 2012). 7 Things You Should Know About Flipped Classrooms. *Educause Learning Initiative.* Retrieved from: http://net.educause.edu/ir/library/pdf/eli7081.pdf

Foertsch, J., Moses, G., Strikwerda, J., & Litzkow, M. (2002). Reversing the lecture/homework paradigm using eTEACH web-based streaming video software. *Journal of Engineering Education,* 91, 267-274. doi: 10.1002/j.2168-9830.2002.tb00703.x

Gobry, P. E. (2012, December 11). What is the flipped classroom model and why is it amazing? *Forbes.* Retrieved from: http://www.forbes.com/sites/pascalemmanuelgobry/2012/12/11/what-is-the-flipped-classroom-model-and-why-is-it-amazing-with-infographic/

King, A. (1993). From sage on the stage to guide on the side. *College Teaching,* 41, 30-35. Retrieved from: http://www.jstor.org/stable/27558571

Krathwohl, D. R. (2002). A revision of Bloom's Taxonomy: An overview. *Theory into Practice,* 41, 212-218. doi: 10.1207/s15430421tip4104_2

Lage, M. J., Platt, G. J., & Treglia, M. (2000). Inverting the classroom: A gateway to creating an inclusive learning environment. *Journal of Economic Education,* 31, 30-43. Retrieved from: http://www.jstor.org/stable/1183338

Mesmer-Magnus, J. R., & Viswesvaran, C. (2007). Inducing maximal versus typical learning through the provision of a pre-training goal orientation. *Human Performance,* 20(3), 205-222. doi: 10.1080/08959280701333016

Oken, B. S., Salinsky, M. C., & Elsas, S. M. (2006). Vigilance, alertness, or sustained attention: Psychological basis and measurement. *Clinical Neurophysiology*, 117, 1885-1901. doi: 10.1016/j. clinph.2006.01.017

P. Stubbs. (2013, September 23). Is the traditional lecture meeting the needs of connected learners? Retrieved from: http://www.flipyourthinking. net/precision-teaching-blog/2013/9/23/ is-the-traditional-lecture-meeting-the-needs-of-connected-learners

Strayer, J. (2007). *The effects of the classroom flip on the learning environment: A comparison of learning activity in a traditional classroom and a flip classroom that used an intelligent tutoring system*. Retrieved from OhioLINK Electronic Theses & Dissertation Center. (osu1189523914)

Wilson, R., Majsterek, D., & Simmons, D. (1996). The effects of computer-assisted versus teacher-directed instruction on the multiplication performance of elementary students. *Journal of Learning Disabilities*, 29, 382-390. Retrieved from: http://www.ncbi.nlm. nih.gov/pubmed/8763553

FIGURE 1

Traditional v. Flipped Classroom

TRADITIONAL CLASS	FLIPPED CLASS
In class: Teacher instructs in class & students take notes	**Before class:** Teacher instructs lesson via video, website, book, etc.
After class: Students have homework; typically work on their own to attempt to gain deeper understanding of concepts and applications	**In class:** Students work together under guidance of instructor to gain deeper understanding of concepts and applications; students receive support as needed
Disadvantages: Students can't easily ask questions; mistakes aren't quickly identified	

ROBERT BOYCE
SCHOOL OF HEALTH AND APPLIED HUMAN SCIENCES

Embracing the Future: How I Overcame My Fear of Technology and Learned to Love e-Learning

Since 2003 I have taught at the University of North Carolina Wilmington, where I am currently an associate professor in the School of Health and Applied Human Sciences. I teach Human Anatomy and Physiology and Exercise Physiology and my research focuses on Occupational Physiology. In addition to my lecture courses, I also direct the supporting labs and I have made a practice of including undergraduate students in many of my research projects.

To illustrate what a significant development e-learning has been to me you have to understand where I come from. I was born in 1946 and grew up on a farm outside Gastonia, North Carolina. I received my Ph.D. in 1975, so clearly computers and today's modern modes of communication and social interaction were not in evidence during my early educational development and career. In fact I had to hire someone to type my doctoral dissertation on a typewriter because I hadn't learned how to type. My father, when I wished to enroll in a typing class, discouraged me because at the time it was considered the domain of secretaries and support staff. Many of the tools I use daily in my teaching and my research were not developed until many years after I completed my education. In fact, my typing skills are still a hindrance to me and to be absolutely honest, I just don't track on a computer anywhere near as quickly as the Millennial generation students I work with daily. You can imagine my initial trepidation when it was suggested that I incorporate e-learning methods into my regular teaching practices.

However, my background includes raising two children and putting them through college and graduate school as well as many years of teaching secondary school and college. This provided me an ability to communicate well with young people which ultimately contributed to my recently receiving the Chancellor's Teaching Excellence Award from UNCW. I have also worked in the area of health promotion for large organizations such as the Police Department in Charlotte, NC and the William Beaumont Hospital in Royal Oak, MI. For a number of years I had my own business which provided ergonomics, exercise physiology and health promotion consulting to increase productivity and reduce workplace injuries in business and industrial settings. Throughout my career, I have often capitalized on the synergy of skills and knowledge that comes from integrating others in the development of new programming. I work well in a team environment and find that productive interactions of several disciplines can ultimately facilitate positive outcomes in a variety of settings.

When I began my job at UNCW and was assigned to teach the Human Anatomy and Physiology (A&P) courses I had to develop my own style of presenting the information in a dynamic and lively fashion. This was my first experience teaching this broad and complex subject. My teaching style is very physical and interactive; think carnival barker, inspirational speaker and mediocre comedian all rolled into one. In fact, one of my teaching reviews by a less than complementary colleague referred to my presentation as a "dog and pony show." However, my student reviews reflect that I am making the desired impression. I make it a priority to personally connect with each of them; I want to shake them up, wake them up, and get them to interact with each other and with me. We dance, we laugh, we shout out the "words of the day" and we work together to delve into this complex information and to maximize their retention and understanding of the materials.

My A&P courses are offered as part of the University Studies program. I have students from numerous disciplines. For many of them this is their first (and sometimes only) encounter with A&P and it can be overwhelming if not presented well. This was new course preparation for me and obviously there was a tremendous amount of course materials to cover. My classes are offered at 8:00 a.m., which also presents a challenge. How does one wake students, engage and imprint them with a course that involves so many complex systems and information? It is like teaching a foreign language that includes intricate processes such as chemistry and bio-mechanics.

To prepare my A&P course I chose to incorporate materials from a variety of sources, depending heavily upon the multi-media options provided by my textbook publishers. In the course of a standard lecture I might use the following materials:

- Two screens simultaneously showing:
  - Power point slides
  - An overhead projector with transparencies
  - Interactive videos and animations
- Verbal quizzes, quick on-the-spot assessments that let me know what they understand
- Electronic interactive animations with quizzes shown on the overhead screens
  - multiple choice questions
  - labeling anatomical diagrams
- Students have their textbooks, a handbook of the powerpoint slides and an interactive CD they can play on their laptops
- At the end of each session, students write down their "Golden Nuggets" (three things they learned that day) in their slide handbook
- Anatomical models
- A good, old-fashioned dry-erase board
- Group study sessions, outside of class times, to prepare for big tests

Obviously there is only so much than can be accomplished in our limited lecture and lab time. The responsibility rests on the students to do the homework and prepare outside of class. I was searching for an effective way to aid them in their home studies and in so doing support our interactions in the classroom. When my publisher's representative approached me about incorporating "Mastering A&P" into my course, I was interested if somewhat skeptical about its efficacy. My courses have a large student load and while I strive to be the best teacher I can be, I have a lot of work to do now and was not excited about adding more tasks to my day. Learning a new computerized system can be a challenge, especially to a "Baby Boomer" like me, as computer literacy is not my first language.

Let me backtrack just a moment. Over the past nine years at UNCW I have worked closely with 26 students in Directed Individual Studies, providing them with the opportunity to participate in my research, publish our work in peer-reviewed journals and to present at a number of professional meetings. Therefore, it seemed natural to utilize my established practice of undergraduate research to jump into the e-learning arena. I did so by preparing a pilot project to track and evaluate the outcomes of using "Mastering A&P" with the intention of involving some of my student researchers in research design, data-collection, analysis, writing and ultimately presentation and publication of the results.

My initial expectation regarding e-learning was that it would risk promoting separation and isolation. It contradicts my philosophy of interpersonal connections and puts the emphasis on one-on-one interaction with a computer. I approached the e-learning systems with a great deal of trepidation. I felt that it might impede my ability to personally direct my students through the course materials personally and that it didn't seem to be a natural teaching style for me. Fortunately, this was not the case and I came to see multiple benefits from the system.

By involving my student researchers in the pilot project, I quickly discovered that my Millennial students possessed the computer skills necessary to make this transition successful. My publisher's representative (another Millennial, by the way) also provided terrific support through her extensive experience and knowledge of the product. Pearson Education took a very active role in supporting our pilot project as they were keenly interested in how this program could be broadly adopted and also adapted to other disciplines. I was impressed with how quickly they utilized our results to fine-tune their program, making changes to improve the system and to identify best practices for implementation. Their responsiveness made this project a pleasure and all involved received many benefits from their participation. It reinforced my central philosophy of group interaction and opened my eyes to the possibilities of utilizing these interactive computer programs to further learning and enhance the teacher-student relationship.

One big thing I have learned in this process is that if one doesn't constantly evolve, one is soon left behind. Textbook publishers must keep innovating to keep up with the incredibly rapid pace of technology, and they must involve the teaching community in order for their systems to become widely adopted. It is so exciting, as a teacher, to be an active part of this development process. Using these teaching modules in my classes is where the "rubber meets the road" and to see my input result in rapid and specific improvements was intensely gratifying.

It is important to note that how you begin this process is critical. Every instructor who intends to utilize such an e-learning system must take the time to pick and choose the content that best supports the class directives. In this section I will cover how we designed our pilot study and eventually moved to full implementation of the e-learning system and discuss the outcomes. As I stated before, my philosophy is based on total inclusion and maintaining great relationships and communications. It rests on the complete involvement and participation of all parties: the students (researchers/

observers and the participants), the publisher, the UNCW Office of e-Learning and myself.

When Pearson first approached me, they wanted me to adopt the program and move immediately into full implementation. I'm conservative at heart and wanted to know more about what I was getting involved with before making that commitment. First I spent time with the Pearson representative and the UNCW bookstore to evaluate costs, ensuring that it would be cost-effective for the students to use. Even though the Mastering A&P e-learning system had a cost of its own, above and beyond the cost of the class textbook, we learned that the e-learning materials could potentially save the students money as they had the option to go completely virtual with their texts and/or use a loose-leaf version of the text at a great savings from the traditional hardcover book.

However, if students purchased their textbooks from other sources than the UNCW bookstore (such as Amazon), they could often get them at a lower cost, but unfortunately they could not get access to the Mastering A&P program unless they purchased it separately. In that circumstance, they might not realize any cost savings and in fact the complete materials might be a bit more expensive. It is evident that in the not-so-distant future materials will become virtual and there will be no more textbooks. The publishers are preparing now for this reality. In the past year I have already observed a dramatic increase in students coming to classes with laptops, notebooks and tablets. In that short time I've already seen programming adapted to incorporate the different operating systems such as Android and iPad.

My next step was to identify a student research partner and together we prepared a directed individual study with the focus being the creation of a pilot study to review the efficacy of implementing the Mastering A&P program. The design of the pilot study included developing a research protocol and identifying volunteer participants from my current A&P course. In the fall of 2011, after the first exam, I sent an email to all the students in the course asking them to take part in a Mastering A&P pilot study. I offered them an incentive of 1 point added to their final grade if they completed 100% of the assignments in the time allotted. Participants were required to attend two optional evaluative interviews and complete a series of surveys. The final survey included questions about their experience using the program. We used Survey Monkey to conduct our surveys electronically and found this to be most helpful. It is interesting to note that as the study progressed, and the volunteers shared their experiences with the other students, more volunteers joined the program. By the end of the semester 20 students – 34% of the class – were involved. Of those students, 11 completed 100% of the

Mastering A&P assignments.

During the course of the pilot study, the student researcher and I managed to stay about one step ahead of our volunteer participants. We would meet three times each week and review each module, selecting the portions that best supported my specific syllabus. At my suggestion, Pearson Education underwrote the cost of two pizza parties to attract the participants to provide their feedback through mid-term and end-of-course evaluative interviews. Five to eight students came to each evaluative interview. The end-of-course survey was completed by over 90% of the participants.

At the end of the initial pilot study I reviewed final course grades and compared the Mastering A&P participants to those who did not utilize the e-learning system. The grades revealed a positive benefit for those who completed over 50% of the assignments. Additionally, the student volunteers were overwhelmingly favorable in their feedback about the experience. Out of a class of 59 students, 39 did not participate in the Mastering A&P pilot study, 14 participated and completed at least 50% of the assignments and 6 participated and completed less than half of the assignments. As shown in Figure 1, all of the students who completed more than half of the assignments successfully completed the course and had the highest percentage of A grades. The results reported in Figure 1 include scores from all tests (73%), class participation points (2%) and laboratory grades (25%).

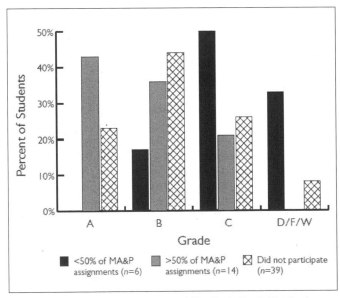

Figure 1. Human Anatomy and Physiology I Pilot Study Grade Distribution, Fall 2011

Based upon the positive impact on the student's grades and the favorable response from the participants, I opted to fully implement the Mastering A&P system on a mandatory participation basis in spring of 2012. Before adopting Mastering A&P, I modified the assignments based upon the feedback of the students who completed the evaluative interviews and surveys in the pilot study. One thing I particularly like about the system is that the publisher intends for instructors to "tweak" the systems to best support their courses. The course included the following units: human integumentary, skeletal, muscular, circulatory, and respiratory structures and functions as related to health and movement. Mastering A&P provided electronic homework, tutorials, and end-of-chapter questions for each learning unit. The students were graded on each assignment, giving them on-the-spot feedback regarding their understanding of the course material. My A&P1 course grade assessments included five unit exams (62.5%), laboratory assignments (25%) and the Mastering A&P homework assignments (12.5%). The 12.5% grade weight was suggested by both the publisher and the student pilot study volunteers. They agreed that this percentage was significant enough to motivate serious participation.

One unintended benefit of adopting Mastering A&P that semester was that I found it no longer necessary to host extra study sessions, as had been my practice, since the students were busy working on their Mastering A&P homework and very few attended the extra sessions. This had the positive outcome of freeing up my time while the students still received significant support in achieving good test scores.

The results of this first semester of fully incorporating Mastering A&P mirrored the pilot study results. The percentage of F grades remained the same between the two groups. A significant ($p \leq 0.001$) increase was observed in mean test grades from spring 2011 (71.8 ± 7.8) to spring 2012 (77.9 ± 10.6). The average Mastering A&P scores (82.0 ± 14.3) were significantly ($p \leq 0.01$) and positively correlated ($r = 0.60$) with the average test scores (see figure 3). There was a shift in the grade distribution favoring those in the spring 2012 class, such that the percentage of C and D grades decreased, the percentage of B grades increased from 11% to 20% and the percentage of A grades increased from 0% to 6% (see figure 2).

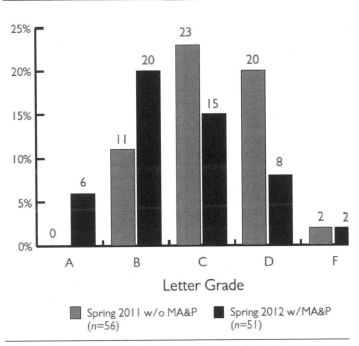

e 2. Human Anatomy and Physiology I Grade Distribution, Spring 20
Spring 2012

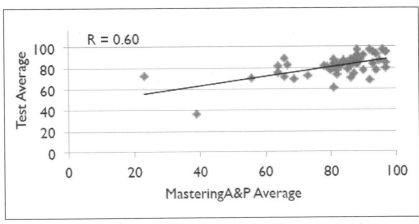

Figure 3. Correlation between MasteringA&P Scores and Average Human
Anatomy and Physiology I Test Scores, Spring 2012

When comparing mean test scores between 2011 and 2012 we found a significant increase (p ≤ 0.001; see Figure 4). Thus introducing Mastering A&P into my course curriculum produced a demonstrable positive outcome. However, we will continue to monitor and evaluate this process. The surveys provide valuable feedback for a continuous improvement model allowing the program to evolve constantly in order to meet the ever changing needs of the course and my students.

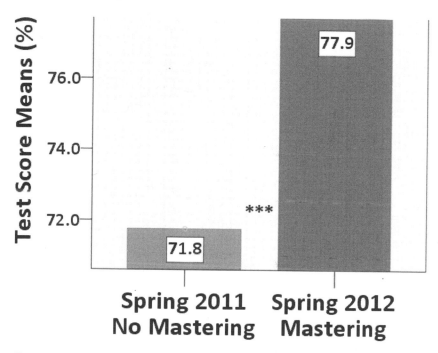

Figure 4: Mean Test Scores of No Mastering vs. Mastering

In the future, I would like to collect enough data over numerous semesters to be able to evaluate the outcomes while controlling for the student's GPA, year in school and gender. We suspect, at this time, that the students that benefited the most from Mastering A&P are those students who have GPAs in the middle to lower percentages. We also expect that the higher performing students will not realize such a significant impact from the introduction of Mastering A&P on their test grades, but this remains to be demonstrated by more data collection.

The end-of-course survey in spring 2012 indicated very positive experiences by my students. This mirrored our surveys from the pilot study. Their responses are outlined in the graphic below.

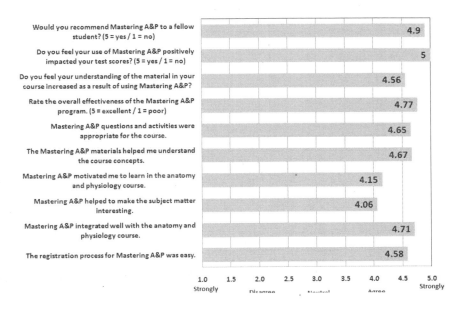

At this point I am in the third semester of implementation of Mastering A&P (including the pilot study). Taking what I have learned to date from student interviews and surveys, I have arrived at the following best practices for utilizing this e-learning system for my particular application.

Best Practices

- **Grade Weight**: Give the e-learning homework 12% weight of the final score (one test grade level). Student and publisher feedback suggested that this was sufficient to motivate students to commit to completing the assignments.
- **Expectations:** Make sure students clearly understand the course expectations in regards to Mastering A&P.
- **Registration Issues:** Walk your students through the registration process so they can utilize the homework program as soon as possible with minimum confusion and frustration.
  - For example, some of my students purchased the international edition by mistake, which meant they did

not receive the correct access code for our Mastering A&P.

- Make sure your students know exactly which edition is supported for your course.

- **Pick What Works Best For You:** Mastering A&P has some modules that involve the students writing long answers. I opted not to include these in my class preparation as my classes are typically quite large and I do not have sufficient time to take on grading more papers. I appreciate that Pearson makes it possible for me to fine-tune the homework to suit my needs.

- **Preferred Formats:** I found that the students' preferred homework formats included:
  - Tutorials (both reading and animation)
  - Drag and drop exercises (attaching names to diagrams)
  - Multiple choice quizzes

Note: Be cautious when using quizzes that require students to fill in the blanks. This because there are often multiple ways to respond correctly (kidney versus kidneys). The system doesn't always recognize these variations leading to inconsistent results which could lead to lower test scores which frustrates and upsets the students. Pearson is striving to address this, such as having the system accept multiple correct variations of an answer.

- **Assignment Length:** Students liked the 30-minute assignments even if they opted to complete more than one assignment in a single sitting.

- **Timing:** Make assignments due at test time.

Having the students complete the homework projects right before the test appeared to support higher test scores.

- My students stated that they preferred to do the Mastering A&P assignments following my lecture on the topic. Hearing me pronounce vocabulary and place the concepts in a meaningful context supported their understanding when completing their homework assignments. Remember, for many of these students in their first encounter with A&P, so it is like learning a

foreign language.
- **Professional Support:** Be sure to take advantage of the expertise and advice of your publishing representative to best organize your details before implementing a similar program.

This process of evaluating and implementing Mastering A&P has led to the following positive outcomes for my student researchers above and beyond the benefits received by my classes. Through their participation in designing, implementing the pilot study, preparing the results, etc. they have been able to present their findings at a variety of professional venues including the Southeast American College of Sports Medicine, American Association of Health Physical Education Recreation and Dance, Student North Carolina Undergraduate Research Symposium, and other regional and local student research events. They have been recognized by UNCW's CSURF/ Honors Program with travel awards of over $1500. Their work has been published in White Papers by the Pearson Publishing Company and abstracts have been published in peer-reviewed journals such as the Southeast American College of Sports Medicine. They also had opportunities to interact with and be mentored by the publisher's representative (exposing them to yet another employment option in their chosen field).

In conclusion, my experience with the process of implementing an e-learning homework system to support my A&P courses has been a positive one, leading me to be more open to new electronic learning systems. I am aware that there are other e-learning options available but at this point I can only speak to my specific experience with Pearson Education. Mastering A&P continues to open doors for me as I am currently in the process of implementing it in my A&PII course and am investigating utilizing the system for my A&P laboratories. I have found that embracing the cutting edge in electronic learning gives increased credibility to my teaching and courses. My students have benefited from their exposure to these systems and Mastering A&P has provided me with an efficient, time-saving method to monitor their progress and motivate their learning process.

BRAD WALKER

DEPARTMENT OF ELEMENTARY, MIDDLE LEVEL, AND LITERACY
EDUCATION

Communities of Learners: Empowerment Through Principles of Learning

As we endeavor to create communities of learners in our classrooms in order to empower our students as learners, we might benefit from looking at principles of learning that have been identified in other settings. Three such settings will be explored in this essay — Frank Smith's sense of "clubness," Brian Cambourne's principles of learning, and Donald Graves's notion of "slowing down so learners can hurry up." While these three settings are focused on supporting children in their literacy growth, they present powerful principles that can help us in our work at the university.

Frank Smith — Learning Clubs

Frank Smith (1994) has created a portrait of an effective community of learners in the area of literacy by comparing a community of learners to a club — similar to several clubs we might join in our lives. As we look at how clubs operate, we can identify principles that might effectively support the learning that we desire our students to do.

Smith (1994) suggests that children learn to read and write because they eventually are invited into and join what he calls the "literacy club." As with other clubs, children can join the literacy club with a "single unqualified reciprocal act of affiliation. There are no dues to be paid, no entry standards to be met" (p. 217). There is a mutual acknowledgement of acceptance into this group in which all members use written language as a way of knowing and communicating. There is a high level of expectation when one joins the club. New members join and fully expect that they will eventually be able to read and write like the more experienced members of the group. In a similar vein, the more experienced members of the group know that the new members will, eventually, learn to read and write as well as they do. Smith points out that this notion of expectation is very powerful. It sets a purpose for the activities of the club and gives hope to new members. It builds a realization of authentic engagements. There is purpose to the activities of the club, and there is hope and expectation that all members of the club will be successful. These expectations create trust in the abilities of all members of the club. More experienced members of the club conduct their business from a perspective of trusting the newer members. They operate as if the newer members of the club will be successful. This trust and confidence does much to support the growth of newer members.

Other principles of the club also help us identify aspects that we might want to establish in our classroom communities. Members of the club engage in the activities for which they have formed. In this case, they read and write for authentic purposes. This presents a powerful demonstration showing what those engagements will do for members. It reinforces the reasons for the engagements and promises results that the members value. There is an element of invitation, allowing new members to enter the engagements when they feel ready. Force is not a part of the club. Members of the club operate from a position of tolerance, never criticizing members because they lack the skills or the sophistication of more experienced members of the club. It is very acceptable to be an amateur. Members of the group help each other to grow towards proficiency. Mistakes are looked upon as a natural part of the process and are to be expected, not avoided nor penalized.

Is it possible to use these same principles in our classrooms? Could we create biology clubs that focus on ways of knowing the world through the eyes of the biologist or history clubs that focus on ways of knowing the world through the eyes of the historian? Let's use the perspective of history as an example. What might happen if we created a community of learners in our classroom that looked like a history club? The club would welcome the new students as valued members. Students would join through the act of affiliation, the act of enrolling in the course. They would know that we valued their membership, that we didn't expect them to be proficient historians from the start, and that we knew that in time they would become proficient at understanding the world from the vantage point of a historian. We would invite them into a wide range of engagements through which they could come to know what the study of history and the techniques of the historian could do for them. We would organize the engagements in our classrooms so that they were authentic and so that they sent the message that we trusted our students to learn and grow and that we were sincerely interested in supporting their learning and growth. The engagements and interactions in the class would invite our students to become engaged in the course at a level of significance for them.

Students would soon learn that they are very able to participate in these engagements, regardless of their proficiency in the various skills and processes that we will help them learn. They would understand that they are able to engage at their level of expertise. They would come to value this way of knowing. They would know that the mistakes they will inevitably make in their efforts to engage in learning through the tools and perspectives of the historian are expected and are a natural part of the process. They would know that they would not be penalized for their mistakes, but that we would help them learn from their miscues. They would come to know that we are committed to ensure that they are successful and that they begin to feel the excitement that comes from understanding the world through this historical perspective. They would feel welcome, wanted, supported, and complimented. They would feel and begin to act as an important member of our class, our community. They would enjoy being with others in the history club because they would have started to develop a shared sense of community and have felt the excitement that comes from learning. They would be able to see their successes and begin to want more. The class would no longer seem like a class. It would be a community of learners, and our students would feel empowered. The principles of learning clubs could add much to our efforts to empower our students as learners.

Perhaps the following chart might serve as further illustration of the power of "clubness" in our classrooms. The blank in each statement is the place in which we can substitute any discipline we teach. I have included possible insertions from the field of literacy in quotation marks and some generic insertions from geology in parentheses to illustrate the points.

Advantages of a Club:

1. Members identify themselves as _____ "readers, writers, learners, literate individuals," (geologists: as scientists, as learners).
2. Members see what _____ "written language" (geology: looking at the world through the lenses that geology offers) does for them and how it works.
3. Members are admitted as amateur members; they aren't expected to _____ "read or write" (know and do geology) like more experienced members.
4. Members help newcomers become experts. There is no specific instruction, no deadlines. Most of this is handled through informal demonstrations and collaboration in doing the work of the club.

5. More experienced members help new members _____ "read what they are trying to read" (Do the geology they are trying to do). Help is always relevant.
6. Members are quickly admitted into a full range of club activities.
7. Risk taking is fully supported in the confines of the club. The price of being wrong is very minimal.
8. Learning itself is taken care of; there is no need for meaningless effort. Learning happens in the course of doing what the club does.
9. Members benefit from the power of seeing themselves as _____ "readers" (geologists).
10. It is the _____ "reader" (budding geologist) who demands the feedback: "How do you know what it will say next?" (How do I know what to look for? Where to look? To what do I compare this data?)
11. Motivation is not a problem because time in the club is fruitful, productive, and enjoyable

What a club looks like in a classroom:
Professors letting go,
Professors trusting students and their innate desire to learn,
Professors giving ownership,
Professors empowering students,
Time, time, time — time for learning to happen,
Time to think and reflect,
Time to explore and ask questions,
Time to talk about the focus of the club with individuals and small groups,
Time to learn,
Exploration groups organized and
    learning about the world,
    answering authentic questions,
    sharing significant learning with others, and
    helping and pushing.
Professors realizing that they can't teach everything,
Professors organizing engagements, so that children learn everything.

Brian Cambourne — Principles of Learning Language

Additional principles have been identified by Brian Cambourne (1988), a professor in Australia. He searched for the principles that supported young children in their efforts to learn to speak. He reasoned that most, if not all, children learned to speak, and they learned it very effectively. Some of these same children, however, struggled with learning how to read. His question was, "Why?" If these children can speak so well and communicate so effectively, why do they struggle as they learn to read? As he observed hundreds of young children in their efforts to learn to speak, he was able to identify seven principles that seemed to be in place that supported these children in this process. His conclusion is that if these principles were in place in our schools, as they are in the child's natural life outside of school, children would not struggle as many of them do in learning how to read. I argue that these same principles support learning in any situation, at any level. Perhaps university professors can also benefit by looking at the principles and reflecting on their use in the communities of learners that we build. Cambourne's principles are discussed below with possible applications to the classrooms we create at the university level. I have included an example of ways I try to incorporate each principle in my undergraduate reading methods class.

Immersion. Learners need to be immersed in text of all kinds. Children learn to speak because they are immersed in an environment saturated with spoken language. Almost everywhere they look, they hear language being used for meaningful purposes, and they see the meaningful contexts in which it is being used.

The learners we work with will learn more effectively if the communities we create are smeared with numerous opportunities to use the skills and the perspectives of our discipline to make sense of the world. We can't hold back. Students will benefit from being immersed in the field of study. This includes many opportunities to jump into various ways of knowing in that field including text books, journal articles, computers, multimedia presentations, research projects, seminars, discussions, and interaction with experts in the field (historians, psychologists, scientists, anthropologists, educators, etc). Immersion provides opportunities for our students to learn, ponder, and question their world through the perspectives of our disciplines. These engagements must be authentic and meaningful.

Ways in which I endeavor to immerse my students in the discipline are to smear the environment with texts such as the text books for the class, children's picture books, case studies of young students learning to read, journal articles, student reflective journals, Web sites, and video clips. I read a children's picture book at the beginning of every class, and we talk about ways to use it in our teaching, as well as connections we make to the story of the book and how it helps us understand our craft of teaching more deeply. For example, one book I read is More Than Anything Else by Marie Bradby (1995). It is the story of Booker T. Washington and how he wanted to learn to read more than anything else. We read the book, and I ask students to share implications they see for our work with students and facilitating students' learning since they, too, come to school wanting to learn more than anything else. Every other week I invite students to share their reflective journals with students at their tables to provide more text dealing with the topics of the class.

Demonstration. Learners benefit from numerous demonstrations of how oral language is used to communicate and to get our needs met. These demonstrations must come from those significant in their lives and must be constant. Children watch parents, siblings, and others in their lives, use oral language to communicate and to satisfy their wants. They always see the meaningful context in which the language is used.

Demonstrations help students come to know what the engagements will do for them and will help them see how to use the skills and perspectives to facilitate their own learning. Our students will benefit from demonstrations showing how we use the skills and perspectives of our discipline to create knowledge, solve problems, communicate and, mediate the world. These demonstrations must be from those significant in their lives. In other words, they must come from us, our colleagues, and from other students. Taking advantage of opportunities to share our work and the ways in which we used the tools of our discipline to come to know what we know or how we chose to use a specific tool in order to pursue understanding or to express our feelings can be very supportive of learning. Allowing students to use the tools in authentic ways will allow them to be demonstrations for each other. Time to share insights and what we have learned can be most productive. Student work can become a very effective demonstration if it is shared with other students, instead of simply being turned into the professor, graded, and returned, without other students benefiting from the demonstration it could provide.

I try to enhance demonstrations in our classroom by asking students to share specific challenges/successes they are having with their tutoring. Students tutor a child who is struggling in learning to read as part of the lab attached to this course. The demonstrations they create as they share what they are doing, and the decisions they are making as they tutor can be strong support to the learning we are all doing. Another demonstration is called "Behind the Glass." We have a one-way mirror set up in our building as part of our Reading Recovery Training experience. Students in that program watch one of their classmates tutor a child. Because they are on the other side of the mirror. which is also soundproof, they can observe and discuss the tutoring session while it is happening. I ask my students to join that class at least two times during the semester. Watching someone else teach is a marvelous demonstration, but it is also powerful to join the conversation about what is going on. Since I teach in the education department, my teaching must be a solid demonstration of the concepts, skills, and dispositions I am helping my students to learn. They should be able to learn as much about teaching from watching me teach as they do from the learning engagements in class.

Expectation. Expectations of those around us provide a powerful support for our learning. Children learn to speak because we naturally expect them to be successful. Seldom do we ever express concern that a child will not learn to speak. We simply expect that it will happen and go about our business in that way. Our interactions with children are such that we treat them as capable, competent learners who will learn to speak. In many ways, we communicate with them as if they were already proficient. As learners we achieve what we expect to achieve, and we fail if we expect to fail.

High expectations are important, but sending a strong message of confidence in our students and their ability to be successful is also part of this element. This is very subtle. It is more than just telling students of our confidence in them. They see it more in the ways we interact with them than in the specific words that we share. Trust is also a huge part of this element and must be in place. As instructors, we must trust our students as capable, competent learners. We invite them to learn with us, and we treat them as proficient learners, knowing that they will get to that point. Fear is not part of expectation. Holding grades over students' heads is never helpful in the long run. We set high expectations and then trust them to reach and meet those expectations. Expectations suggest that we do not talk down to our students. We do not belittle them, nor do we patronize them. We treat them as the capable, competent, motivated learners that they are and/or that they can become. Expectations would also suggest that we bond with our students and that we share ourselves with them. Often we choose not to operate from this perspective for fear that students will cheat or that they might try to take advantage of our position. We must treat them as they can become. This requires a letting go of some of our control. It requires us to trust them and let them do what we are asking them to do — to rise to the expectation that we have for them. Too much control can be damaging to the learning process. Students might learn the specific facts and concepts we are presenting, but they might also learn to dislike the discipline and choose not to learn in this area again.

One way I try to show my trust in my students and to treat them as learners is to organize our class discussion, so that we are a group of professional educators exploring and learning together, earnestly trying to understand our craft. I work to ask authentic questions and listen intently to their answers. I participate as a co-learner. I endeavor to send the message that I am also learning by sharing things that I learned and connections I am making as a result of the discussion. I find that questions that are focused to a right answer are less effective than more open-ended questions. A good follow-up question might be, "That is an interesting perspective. Tell us more."

Responsibility. Learners need to make their own decision about when, how and what 'bits' of information to learn in any learning tasks. Children learn language because they have the responsibility to decide which aspect of the demonstration they will attend. They choose what aspect of learning to speak to which they will attend. They might be in a room in which they hear many voices and observe many contexts in which language is being taught, but they are the only ones who determine which demonstrations on which they will focus. They are the ones who have the responsibility to determine the aspect of language they will attempt to learn. Learners who lose the ability to make decisions are not empowered.

Our students will be empowered and supported more effectively in their learning to the extent we can give them ownership — to the degree in which they take responsibility. When we have a discussion or a lecture in class, we might think we know what students are learning, but it is their right and their responsibility to determine the specific aspect of that lesson to which they will attend. They know their level of understanding and the questions with which they are dealing. They know the connections that are exciting them and to which they wish to attend. We cannot control this. If we try to direct it too much, we teach them to not take charge, that their questions are not important, and that we, not them, are in control. We cannot effectively control them anyway. Even if we force their attention at a specific time, it will not be lasting. We can be consistent with this element of learning as we allow our students to help make the curricular decisions in our classroom. This could include choice in assignments completed, choice in ways to learn, choice in ways to share or present learning. We can help them with their responsibility as we invite them to ask questions or to share the connections they are making to the concepts discussed in class.

Another way to describe this principle is giving students ownership. One way to make this happen in my class is to provide alternatives to assignments and exams. For example, for the midterm I often give students three choices on what they would like to do for the midterm. They can spend three hours researching a topic about which they would like to learn more and then sharing what they learned; they can take time to read through the online discussions and posted assignments from other students and then summarizing significant points discussed; or they can identify another way to share what they have learned that is more meaningful to them, discussing it with me, and then completing it.

Use. Learners need time and opportunity to use, employ, and practice their developing control in functional, realistic, non-artificial ways. Children will not learn to speak unless they try to speak and use their developing control of oral language in meaningful, authentic ways. They learn to speak so quickly because they use language to get their needs met. Their use of language is 100% authentic. If they see no purpose in using language, they simply will not use it.

Our learners need to use the information they are learning for real purposes. Authentic engagements allow them to come to know what the discipline will do for them — right now, not after they graduate. They need the opportunity to act like geologists, sociologists, psychologists, teachers, nurses, and businessmen/women. They need the opportunity to engage in real uses of their skills and knowledge. Putting their knowledge to work will be a marvelous opportunity for them. We don't have to create artificial ways to use their knowledge. This is not motivating for anyone. Involving them in ongoing projects, allowing them to interview participants in an exciting research project, service learning, and internships are all effective ways to help our students use what they are learning and learn through their actions.

In our class, students must tutor a child who is struggling with reading. This is authentic use of the knowledge they are gaining. They work with a real student who faces real challenges. The learning of my students is enhanced as they face real challenges and make curricular decisions in working to support the learning of their student. One of the assignments in our class is for students to create a reading profile for the child they tutor, which includes strengths the child has, challenges he/she is facing, and next best-steps the tutor will try to help the child take.

Approximation. Learners must be free to approximate the desired model — mistakes are essential for learning to occur. If children were always corrected and lectured each time they made a mistake in their use of language, they would soon stop using it. If our efforts to help them learn the conventions of our language get in the way of getting their needs met, they will not listen. Children all know that mistakes are to be expected. That is why they can learn to speak another language so quickly or learn to use technology faster than most adults. They are not concerned with making mistakes. They are willing to take the risks that are a natural part of learning. They will try new language structures because they think it will help them meet their needs more effectively or because they have become intrigued with the specific use of language. They will risk trying because they know mistakes are not to be avoided, but are a natural part of the learning experience.

We might ask ourselves if there is room for approximation in our classrooms. Are mistakes looked upon as a natural part of the learning process? Do we help our students understand that mistakes are not something to be avoided, but something to learn from? Does our grading policy support our students in taking the risks necessary to effective learning?

We must provide our students with rough draft time. This is time to think through the concepts and try them out without penalty of being wrong. If the consequences of being wrong are too severe, students will pull back from taking risks. They will take the safe route, the route that will result in no penalties. It might not be the most productive or supportive route. If student homework is always graded on whether or not it is correct, then students lose assignment time as rough draft work time.

One effective way to create rough draft time is to provide the answers to the problems we ask our students to solve. Students could try to solve the problems or answer the questions and then check their work. It they have the correct answer, they move to the next problem. If they don't, they study their work to determine what went wrong or aspects they need to consider. Many professors shy away from this, concerned that students will cheat. This is where the trust comes in. We must trust our students to learn. We might consider structuring our class experiences to benefit those students who are learners, rather than always structuring experiences to catch the students who will cheat or not live up to their potential. The trust we give students will be a big factor in motivating them and will be a strong invitation into the learning communities we are creating.

In my classroom, I often tell students that this class is about learning and developing as effective teachers of reading. It is not about strict due dates and timelines. It is not about getting high scores on the tests. I hope this helps create a more relaxed, but more supportive, environment in which to learn. Students can redo assignments after receiving feedback from me. Our tests are focused to knowledge learned, not scores. I talk with students about the difference between a student and a learner. Basically, students come to class, listen, take notes, do the assignments, complete exams and move on. Learners do all of that but they take advantage of other opportunities to learn, explore, and discuss issues with me and other students. They monitor their learning, identify gaps, and then pursue information that will help them fill in those gaps. They ask questions. I try to create a grading structure that supports students in taking the risks necessary for learning to happen.

Response. Learners must receive feedback from exchanges with more knowledgeable others. Response must be relevant, appropriate, timely, readily available, non-threatening, with no strings attached. It must be real and honest. Children who attempt to say new things or use new words or structures receive feedback in positive, supportive ways. Most often, when we hear a child trying to communicate, we respond in ways that allow us to continue to communicate. If a child says, "We goed to the store yesterday," we typically don't give them a quick lesson on irregular verbs. Instead, we respond as we would in normal conversation saying, "Yes, we went to the store, and we bought some milk and bread." We basically leave it up to the child to start to make the connections between the conventions of our language and what they are doing with it at the time. That feedback is honest, and it is authentic. It is most supportive.

To give the kind of feedback required for learning requires time. Instructors must know their students and be able to identify the kind of feedback that is most needed at that particular moment. Feedback must be more than a simple grade or even a simple check on a paper. It is more than simply correcting a paper or a test. Feedback is most effective when it is part of an ongoing dialogue between participants. Feedback is very supportive when it comes in the form of collaboration where all participants are committed to supporting the learning and growth of others, as well, and the challenging of thoughts and beliefs.

During a faculty meeting one day, I was responding to papers my students had written. A colleague leaned over and said, "You are writing too much. They never read our comments anyway." I disagreed. I devote a good deal of time to give feedback to students. Providing significant feedback is a good way to support their learning. My feedback usually comes in the form of written comments on exams and assignments, as well as verbal comments in class and as I observe them teaching. It comes in our discussions. In my comments, I try to show them the progress they are making, further illustrate the principles they are learning, and help them see ways of talking about our craft of teaching. Comments such as, "You can see how important it is to come to know our students as readers before we can help them. You now know that John can …," "Another way to handle that situation is to…," "I would have made the same decision you made. I know other teachers who might have approached that situation from this perspective…," "Good job by you. Your work has helped him gain new strategies to use when he comes to something he doesn't understand as the reads. He might be ready for _____ at an upcoming lesson," "Have you thought about ...?" or "Good job by you. As I read your comments, I made this connection..." can be supportive.

Donald Graves — Slowing Down

Donald Graves (1990) said, "Schools need to slow down, so kids can hurry up." I argue that this applies just as much to universities as it does to elementary schools. In our efforts to "cover" the curriculum and to ensure the greatest amount of learning possible, we might actually be hindering the learning we desire. One of our challenges is to stay out of the way of our students as they learn. As we work to create communities of learners, it can be helpful to look for ways to slow down so that students can hurry up. We want them to use their time in the most productive manner. This might include time to reflect, time to discuss, and the rough draft time mentioned earlier in this chapter. Instead of assigning four 15-page papers during the course of the semester, perhaps we could slow down by having students submit a list of the 15 top connections they have made about a particular topic in lieu of one or two of the papers. Perhaps our midterm exam might be a written conversation between pairs of students discussing a salient point covered in class and asking them to extend the thinking to possibilities or other conclusions. Perhaps cutting back on reading assignments and providing time for more authentic work in our classrooms would also help us slow down. Slowing down so students have more time to use the knowledge, skills, and dispositions they are learning in our classroom to solve authentic problems in our discipline can be most supportive. An effective practice is to consistently reflect about the learning engagements we have created for our students and the manner in which we have organized our courses to see if we are getting in way of their learning. More is not always better. Perhaps slowing down can be a better source of rigor than piling it on.

The establishment of learning communities can be very helpful in our quest to effectively support the learning of our students and help them become lifelong learners. The principles of learning established in other disciplines can present us with a perspective from which to create the communities of learners that will empower our students. The principles set forth by Smith, Cambourne, and Graves can be effective tools in our work.

REFERENCES

Bradby, M. (1995). *More than anything else.* New York: Orchard Books.

Cambourne, B. (1988). *The whole story: Natural learning and the acquisition of literacy in the classroom.* Auckland, New Zealand: Scholastic.

Graves, D. (1990, May). Presentation given at the International Reading Association Annual Convention, Atlanta, GA.

Smith, F. (1994). *Understanding reading: A psycholinguistic analysis of reading and learning to read.* Hillsdale, New Jersey: Lawrence Erlbaum Associates, Publishers.

Smith, F. (2006). *Reading without nonsense* (4th ed.). New York: Teachers College Press.

KATHERINE BRUCE
DEPARTMENT OF PSYCHOLOGY
HONORS COLLEGE

Fostering Transformative Undergraduate Experiences

Preparing for a family reunion recently, I came upon a photo of myself soon after coming to UNCW and tried to reconnect with the ambitions, goals, expectations, and fears of that young 26-year-old with a newly minted Ph.D. While I had taught as a graduate assistant, I remember walking into those first few classes and how different it was being an official assistant professor. Those first classes began the long process of shaping my teaching style and philosophy. I recall I had a MWF 4-4:50 p.m. Introduction to Psychology class (the timing did not help my long-distance relationship at the time) that was a small section of students who also had drawn the bad schedule card. Because it was a small group that included engaged and committed students who did come to class on Friday afternoons (there were several nontraditional students in the class and also Rick Olsen, now chair of Communication Studies), we were able to connect and discuss the course topics and get off topic, as well. Now, almost 30 years later, I still enjoy that type of class best.

In that first semester, I found myself drawing on my own positive experiences in college, trying to model effective teaching practices that my professors at Rhodes College in Memphis, Tennessee (née Southwestern at Memphis), had used. And now I understand that I have continued this process, especially in my role as UNCW Honors College director and founder of the UNCW Center for the Support of Undergraduate Research and Fellowships. As we design new seminar topics or research opportunities, I think of particular transformative experiences that I had as an undergraduate that opened up possibilities, that made me think outside of the box, and that helped me develop confidence to begin to master my own academic passions as a scientist. There are four in particular that stand out, and they continue to influence my teaching and my impact shaping the Honors College vision at UNCW over the past 15 years.

But, let me begin with full disclosure – I am not an honors graduate myself. I came to Honors at UNCW through mentoring some talented students early on with their capstone departmental honors projects in psychology: Mary Matthews Behan, Chris Trefethen, Wanda Grace White. Once sociology professor Diane Levy and crew developed the four-year Honors Scholars Program in 1994, I came on board teaching an "honors enrichment/experiential seminar" on Observing Animal Behavior that I continue to teach on occasion in different venues. And, while I am not an honors graduate myself, I did marry one, and that has to count for something.

I did, however, take advantage of several types of undergraduate experiences that feature the types of teaching pedagogies so important for honors or enriched academic engagement: peripatetic teaching, faculty-mentored independent research and internships, and an interdisciplinary approach. One more ingredient, intrinsic to the student and related to these three pedagogies, is essential for this mix – an openness to step outside the box and try something new.

Peripatetic teaching

The essence of this teaching format is that learning is best when one travels to a particular location and is immersed in the study of the topic – on location. My own experience from college was a month-long Maymester (we called it "Third Term") spent in New York City, living in Chelsea. The class was set up to spend two weeks each with History and Art professors to earn interdisciplinary seminar credits; the other credits were in the form of Directed Independent Study (DIS). We spent each day with a short seminar on Modern Art or American History, then studied the originals in different art galleries or went on location to discuss historical themes and people. We also had open time to study our DIS topics or just explore The City.

The peripatetic seminar is a critical feature of the honors curriculum at UNCW, and, indeed, for many types of applied learning. From the annual Honors Lyceum to Washington, D.C., to Honors International Splashes, our signature Honors enrichment seminars that include short, concentrated study abroad travel learning over spring break or summer, we emphasize the importance of themed peripatetic teaching. This has several intended consequences: to help students develop a lifelong travelling style that includes immersion in the rich history and fabric of a place before they travel to enrich the actual travel experience; to help students develop confidence as they travel to a new place, so that they may consider even more intense study abroad opportunities; and, finally, to offer faculty the chance to enrich their own teaching by including this type of pedagogical experience.

As academically meaningful as my experience was in NYC, just as important was the chance to get lost on the subway and recover, to meet chess-players in Washington Square and hear about their lives in The City and what they thought about Southerners, and to stumble upon an off-off-Broadway play that made me think differently about "creativity." These experiences were key in helping me develop a sense of confidence, independence, and wonder – truly transformative.

And seeing that now as a teacher is amazing. I think I have learned as much or more from teaching this type of class as my students have from taking the class. Travelling with students is a remarkable experience, both in terms of observing their personal growth that can take place so rapidly and seeing their expressions as they encounter something "in person" that we had read about in a book. Looking through their eyes is seeing from a fresh perspective. For example, my spouse and colleague Mark Galizio and I have taken students to Ecuador to study and observe animal behavior and evolution in several settings, from the cloud forest and the Amazon River basin to the Galapagos. The seminars always developed on our own visits to the locations when we realized what an incredible learning venue the site was. We wanted to share it! In each class, the students would research specific animals, make presentations about the unique behaviors to the class before the trip, then serve as the experts on the trip. And then, as they saw a blue-footed booby mating dance in the wild, for example, it was great to see their eyes open wide in delight. Further, the pride that each student showed as "expert" in the field has got to have been instrumental in helping them develop their own academic self-confidence.

As far as building confidence, I have to single out Dr. Melissa Meadows (BS Biology Honors, '04). Melissa's first plane trip was her flight from Raleigh to Miami, en route to the Galapagos. After an eventful first day that included misplacing her passport and causing us to miss the flight from Miami to Quito, Melissa did make it to Ecuador with me the next day. She went on to become a model student on the learning trip. I recall her delight identifying invertebrates while snorkeling, and she later accompanied us back to Ecuador to the Amazon basin. Several years later, as part of her doctorate in Biology from University of Arizona, Melissa landed a competitive position at the Smithsonian Field Station in Panama and is currently immersed in post-doctoral study in Germany.

Because of students like Melissa, I embrace this type of learning wholeheartedly and have encouraged colleagues on and off campus to incorporate travel into their teaching as is possible (Bruce, 2005; Bruce, Horan, Kelley, & Galizio, 2009).

Faculty-mentored independent research and internships

Perhaps the most compelling experience for both student and teacher is one-on-one, faculty-mentored undergraduate research. Mentoring an undergraduate in an authentic research experience can combine the best of the teaching and research expectations we have as professors. Participating in extended DIS experiences or challenging themselves with honors capstone projects or departmental honors are opportunities for students to practice and hone research skills in the discipline that will be critical in a post-baccalaureate setting.

As an undergraduate myself, I had two very different DIS experiences, as well as a research internship that clearly shaped my skills as a scientist and scholar. I still think of the faculty who mentored me, all such different individuals but with several common characteristics as you would expect. The first DIS was after a semester in which I took classes in both animal physiology and psychophysiology, and my animal physiology professor offered me the chance to follow up on a result from a lab that combined the two classes. I researched a finding that allowed me to delve deeper into the study of hormones and behavior, the topic that hooked me into my undergraduate major, psychobiology. I learned a lot in that DIS, from conducting a literature review and to designing a study to running the stats, but one particular afternoon stands out to me. In addition to meeting after classes on a regular basis, Professor John Mugaas came in on a weekend or two to help me with a particular aspect of the research and to help me work with the animals I was studying. And one of those Saturday afternoons is the flashbulb memory I have of the DIS. Of course, Rhodes College is a small liberal arts school, and one might expect this type of commitment there. But, as at UNCW, supervising DIS was not required or compensated; Prof. Mugaas was just going the extra step as a mentor. I now see this every day at UNCW; I even expect it of myself and my colleagues. I have come to expect it because I know how important diving into a mentored research experience is; it creates the transformation of student to junior colleague. This experience is heralded by the American Association of Colleges and Universities as a High-Impact Practice (AACU, 2008) and is championed by the Council on Undergraduate Research (CUR, 2011).

Research internships can be the same. My internship experience grew out of a clinical partnership my Abnormal Psychology professor had with a research team who were studying the effectiveness of different psychological interventions via the "SPU- Special Problems Unit" at the University of Tennessee medical school. (Interestingly, my professor provided the psychoanalytical comparison to the behavioral therapies used at the SPU.) And "Special Problems" was right on the mark; my internship summer experience included collecting data related to several studies: behavioral interventions for autism, behavioral therapies for "sexual-aggressives," behavioral strategies used by attempted rape victims to thwart a rape, and diagnostic evaluation of erectile dysfunction in a sleep lab. I still share examples of these unique experiences in my classes.

Again, several of the research scientists took an interest in and a chance on me, a rising senior in college. That summer, I interned every day as a volunteer, and the position morphed into a part-time job the next year. I was allowed to collect data for large-scale NIH grants, run statistics, search for references, and, ultimately, become an author on two publications. When the SPU moved to New York City the next year, they hired me for a summer to work in the sleep lab. I also used that opportunity to take a graduate class on hormones and behavior at New York University, see Judy Collins and Poco in concert in Central Park, and learn to navigate to any location on the New York Transit System with one token.

Interdisciplinary Approaches

Learning to examine topics from multiple perspectives is essential in most disciplines. In fact, at UNCW we value this approach so much that our current University Studies program requires participation in Transdisciplinary Clusters of courses that examine a theme from multiple perspectives. My undergraduate major was a blending of biology and psychology into what was then called a "bridge" major: psychobiology. Thematic interdisciplinary senior seminars were expected, as well as qualifying exams with integrated items written by both psychology and biology faculty.

Interdisciplinarity is a key feature of the Honors College seminars and one that allows faculty to be creative in their approach to a topic. It is also a format that allows for effective and engaged team-teaching. Students in these honors interdisciplinary seminars are often surprised to learn about connections across disciplines and comment that they feel academically stretched and challenged to think outside the box. For example, the Mind, Morals and Evolution seminar featured philosophy, biology, and psychology. Many biology majors commented that they just had never considered that evolution could apply to how we interact with one another (James & Bruce, 2009). Another example of a serendipitous connection for many students was the biology-theatre seminar on HIV/AIDS taught from a virology, as well as a social commentary, perspective.

Trying something new

Being open to take an academic risk by taking multiple classes outside one's special interest is difficult. Certainly University Studies encourages a sampling of a classical core liberal arts curriculum along with courses designed to push the limits in terms of consideration of diversity and a global perspective, but it does create some angst at first on the part of goal-oriented students. The risk can come from unfamiliarity with or even disinterest in the topic or discipline of the class or from the expectations to demonstrate student learning outcomes, for example, class presentations or creative work.

One of my experiences trying something new came in the form of the DIS I enrolled in to meet the DIS requirement of my New York mini-term. I remember trying my best to develop a DIS idea that involved psychiatry, and it just did not pan out. Someone suggested that I talk to Dr. Richard Wood, the professor of my required English Lit class that semester. The topic was folklore, and I remember it included a visit to a Sacred Harp worship service and William Faulkner's home in Mississippi (peripatetic learning strikes again). Doc Wood had a reputation for being accommodating, and I hoped he would agree to a DIS so that I could go to New York! His idea was that I would write a set of critiques of off-off Broadway shows and keep a reflective journal. This was not up my alley, and I am really not sure how or why I agreed to it, but I did. I do recall being at a loss to find off-off Broadway shows at first, but I enlisted a friend or two who accompanied me. I am sure my critiques were, well, sophomoric, but it gave me practice in reflection and was definitely a reach. Doc Wood read my essays and journal and found something to like in my writing style, if not my critical reviews. I published a poem in the campus literary journal entitled "Walking Manhattan" that was part of the journal, and I ended up taking another DIS with Doc Wood on Virginia Woolf because he said he thought I'd like her – and I did.

Now as Honors director, I am in the enviable position of watching students blossom across the four years of college. The ones who take a chance find a depth in themselves that they could have easily missed.

Pay it forward

It takes a community of dedicated teachers to foster these critical life experiences for students, from travel learning, research mentoring and interdisciplinary course design to effective advising that challenges students to take some academic chances. In my role as Honors director, I count on my colleagues to engage students in this way and to show their own excitement about thinking outside the box. I count on them to remember what motivated them while undergraduates.

I don't think I ever properly thanked John Mugaas or Doc Wood or Alan Battle, my abnormal psychology professor, for their inspiration, patience, and time. But in my role as Honors director, I have been privileged to pay forward their kindness throughout these years in creating high-impact educational experiences for undergraduates. Now, 1,800 honors students later, what I see when a student receives an Honors medallion to signify completion of the Honors College requirements is not only a capable university graduate but also a confident world traveler or a self-assured budding scientist or a questioning and creative scholar.

REFERENCES

American Association of Colleges and Universities. (2008). High-impact educational practices. Retrieved from: http://www.aacu.org/leap/ hip.cfm

Bruce, K. E. (2005). Travels with Charley and Mike and Becky and Nina and Melissa and Tauheed and Johanna and Matt and John and… In *Peterson's Honors Programs and Colleges* (pp. 34-35). Lawrenceville, NJ: Thomson Peterson's.

Bruce, K., Horan, J., Kelley, P., & Galizio, M. (2009). Teaching evolution in the Galápagos. *Journal of Effective Teaching*, 9 (2), 13-28. Retrieved from: http://uncw.edu/cte/et/articles/Vol9_2/index.htm

Council on Undergraduate Research (2011). CUR Mission statement. Retrieved from: http://www.cur.org/about_cur/

James, S. M., & Bruce, K. E. (2009). Evolution and human nature: Comparing honors and traditional pedagogies for the new science of the mind. *Journal of the National Collegiate Honors Council*, 10 (2), 93-102. Retrieved from: http://connection. ebscohost.com

MICHAEL WENTWORTH
DEPARTMENT OF ENGLISH

"Only Connect": The Continuing Value and Relevance of the Liberal Arts

"Having recognized the need for education within a democracy, we need to determine the appropriate content of that education. In addition to an understanding and appreciation of the democratic system itself, what knowledge, skills, and values are necessary to enable individuals to live intelligently and responsibly as free persons in a free society?"
— Stephen Cahn (2003)

"It is time that we had uncommon schools, that we did not leave off our education when we begin to be men and women. It is time that villages were universities, and their elder inhabitants the fellows of universities, with leisure ... to pursue liberal studies the rest of their lives."
— Henry David Thoreau (1910)

A number of years ago, a colleague in political science called and left a message in my mailbox in the English Department that went something like this: "Mike, wouldn't you like to speak on the value of the liberal arts at the upcoming dinner honoring the newly inducted members of the Phi Eta Sigma Honor Society? Nothing fancy or elaborate. Fifteen to twenty minutes should cover it."

I read the message to its conclusion with an accelerating sense of panic, and suddenly I saw myself in high school speech class standing in front of my fellow orators, including the love of my life at the time, who was in love with some four-letter ace who drove a flaming crimson, gorp-heavy Bonneville convertible and had everything going for him, unlike me, who stood dumbfounded and goofy like the scarecrow in *The Wizard of Oz*, frantically restuffing his innards after the attack of the flying monkeys. I don't remember the topic of the speech, but like every other speech that fateful year, I – elocutionally challenged – stammered through to the end.

Returning to the present, I sadly acknowledged the fact that there was no way out of this one; for no apparent reason, my colleague in political science obviously had it in for me. He was clearly evening some score I wasn't even aware of. Compared to the current proliferation of construction projects and the escalating student enrollment, it was a much smaller campus at the time and, like the song goes, there was "nowhere to run, nowhere to hide." And besides, I could hardly refuse. The word would get out that "Wentworth over in English doesn't even know the value of the liberal arts." Yes, I was definitely stuck all right.

Morosely, I went home, overcome with a shuddering fit of the shakes. I somehow managed to eat dinner and afterwards turned on the TV, flipped a few channels, and there it was: *Jeopardy*. The first-round categories had already been revealed: history, philosophy, the planets, bodies of water, presidential elections, and the Wild West. "No sweat," I thought, as I proceeded to answer question after question with a mounting sense of self-satisfaction and realized that, at least on this particular evening, I would have outscored the contestants and walked away with the big money. Then, with a sudden flash of inspiration, I sensed a possible connection with my topic — the value of the liberal arts — and the diversified information base of the successful *Jeopardy* contestant. Just for the fun of it, I jotted down a number of answers:

- According to the World Almanac, he's the last U.S. president to run with no opposition (That's right, "no opposition"!).
- The axiom "Cogito ergo sum" ("I think, therefore I am") is his most famous formulation.
- This Wild West horse thief with a glamorous name was dubbed "the female Robin Hood" by the popular press.
- She was known as Rebecca Rolfe when she died in England of a sudden illness in 1617.

Well, by the time the show had ended, I began to have second thoughts, triggered perhaps by the fact that I had missed the Final Jeopardy question and, consequently, lost all my imaginary earnings (naturally, I had risked everything). No doubt chastened, I began to realize that the value of the liberal arts very possibly involved more than a flashy display of erudition, and erudition that relied more on the reflexive regurgitation of stored facts (the modus operandi of one Thomas Gradgrind, sir, and his trusty and trusting protégé Mr. McChoakmchild, so wonderfully pilloried by Charles Dickens in *Hard Times*) than any measure of judgment and genuine problem-solving. The whole "*Jeopardy* trip," not to mention any number of evenings when I'd "run the table" in "Trivial Pursuit," suddenly struck me as pretty mercenary and self-serving.

"Come on," I told myself. "You know the value of the liberal arts." Well, sure I did, didn't I? Evidently not, as I spent several uninspired hours at the drawing board. Reassured by the fact that if worst came to worst, I could always fall back on the official UNCW catalogue (Surely, there would be something in there!) or Cardinal Newman's *The Idea of a University* – which admittedly I'd never read, and still haven't – though I could handle the relevant *Jeopardy* question, I finally went to bed. I fidgeted about for maybe six or seven hours, but eventually dozed off and had this weird sort of dream – or it seemed weird at the time. I don't remember all the details, but it went something like this: There's a shipload of people (the ship looked like something out of some pirate movie with Bob Hope and Virginia Mayo I'd seen as a kid), and the people looked like they had maybe shopped off the back rack at some Army-Navy surplus store before there even were Army-Navy surplus stores. Well, they arrive and disembark at their destination, some uncivilized wilderness they'd only heard or dreamt about in their worst nightmare.

There were no houses, schools, or hospitals, no malls, no video rental stores, no buy-one-and-get-one free pizza franchises, and, perhaps most distressing, no Krispy Kreme donut shops. The climate, together with much of the vegetation and wildlife, was equally strange and unfamiliar. Shortly after landing, our ragged crew came into contact with what appeared to be native residents, though they, too, seemed strange and, evidently unfamiliar with the Queen's English, spoke a language totally incomprehensible to our landing party. It wasn't long before one faction among the party had seen enough and was determined to head back home even though things weren't much better there. But the leader of the group, with rhetorical pluck that would have made Dale Carnegie proud, somehow convinced everyone that "we can make this work." Then, somewhere off-stage, a disembodied, but authoritative, voice (amazing that disembodied voices often assume an authoritative register) pronounced, "And so they did."

Before "The End" flashed up on the screen, the alarm sounded, and I awoke in a feverish sweat and a high state of agitation before discovering that, unlike the alien wilderness of my dream, I was lying in my bed, right here in Wilmington, North Carolina, the very nexus of comfort and civilization.

I didn't think much of this dream until I arrived at the university to teach my first class of the day: American Literature to 1870. Then, as I opened my dog-eared anthology to the assigned text, there it was: Anne Bradstreet's poem "To My Dear and Loving Husband." Bradstreet and her husband were members of a party led by John Winthrop, who left England for the New World of "America" in 1630 to escape religious persecution. Though beset throughout her life by a series of misfortunes, ranging from rheumatic fever and smallpox to lameness, fever, and frequent fainting spells, Anne, much to the disapproval of local townswomen, managed to write poetry in her spare time and produced, as it turns out, the first published volume of poetry in colonial America. Not only Anne, but her fellow colonists, were afflicted by every conceivable form of discomfort and personal tragedy upon landing in a wilderness where, according to Anne's father, "many died weekly, yea, almost daily."

Yet, whatever the personal adversity and hardship, they made it work. And beyond their courage, stamina, and vision, the eventual success of their enterprise was enabled by an assiduous application of — and, yes, you're probably five steps ahead of me — nearly every one of the liberal arts included in your typical college catalog. Try building a house, a church, a community center without some knowledge of mathematics, physics, engineering, and architectural design; try designing an equitable form of government without some knowledge of political and social philosophy; try establishing an agriculturally based economy without some knowledge of natural science on the one hand, and marketing and economics on the other; try operating harmoniously and purposefully as a society without some awareness of the dynamic sociological principles that define any functional social community; try preserving the triumphs and failures of any social experiment without an understanding of history as the recorded measure of human achievement; try surviving the accumulated rigors of life in a strange land without the recreational, but nonetheless essential, diversion of music, storytelling, and the visual arts and crafts; try negotiating amicable relations with indigenous cultures (which, regrettably, with the notable exception of Roger Williams, we more often than not failed, and are still failing, to do) without the anthropologist's respect for cultural relativism or the linguist's concern for language as the fundamental basis for human communication and understanding.

The point, of course, as I myself realized at the time, is that nothing less than American civilization and the cultivated understanding of its diverse peoples and folkways, its landscape and physical resources, its continuing evolution as a social experiment should convince the most smugly snickering of skeptics about the value of the liberal arts. Amazingly, such an achievement, in terms of early American history, was more a matter of natural aptitude and acquired skill than formal education. True enough, such early colonial leaders as John Winthrop, Samuel Sewall, and Cotton Mather had graduated from university, though educational historians would be quick to point out that such graduates would have been totally unfamiliar with the modern liberal arts curriculum.

Consider, for example, the rigidly classical curriculum at Harvard College in 1636 when first-year students — all men, by the way — would have been expected to take logic, Greek, Hebrew, rhetoric, and theology in addition to more familiar courses in history and plant biology. As recently as 1916, North Carolina novelist Thomas Wolfe's first semester of study as a freshman at the University of North Carolina at Chapel Hill included Greek, Latin, philosophy, and English literature. Still, however unselfconsciously, the early colonists must have intuitively understood the value of what we now recognize as the liberal arts in domesticating what was often described as a "savage and desert wilderness." In fact, it's not entirely fanciful to think of the earliest colonial settlements as open classrooms or informal campus communities, though daily assignments involved a constant array of unanticipated problem-solving situations, and a passing grade was more often than not survival itself.

But what about the value of the liberal arts for the contemporary college student? Several years ago, I conducted a survey among my undergraduate classes to see what they thought and was disappointed, if not entirely surprised, to discover that many didn't know or viewed general education requirements as a waste of time or something to get out of the way (like cleaning the attic or mowing the lawn). Other responses were more encouraging and ranged from such profound insights as "The liberal arts enable you to interpret life in terms that reflect 'the poetry of being'" to a more typical response: "I believe that a liberal arts education allows you to broaden your horizons and get a different view of life. You become a well-rounded person who is able to carry on a conversation about anything." Now, I'm all in favor of conversational facility though I'm wary of a further proliferation of talk-show hosts in an already glutted media market, and far be it from me to quibble with the notion of well-roundedness, though here again I'm uncomfortably reminded of my expanding waistline or some department-store Santa Claus.

So, let me suggest a number of additional advantages. Students will expectedly and rightfully continue to question the value of the liberal arts until educators and administrators make a convincing and compelling case for the liberal arts as a coherent, interrelated, intrinsically <u>and</u> extrinsically meaningful system of knowledge, the individual components of which should complement and reinforce one another. Even the most comprehensive curriculum, even the most inspired classroom instruction will inevitably fail unless students are encouraged to discover the connections between and among disciplines and the relevance of other disciplines to their own chosen field of major concentration.

As novelist and cultural historian David Madden (2000) observes,

> The premise behind interdisciplinary studies is that just as no person is an island, no subject exists in isolation from all others; that a complex examination of a subject is rewarding; that several disciplines provide the milieu for that relationship; and that each discipline is enriched and made more powerful by interaction with other disciplines. (p. 2)

It's impossible, for example, to fully appreciate the poet William Wordsworth's autobiographical narrative *The Prelude* without some understanding of the role of the French Revolution in the formative development of Wordsworth and his contemporaries, and it's likewise impossible to fully appreciate the romantic spirit of the age without an awareness of such philosophers as Locke and Rousseau, such composers as Berlioz, Beethoven, and Chopin, such painters as Constable, Turner, Gericault, and Delacroix. It's impossible to understand our good friend Anne Bradstreet's poetry in isolation from matters of history, economics, and religious beliefs that provided the practical and ideological frame of reference for her personal history, and, of course, it's no less shortsighted to ignore the social, political, philosophical, and cultural variables that frame our own personal histories.

In short, it's all a matter of "making connections," in regard to which the titular heroine in Willy Russell's (1986) popular drama *Educating Rita* (the basis for an equally popular film featuring Julie Waters and Michael Caine) provides a revealing and telling case in point. Russell's drama, inspired by his own working-class background outside of Liverpool and, as such, his own unlikely educational aspirations, involves the working class hairdresser Rita (at one time, Russell himself was a hairdresser), who undertakes an "open university" course in literature at "a Victorian-built university in the north of England," with a cynical burnt-out alcoholic English professor, Frank.

Following their introductory tutorial, Frank lends Rita, whose taste in literature runs toward Rita Mae Brown and Harold Robbins, a copy of E. M. Forster's *Howard's End*. During their next tutorial, Rita dismisses *Howard's End* as "crap," an estimate based on what she perceives as the elitist orientation of the novel and later raises the question, "Does Forster's repeated use of the phrase 'only connect' suggest that he was really a frustrated electrician?" (p. 189). Frank, who has been invigorated by Rita's wit, humor, spontaneity, and unrehearsed charm, for the moment lets Rita's question ride. Rita doesn't catch up with the actual import of Forster's phrase until later when she provides a probing analysis of the lack of meaning in her working-class milieu:

> There's somethin' wrong. An' like the worst thing is that y'
> know the people who are supposed to like represent the people
> on our estate, y' know the *Daily Mirror* an' the *Sun*, an' ITV an'
> the Unions, what are they tellin' the people to do. They just tell
> them to go out an' get more money, don't they? But they don't
> want more money; it's like me, isn't it? Y' know, buyin' new
> dresses all the time, isn't it? The Unions tell them to go out an'
> get more money an' ITV an' the papers tell them what to spend
> it on so the disease is always covered up" (p. 195).

Rita then observes that her husband, Denny, who resents her ambition "to sing a better song,"

> tried to stop me comin' tonight. He tried to get me to go out
> to the pub with him an' his mates. He hates me comin' here. It's
> like drug addicts, isn't it? They hate it when one of them tries
> to break away. It makes me stronger comin' here. That's what
> Denny's frightened of (p. 195).

Frank then remarks, "Only connect," to which Rita responds, "Oh, not friggin' Forster again." Frank then identifies various connections she's unselfconsciously expressed: "Your dresses/ITV and the *Daily Mirror*. Addicts/you and your husband." In a clarifying moment of illumination, Rita reflects, "An'—an' in that book, no one does connect." She then asks Frank, "Why didn't y' just tell me from the start?" in response to which Frank explains, "I could have told you, but you'll have a much better understanding of something if you discover it in your own terms" (p. 195).

Frank's response to Rita's question reveals an enlightened pedagogy that creatively, by way of a calculated reticence and faith in Rita's innate intelligence, facilitates learning on students' "own terms," though the risk, of course, is that students may fail to successfully meet such a "deferred pedagogical agenda," but that's the challenge confronting any teacher at any level. No less tellingly, the exchange between Rita and Frank models the self-educating process of making connections between the social and cultural variables that define students' backgrounds and their own personal aspirations, as well as making connections between "book learning" (Forster's novel, in Rita's case) and the "real world" that should underscore and characterize the learning experience of students in the college classroom. This, in no small measure, constitutes a primary outcome of a liberal arts education.

But beyond promoting such a facility – no inconsequential achievement in itself – any authentic, meaningful liberal arts curriculum should promote an informed, active citizenship in assessing and responsibly responding to various local, regional, national, and global concerns. Ralph Waldo Emerson (1960), in "The American Scholar," often regarded as America's "intellectual declaration of independence," identifies and discusses the "main influences" on the mind of the scholar, or "Man Thinking." First and foremost is the "book of nature," followed by "the mind of the Past," as recorded and preserved in books. Yet Emerson ultimately holds that knowledge, whether acquired through the direct and studious observation of nature or through the assiduous study of the "inscribed" genius of the past, must culminate in "action," which, for the "true scholar," as opposed to the cloistered "recluse," is "essential," for "without it he is not yet man." Emerson (1960) then elaborates:

> I do not see how any man can afford, for the sake of his nerves and his nap, to spare any action in which he can partake … . The true scholar grudges every opportunity of action past by, as a loss of power. It is the raw material out of which the intellect moulds her splendid products (p. 70).

The "true scholar's" necessary commitment to action is aptly illustrated by Henry David Thoreau, Emerson's friend and neighbor. Like Emerson, he was a Harvard graduate, who, in his refusal to support the Mexican War – a war he viewed as an immoral pretext to extend institutional slavery to the American West – withheld a proportionate portion of his assigned tax as a result of which he was arrested by local authorities and spent a night in jail. The philosophical, ethical, and political considerations that informed Thoreau's defiance are eloquently articulated in his well-known and influential essay "Resistance to Civil Government."

Thoreau's principled resistance is as relevant and timely today as it was more than a century and a half ago in illustrating the ethical dilemma of those singular individuals who choose to turn their backs to a government whose policies they find oppressive. Thoreau's example would later prove instructive to Gandhi in India and Martin Luther King, Jr., in the American South, both of whom applied the lesson of Thoreau's passive resistance and civil disobedience to pressing social inequities of their own day. Yet Thoreau's passive resistance was hardly an original concept or stance since he had been anticipated nearly two thousand years before by Jesus Christ and even earlier than that by the titular heroine of Sophocles' *Antigone*. What was true for Antigone, Jesus, Thoreau, Gandhi, and Martin Luther King, Jr., is no less true for those students with whom we come into contact on a regular basis.

To summarize, then, any set of general education requirements should validate the value of the liberal arts by stimulating the sort of critical thinking that facilitates the discovery of connections among disciplines, encourages meaningful links to the real world, both on and off campus, and promotes an informed and principled notion of active citizenship. For philosopher of education Stephen Cahn (2003), an integral component of liberal arts education is developing an "understanding of public issues," culminating in such a notion of "active citizenship":

> In a democracy public issues cover an enormous range of topics, for every action of a government is an appropriate subject for open discussion, and such actions typically involve social, political, economic, scientific, and historical factors. Consider some of the critical issues confronting the world today: poverty, overpopulation, pollution, ideological conflict, the dangers of nuclear warfare, and the possible benefits of space research. How can these matters be intelligently discussed or even understood by those ignorant of the physical structure of the world, the forces that shape society, or the ideas and events that form the background of present crises? Thus, substantial knowledge of natural science, social science, world history, and national history is required for all those called upon to think about public issues, and in a democracy such participation is required of everyone (p. 202).

In this spirit, the University of North Carolina Wilmington has recently revised its longstanding basic studies requirements and adopted a more current, relevant, integrative set of "University Studies" requirements, which, beyond an overarching agenda "to cultivate [the student's] skills and capacities [within and across disciplines] to respond to and anticipate the complexities of modern citizenship in an inclusive and creative manner," incorporates a number of additional innovative features. Students, for example, are required to take a three-course sequence within a self-selected "transdisciplinary cluster," the purpose of which is to engage students "in the type of cross-disciplinary study that will help them to seek creative solutions to difficulties they will encounter when dealing with the complex problems that shape our modern world." Representative clusters not only include such traditional topical themes as ancient thought and culture and Judaism and the Jewish people, but such timely topical themes as immigration, climate change and society, gender and social justice, global diversity, and evolution, which address current social, ethnic, gender, legal, environmental, and scientific issues that require a well-informed, well-reasoned measure of critical judgment and discrimination.

In a similar vein, UNCW has also developed a wide range of area studies minors that illustrates the sort of integrated curricular enterprise I've previously described. Such area studies minors include African-American Studies, Asian Studies, European Studies, Latin American Studies, Middle East/Islamic Studies, Native American Studies, Postcolonial Studies, and Women's Studies, thereby reinforcing UNCW's commitment to globalism, cultural diversity, and cross-disciplinary studies, though other more professionally oriented area studies minors include Digital Arts, Forensic Science, Information Technology, and Journalism.

I myself have adopted an interdisciplinary approach to various special topics courses I have taught in the past. In "America and the Great Depression," for example, students are invited to examine the Great Depression from a variety of disciplinary perspectives, ranging from literature, photography, popular music, and popular film to sociology, transportation geography, climatology, agronomy, politics, economics, public health, and education. Thus, in addition to John Steinbeck's *The Grapes of Wrath*, the reading-viewing-listening syllabus for the course includes Karen Hesse's *Out of the Dust* (a prize-winning young adult novel), Studs Terkel's *Hard Times: An Oral History of the Great Depression*, Jerry Stanley's *Children of the Dust Bowl: The True Story of the School at Weedpatch Camp*, *Dear Mrs. Roosevelt: Letters from Children of the Great Depression*, Timothy Egan's *The Worst Hard Time: The Untold Story of Those Who Survived the Great American Dust Bowl*, Errol Lincoln Uys' *Riding the Rails: Teenagers on the Move during the Great Depression*, Michael Wallis' *Route 66: The Mother Road*, Mildred Armstrong Kalish's *Little Heathens: Hard Times and High Spirits on an Iowa Farm during the Great Depression*, Woody Guthrie's "Dust Bowl Ballads," and *Children of the Great Depression*, a remarkable, often-haunting anthology of photographs by such legendary Farm Security Administration photographers as Dorothea Lange, Walker Evans, Russell Lee, and Arthur Rothstein.

But whatever the focus of the course, I typically incorporate a directive in the course syllabus encouraging students to establish possible complementary relations, as relevant, between assigned readings and 1) the current arena of local, regional, national, and international affairs, 2) other works of literature they have read, either independently or in other courses, and 3) other academic courses they have taken or are currently taking — e.g., American history, psychology, sociology, anthropology, economics, geography, philosophy and religion. The supposition is that a <u>real</u> liberal arts education should be consciously and purposefully interdisciplinary and, thereby, should encourage a sensitivity to the interconnectedness of both major and non-major courses.

However daunting and prohibitive the current tendency toward the "specialized major," students themselves should be encouraged to familiarize themselves with various course offerings outside their major and across disciplines and to assume a resourceful and creative initiative in mapping a meaningful and integrated scheme of courses that corresponds to their own special interests and aptitudes (though, admittedly, upon entering college or university, many students have yet to discover their "own special interests and aptitudes"). Such an initiative, especially for those students in the liberal arts who often enjoy a greater degree of flexibility in regard to elective hours than the more specialized professional major, might lead students to consider a double major, an academic minor, an area studies minor, or certificate program option outside their major.

Aside from a judicious and imaginative selection of distribution and elective courses, students should also be encouraged to broaden their cultural frame of reference by continuing their study of a foreign language beyond the minimal proficiency requirement or by taking a second language. Stephen Cahn notes (2003), in this regard,

> the significant value . . . derived from reading some foreign literature in its original language. Not only does great literature lose some of its richness in translation, but learning another language increases linguistic sensitivity and makes one more conscious of the unique potentialities and limitations of any particular tongue. Such study is also a most effective means of widening cultural horizons, for understanding another language is a key to understanding another culture (p. 203).

Likewise, French professor Michael Randall (2003) advocates the study of foreign language texts in their original language and, more specifically, older texts:

> These texts . . . demand that students drop their understanding of the world based on the present and become part of a reality not their own. . . . If I can draw students into the literary world of 400 to 500 years ago — even briefly — their present can become richer and more complex. . . . A student who has come to grips with a text from a foreign culture from many centuries ago no longer perceives the present in quite the same way. The awareness of the complexity of a difficult text from a foreign culture leads to an awareness of the complexity that marks our present culture. That makes for a less efficient consumer of facile marketing and

political spin; but that inefficiency makes for a richer individual and more responsible citizen (p. 189-190).

Beyond self-enrichment and developing a greater understanding and sensitivity to cultural diversity and a recognition of parallels with the student's own native culture, advanced study in a foreign language carries pragmatic, potential career-oriented benefits, as well. Professional educators, as well as future health professionals, social workers, professional counselors, and public administration officials, among others, might be well-advised to develop an oral proficiency in Spanish, especially in view of the projection that in the not-too-distant future, Spanish rather than English will be the primary spoken language in the U.S. Then, too, given China's increasing economic prominence globally, business majors might consider developing a proficiency in Chinese. Currently, Chinese universities, who are far more progressive – though no doubt driven by pragmatic considerations – than their American counterparts, are anxious to hire English-as-a-second-language teachers — an inviting opportunity for liberal arts students considering the often demoralizing, debt-ridden prospect of "life after graduation."

Students should be further encouraged to involve themselves in the international campus community — which at UNCW currently includes exchange students from more than fifty different countries — and related social and cultural events and to explore travel and study abroad opportunities. The Office of International Programs at UNCW sponsors study abroad programs with "adopted" universities in such countries as Chile, Costa Rica, the United Kingdom, Finland, Sweden, France, Germany, Spain, Italy, the Netherlands, South Africa, China, Japan, New Zealand, and Australia, many – though not all – of which are discipline-specific. Numerous academic departments at UNCW have well-established study abroad programs, most notably, the department of foreign languages, though the Cameron School of Business offers study abroad programs in international business in Bremen, Germany; Marseilles, France; and Valencia, Spain. Just recently, the Department of English has established a dual-exchange program with Nanjing University of Science and Technology in Nanjing, China.

Students should be further aware of applied learning and community-related internship initiatives. Such initiatives are, in fact, a curricular component in many academic departments at UNCW and are particularly meaningful not only in acquiring practical, hands-on experience beyond a formal classroom setting in a student's major and future profession, but in promoting active citizenship, developing social and oral communication skills, and dispelling the "Ivory Tower insularity" and elitism of the academy often held by the "real world outside."

In addition, students should be encouraged to extend the learning curriculum outside the classroom by attending music recitals, poetry and fiction readings, dramatic productions, foreign films, and art exhibits, as well as campus-sponsored lectures and performances, the latter of which can further heighten the student's awareness of pressing social, environmental, and political issues on a global, national, and regional scale, as well as enhancing what Stephen Cahn (2003) describes as the student's "sensitivity to aesthetic experience," for

> an appreciation and understanding of the literature, art, and music of various cultures enriches the imagination, refines the sensibilities, deepens feelings, and provides increased awareness of the world in which we live. In a society of aesthetic illiterates not only the quality of art suffers but also the quality of life (p. 203).

At UNCW, the University Presents series annually provides a wide range of lecture and performance events. Featured events over the upcoming 2013-2014 academic year include professional productions of *The Fantasticks* (the world's longest-running theatrical production of any kind) and *The Graduate* (previously, and memorably, adapted to film, from Charles Webb's novel, by Mike Nichols and starring Dustin Hoffman as an angst-ridden college graduate); Grammy Award-winning saxophonist Branford Marsalis; Mary Wilson, an original member of the Supremes; "Celtic Nights—Journey of Hope: Irish Voice, Music, and Dance"; and lectures by Donna Brazile (veteran political strategist, the first African American to manage a presidential campaign, and one of the *Washingtonian's* "top 100 most powerful women"), Jose Antonio Vargas (Pulitzer Prize-winning author and immigrant activist), and Dr. Daniel Pauly (the world's most well-known fisheries scientist). Various academic departments at UNCW have self-sponsored lecture series of their own, which typically feature scholars with a national and international reputation. By way of cross-disciplinary collaboration, various departments sponsor public symposia and forums on special topics ranging from Islamic culture, terrorism, the endangered coastal environment, elder care, and the local economy.

Finally then, and most importantly, students should be encouraged to avoid overspecialization at the expense of the stimulating range of learning experiences that a liberal arts education is intended to provide and to take advantage of extracurricular learning initiatives. Thus, like Olympic decathletes, students should be discouraged from over-investing in a single event at the expense of the total performance.

If I were to recommend a model – though Thomas Jefferson and Ben

Franklin immediately come to mind – I can think of no better example than Sir Thomas More, the author of *Utopia* and the first lay lord chancellor of England, who served under the most notorious womanizer in English history, Henry VIII. More's interests, ranging from Greek and Latin studies, philosophy, theology, and law to medicine, zoology, music, astronomy, art, and political and economic theory, were so prodigious that the contemporary poet Henry Whittington once described More as "a man for all seasons." Such versatility in a world that increasingly demands nothing less is the ultimate challenge and continuing legacy of the liberal arts. Though their diplomas wouldn't necessarily say as much, upon graduation students should be positioned to take special pride and satisfaction in the fact that they not only leave campus as prospective accountants, teachers, nurses, or chemical engineers but as "men and women for all academic and worldly seasons."

REFERENCES

Cahn, Stephen. (2003). The democratic framework. In R. K. Durst (Ed.), *You are here: Readings on higher education for college writers* (198-205). Upper Saddle, NJ: Prentice Hall.

Durst, R. K. (2003). *You are here: Readings on higher education for college writers.* Upper Saddle, NJ: Prentice Hall.

Emerson, R. W. (1960). The American scholar. In S. E. Whicher (Ed.), *Selections from Ralph Waldo Emerson: An organic anthology* (63-80). Boston: Houghton Mifflin.

Madden, D. (2000). The Civil War as a model for the scope of popular culture, or the United States Civil War Center and the Popular Culture Association: Myriad-minded interdisciplinarians. *Journal of American and Comparative Cultures*, 23, 1-9. doi:10.1111/j.1537-4726.2000.2301_1.x

Randall, M. (2003). A guide to good teaching: Be slow and inefficient. In R. K. Durst (Ed.), *You are here: Readings on higher education for college writers* (188-191). Upper Saddle, NJ: Prentice Hall.

Russell, W. (1986). *Two plays and a musical: Educating Rita/ stags and hens/ blood brothers.* London: Methuen.

Thoreau, H. D. (1910). *Walden.* New York: Thomas Y. Crowell & Company.

Walser, R. G. (1977). *Thomas Wolfe undergraduate.* Durham, NC: Duke University Press.

KATHERINE MONTWIELER

DEPARTMENT OF ENGLISH

Building a Learning Community

Within this essay I reflect on my own experiences, but I try to do so in a way that will help teachers across disciplines. As you'll soon find out, acknowledging the importance of personal perspective is crucial to my pedagogical (and scholarly) practice. By knowing and admitting where we are personally coming from—as students, teachers, and writers—we see and present ourselves as individuals and ideally this leads us to recognize our audience, the people with whom we are communicating in the same way. This is not to say we are narrowly focused or elitist; indeed we can generalize from our experiences, and within this essay, I attempt to do so, so that some lessons I've learned after sixteen years in the classroom might be relevant for you—even if we're not in the same field, building, or campus. Although I occasionally reference texts or lessons peculiar to English instructors, I've attempted to write in a way that will benefit all academics, not just those who teach essay writing or nineteenth-century literature. For my emphasis throughout my classes and indeed throughout much of my life has been on making connections, the practice of building communities. Within this essay I reflect on my own experiences and build on the insights of scholars of pedagogy to offer what I hope is an insightful analysis of one way to teach successfully.

I like to bookend my courses: before they begin and after they end. This work gives me a sense of structure, of opening or starting the term, and of concluding it. The initial bookend is to pose and answer the question: what do I want my students to learn in this course? I frame the answer in two parts: skills and content. And, in answering the question I reflect on my past experiences and consider the future. How, I ask myself, will this course build on previous lessons I've learned as a teacher—and on the work my students will have learned in their previous courses—and how will this course differ from others I've taught, even perhaps those with the same title?

The practice of asking and answering these questions has recently been instituted more formally at many universities, including our own, with the requirement of adding Student Learning Outcomes to our syllabi, and while I bristle as much as the next teacher (okay, probably a little more than the next teacher) when anyone tries to tell me what to do, I firmly believe this exercise helps me as an instructor because I begin to think conscientiously not only about the crafting and trajectory of the course, but also about the students who will be taking it. Indeed the very march towards assessment that makes so many of us shudder has helped me give my courses a clear sense of purpose and has forced me to formalize a process that I previously employed intuitively and haphazardly.

I won't talk here—very much anyway—about the content that I want students to learn, analyze, and fall in love with over the course of the term because as scholars, we already know our individual disciplines better than anyone else who has picked up this volume of essays. As an English teacher, I privilege what Harvey Teres (2011) has termed "the new aesthetics," but before I travel that road, I'd like to spend the bulk of my time (and yours) focusing on skills that I hope to nurture within my students, particularly those skills that transcend disciplinary boundaries. The skills that I hope my class will sharpen for my students include communication (oral, written, visual); self-reflection (an ability to accurately perceive one's work and one's efforts—both individually and as a member of a larger group); analysis; writing for an audience (adaptation); and making connections and understanding the relevance of the work we do (articulating how this course relates to life after the semester's conclusion).

Working within the English Department, I teach a wide variety of classes—from composition and introductory literature courses to advanced seminars for undergraduate or graduate students. Yet although the topic and my students change from course to course and semester to semester, my primary responsibilities as a teacher remain constant: to cultivate my students' desire to learn, to nurture their critical inquiry skills, to encourage them to perceive connections across texts and disciplines, and to foster their development as writers. The specific pedagogical techniques I employ vary depending on the interests and aptitudes of my students, but the most important goals remain the same: facilitating within them an engagement with and intellectual curiosity about the world and their position within it and strengthening their skills as writers. Invariably, I find the best way to accomplish these tasks is by first focusing on building our particular learning community. Through the course of this essay, I'll address ways that I attempt to build community for and with my students because by creating an atmosphere of honesty and respect, we are more willing to address difficult issues both within and outside of the class. First and foremost, students need to recognize that we are here to learn and that genuine learning occurs most profoundly when they take risks and are willing to engage with each other and me not in a facile or superficial way, but by asking serious, pointed questions of the subject, professor, and each other. In a world and at a moment of increasing geographical and emotional distance, classrooms, and, on a wider level, our campuses offer us a specific place to address some of the voids apparent in our post-1950s, suburban fast food nation. Our students, I've found, are skeptical of this notion of community—while many often feel connected to their family and their church—more frequently than not, on my campus, they've grown up in a world structured by play dates, commutes, and organized team practices. In other words, students don't yet know themselves how to build a community—particularly a community that tolerates multiple points of view—and so especially at the early part of the term, I take on an active leadership role in doing so—though as the semester progresses, I step back and let the students take on more responsibility for creating an environment where we encourage multiple points of view.

Concurrent with this idealistic goal of framing our community is the recognition of the importance of humor. This trait is essential for English teachers, and probably for all of us. Whether it's composition ("The 'idea of a university'? Really?"), eighteenth-century British literature ("Did this Alexander Pope guy really put all that stuff into this poem, or are we reading too much into it?"), or critical theory ("But what does the panopticon have to do with me?"), I've found my students often initially resist the texts presented within English classes. This is not surprising of course given how few of our nation's citizens read for pleasure or at all these days. As Gerald Graff (1989) points out:

> The rise of literature as a college subject with its own departments and programs coincided with the collapse of the communal literary culture and the corresponding estrangement of literature from its earlier function in polite society, where it had been an essential instrument of socialization (p. 19-20).

And, so, in many cases, I must begin at the beginning, which requires a lot of humor on everyone's part. It's part of my job to teach my students how to read critically and to recognize that this skill takes time, patience, and concentration, all in short supply for the average 18 year old. So, at the same time that I'm introducing my students, for example, to the German Romantic notion of *Sturm und Drang*, I'm also trying to show them how reading an eighteenth-century novel forces us to slow down, necessarily takes us out of our twenty-first-century comfort zone. Students need to be good humored about this undertaking, and I need to be good humored about reaching my community of learners. Two years ago, juniors in my class on the modern European novel in translation lambasted Twitter after they created Facebook profiles and updates for Goethe's Werther and Charlotte. Last year, nearly all of the students enrolled in my first-year composition course tweeted. We must, of course, adapt to our students, particularly the lightning speed with which they communicate and the learning styles made possible by texting, web surfing, and prezi-ing. They introduce me to Facebook and Twitter. I introduce them to Goethe.

Modeling for my students an excitement about the subject we're studying and a willingness to take myself lightly, I attempt to convey to them that yes, although the texts, the ideas, and the discussions about them are complex, we need not be daunted; rather we can begin with an openness about the challenges, recognizing we need not shy away from those struggles but can appreciate the labor of encountering, engaging with, and analyzing difficult texts and concepts in a shared spirit of inquiry. I include myself in this work—nothing is as boring or as alienating as a self-righteous, pedantic know-it-all—and I've found that many of my students automatically assume I am that person unless I show them otherwise. By encouraging them to be the experts, by letting my students teach me, they are empowered, I am humbled, and we set the stage for an atmosphere of mutual respect. As the Buddhist philosopher Thích Nhât Hanh (2008) writes, "A true teacher…is one who encourages you to look deeply in yourself….The true teacher is someone who helps you discover the teacher in yourself" (p. 14). By letting them teach me, I nurture their self-confidence, their recognition of themselves as intelligent, perceptive members of a community, worthy of respect and with a responsibility to share their wisdom with others.

I believe curiosity is as instrumental for teaching as it is for learning, so even when I teach a course several times, I create a new syllabus and choose new reading. Obviously this is a perk (and a headache) of my discipline, but I believe that even when teaching courses that must necessarily cover a prescribed curriculum, by conscientiously tailoring each course to that particular semester and this particular group of students, we will offer our students the chance to have a more powerful learning experience than if we rely on what is comfortable or easy for us as instructors. Will such efforts demand more of us? Yes. But I believe that that commitment, that freshness, and that energy will ultimately serve our students, our profession, and our community best. The work of curriculum design is laborious but by "keeping it new," the class and the relationship between the texts is (almost) as fresh for me as it is for my students. Through my own willingness to engage with new ideas, new texts, and new approaches, I show my students my curiosity about and enthusiasm for the subject we're studying—and, ideally, life beyond that subject. Establishing rapport with students helps them overcome their skepticism about challenging material, and together we begin in earnest to work on developing their academic skills.

In nearly all of my classes, my students individually craft weekly responses to the reading assignments in the form of thoughtful, detailed questions (usually around 200 words). This process allows them not just to summarize a text, to offer an emotional reaction to it, or to rest in the self-assurance gleaned from reading critical assessments of literature, but sharpens their intellectual flexibility by asking them to think about how the text personally challenges them as well as its more general audience. I use these questions to catalyze class discussion, which then empowers the students by allowing them to take on a proactive role in our classroom. Their questions shape where we go in class that day, and so I learn about their interests, and they learn how to present their insights clearly and eloquently. Slowly, even the most dubious begin to recognize that the texts we're reading are not inaccessible, in spite of the density of the prose or the complexity of the ideas. As Teres (2011) points out, "good books interrogate us. They force us with their incorporeal coaxing, into self-examination, useful doubt, and occasional retractions and confessions" (p. 129). By writing about texts, by asking questions of them, and talking about them, not only do the ideas, aesthetics, and structure of the works we're reading become clearer, but the entire classroom community grows, not only intellectually by wrestling with difficult concepts, but personally and collectively, as well, by taking on new challenges.

An early French novel, a mid-Victorian poem, or a late twentieth-century experimental short story each presents unique challenges for our students. But, as Teres (2011) underscores, reading literature, particularly literature from the past, is crucial if we are to understand who we are as a people and how we have changed; how we have identified, understood, and fought our enemies and whether the quality of our discussions and deliberations has been commensurate with our great need for knowledge and wisdom (p. 54).

After the initial discomfort subsides, once genuine, thoughtful questions begin to be asked, we can move on in class to making connections between texts and across centuries. I provide detailed social, historical context, because I want students to recognize how the works of other centuries and cultures help to illuminate our own position in the United States in the early twenty-first. It's essential to my practice to create an atmosphere of tolerance where lively dialogue and exchanges can take place; we must not be threatened by differences of opinion—though I keep my politics and my personal beliefs close to my chest. I want my students comfortable disagreeing with the writer we're studying, with their colleagues, and with the instructor—articulating my own political convictions might silence those who hold alternative points of view. I concur with Teres (2011) and John Rawls that "the mark of a democracy is robust, respectful discourse among citizens who differ on fundamental values" (p. 173). Ideally, our classrooms can offer such a democratic space and we can encourage our students to disagree respectfully. I believe we ought not to come to consensus, particularly one prescribed by the authority in the room; such a flattening of differences encourages subservience, hardly critical thinking.

But even as I privilege dissent, I also advocate bridge-building. Some of my most exciting pedagogical work has occurred in interdisciplinary classes, in the Learning Communities program, in the Women's Studies program, and in an innovative senior seminar funded by the Center for Teaching Excellence for advanced English and History majors on constructions of gender, power, and sexuality in Modern Europe. Each of these forays has underscored my belief in the importance of a transdisciplinary education, of linking subjects and works, and putting various members of the university community into conversation, so that we can all see how our disciplines speak to and illuminate each other, and how we can provide for our students a way to make connections between and therefore sense of the seemingly disparate parts of their education. Within my discipline-specific classes (whether devoted to the study of composition, literature, or theory), I use a number of methods to help students make these connections, including creative writing prompts, directed self-reflective exercises, analyses of contemporary films or images, or class interviews. While I could enumerate for my students the similarities I see across texts, could make connections between this class and the philosophy, psychology, or communication courses they might be taking, I think it's more valuable and empowering for students to make the connection themselves. So I often offer open-ended essay questions that ask students to explore and explain how a text we're reading relates either to another course they're taking or a current issue facing them as individuals or the United States at this moment in history. Such exercises encourage a thoughtful consideration of the relevance of university studies to life outside the classroom, a meditation not only on the texts themselves, but also, explicitly, on their own intellectual progress. As Cary Nelson (2010) and Gregory Jay (2011) remind us, universities exist "to spend money on making citizens, engineers, writers, and other forms of what is sometimes called 'human capital' and that can also be called the creative capability of always-evolving society" (p. 169). This work ultimately leads to cultivating "reasonable habits of mind" that, according to Teres (2011), create "an effective public democratic culture" (p. 49). Their early work in tolerance, listening to others, and asking critical questions offers a foundation for my students' civic lives as adults.

Writing may be the hardest skill I teach because it takes practice, time, and patience, but it's a skill I privilege. My students write informally often; and we also work together—in small groups and one-on-one—brainstorming, drafting, revising, and editing their longer, formal expositions. Again, good humor is paramount—for everyone involved—as we discuss writing as a recursive process and a practice we are always improving. I work with students individually to meet them at their level and to build on the skills they already have. Not surprisingly, the best writers are often the students most comfortable approaching me for help; I'm delighted to facilitate their development, to stimulate them to demand more of themselves as critical thinkers and sophisticated rhetoricians, so that by the end of the term, their essays show their evolution in complexity of thought and presentation. And while working with advanced writers is a pleasure of its own, one of my greatest joys is helping weaker writers develop their own gifts, realize that they, too, have something original and smart to say, and that with time, practice, and patience, they, too, can communicate clearly and effectively. Deborah Stipek and Kathy Seal (2001) remind us that "the more specific or informational [our] feedback, the better" (p. 65). And, so I try to engage directly with my student writers as unique individuals who have their own strengths (which they might not recognize) and weaknesses (which they might not recognize). Sitting alongside them, we set "intermediate goals to give [them] a sense of accomplishment and competence, which in turn will nourish [their] motivation" (p. 79). My weakest writers don't believe in their own abilities, and I must show them that I trust them and their intelligence, so they can learn to trust it as well. By giving them my time and patience, I hope they learn to give themselves these gifts as well.

At the end of the term, I ask the students to reflect individually on three lessons they'll take with them from the course. This exercise prompts them to realize we have done important work over the semester—whether that's identifying salient characteristics of Romantic-era poetry or the more ineffable qualities of learning to ask good questions, learning to be patient when someone else is talking, learning to build on another's ideas, questioning those ideas (or their own), or sharpening their close reading skills. This practice is, I believe, a way to empower students once again:

rather than the professor listing for them what they have learned, they own their experiences by individually articulating them—and then collectively talking about the class as a whole. I also ask them about the strengths and weaknesses of the course and of my teaching—which activities or readings they thought were the most demanding and most educational—and which should be dropped. My students rally to give feedback, and I subsequently take their suggestions into account when I adapt the course to teach again. This is our last moment as a community—and later, if they don't remember the specifics of the conversation, it's my hope that I've showed them one last time how to have one, how to listen and how to respond thoughtfully. I believe this effort offers one small and yet deeply powerful way we can encourage autonomy and self-confidence within our students and help them to recognize that they have a multi-layered intellectual past and an exciting academic future ahead of them. In other words, by articulating the skills and concepts they've learned in the course, they become more conscientious about their own growth, their own academic career, and, I believe, how their work within the class will lay the foundation for future endeavors. If the students haven't yet addressed the relevance of the course to life beyond the confines of the classroom, I ask them directly how the work we've done might prepare them for a specific career, or, more generally, for their lives as citizens. Usually the students see for themselves that the skills we've been working on through the term, including self-presentation, analytical thinking, question-asking, and listening respectfully, will be ones they'll take with them when they begin, most likely, their management careers; they recognize that creativity, open-mindedness, flexibility, keeping deadlines, writing, revising, and proofreading will all benefit them whether they're working in advertising, the non-profit world, education, or another kind of institution.

But, it's not just about preparation for the workplace, of course. I hope that our class will lead them to a more meaningful, considered life attendant to aesthetics, respectful of others, and involved in the civic polis. Indeed, as a teacher, I believe it's my primary responsibility to show my students that they are not just workers—to help them see themselves as gifted, thoughtful, compassionate people who can help the world through their committed involvement in it—which comes not just from serving the corporations they'll most likely work for—but through active, thoughtful engagement and questioning themselves and others. For the sixteen weeks we work together, I try, as I believe all university teachers do, to, in Martha Nussbaum's (2010) words, "promote a climate of responsible and watchful stewardship and a culture of creative innovation" (p. 10). That lesson is one

I hope they will take with them.

Teaching is a gift; it's a privilege. Over the years my students have revealed their vulnerabilities to me, their struggles inside and outside of the classroom. While they may not even be aware of the trust they've placed in me to help them stretch themselves, they've stretched me, too. Teaching is a demanding job, and yet those demands have helped me to grow—in knowledge of various disciplines from history to literature to women's studies, but also in self-awareness and in appreciation for others. Not only then do I try to teach critical thinking and respectful communication to my students, but I also consciously try to nurture these skills within myself. Following Nussbaum (2010), Jay (2011) claims that to "independently weigh evidence, judge arguments, and resist the dead hand of authority and tradition" (p. 176), to cultivate aesthetic literacy, and to empathize with those who are different from us are at the heart of the pedagogical practice of the liberal arts. Teachers in fact are not so different from students after all. And, so I think one aspect of being a gifted teacher is to demand as much of yourself as you do from your students. We are all learning, and we're learning together. In this attention to community, this eagerness to learn, the recognition of one's limits and the desire to stretch those, I attempt to do so. I ask my students to meet me halfway. If I lead with my example—joyful, engaged, curious, and willing to admit and to work on my limitations—I find they respond in kind.

Together then we create a community of knowledge that transcends us as individuals; the lessons we learn together, about building on each other's ideas, appreciation of disagreement, and the pleasures of challenging work, lead us beyond the class to the greater communities of which we are part. For, ultimately, like Jay (2011), I believe critical thinking and empathy ground the moral life and the maintenance of ethical conduct; without these, democratic society falters and falls; without these, market activity and capital accumulation are free to run amuck, destroying the lives and physical worlds of millions in the process (p. 176).

But our classrooms—and our campuses—offer an antidote. And it is in these very classrooms that we begin.

REFERENCES

Graff, G. (1989). *Professing literature: An institutional history.* Chicago, IL: University of Chicago Press.

Hanh, N. T. (2008). Foreword. In P. Rowe-Ward, & L. Ward (Eds.), *Love's garden: A guide to mindful relationships.* Berkeley, CA: Parallax Press, 13-22.

Jay, G. (2011). Hire Ed! Deconstructing the crises in academe. *American Quarterly 63,* 163-78. Retrieved from: http://www.americanquarterly.org/

Nelson, C. (2010). *No University is an island: Saving academic freedom.* New York, NY: New York University Press.

Nussbaum, M. C. (2010). *Not for profit: Why democracy needs the humanities.* Princeton, NJ: Princeton University Press.

Stipek, D., & Seal, K. (2001). *Motivated minds: Raising children to love learning.* New York, NY: Holt Paperbacks.

Teres, H. (2011). *The word on the street: Linking the academy and the common reader.* Ann Arbor, MI: University of Michigan Press.

TIM BALLARD
DEPARTMENT OF BIOLOGY AND MARINE BIOLOGY

MICHELLE MANNING
DEPARTMENT OF ENGLISH

Tim's Top Ten Tips towards Terrific Teaching to Teeming Throngs Or, Surviving and Thriving in the Large-Class Environment

Editor's Note: When it comes to teachers-as-rock-stars, most of us are playing the cabaret circuit: an intimate 30 to 50 students in a small venue. At the other end of the spectrum, Tim Ballard, anatomy and physiology professor, is playing more to the stadium crowd. When he stands in front of a class, he is looking at, sometimes, more than 300 faces. And over the years, he has figured out what strategies work in small classes and, more importantly here, what works in large classes. He has not only written down his best suggestions, but has teamed with the English Department's Michelle Manning, a previous UNCW Lecturer of the Year winner, to create a current tip sheet informed by the latest research in the scholarship of teaching and learning.

What follows is Tim's and Michelle's interchange; I hope you enjoy it as much as we did. There is great advice throughout — with the backing of both years of hard-won experience and reams of careful research.

Tim Ballard: In 1984 I began my career as a professor at UNCW. As the new, and first, anatomy and physiology professor, I came into the university in support of the new four-year nursing program and, consequently, had an initial class of only 25 students. In 1985 that enrollment doubled and, by fall of 1989, had doubled again. By the turn of the century, my class routinely started with 250-plus students and occasionally as many as 312. As a result of these incremental increases in enrollment over the course of a 29-year career, I've had the luxury of learning how to manage a large class on the fly. However, as UNCW has grown, so too have all of our service courses, and many of them have large enrollments into which new faculty, some of whom are teaching for the first time, are quite literally pitched in. We pull the doors closed behind them quickly and shout, "Go get 'em, Tiger" without much in the way of survival skills. So to that end, I offer you Tim's Top Ten Tips towards Terrific Teaching to Teeming Throngs (pardon the alliteration).

Michelle Manning: Although I do not teach large classes, I have been the "victim" of a large class as a first-year student at UNC Chapel Hill. My 8:00 a.m. Chemistry 101, now subtitled as "The Reason I Am Not a Pediatrician," was held in a dark auditorium filled with more than 300 people. The first day of classes, I was stunned and a bit panicky. Illuminated by a lowly overhead projector, led by a professor with a monotone voice like the science teacher from The Wonder Years, I was invisible, warm, and disengaged; I slept through nearly every class. Because I wrote with an actual ink pen, my notebook resembled a series of Rorschach tests by the end of the semester. I am sure my professor was a nice man, and perhaps he had office hours, and perhaps people went to see him during office hours, but I, of course, never spoke one word to him. Like most first-year students, I was unprepared for a large class and how I should adjust my own habits to be successful in one. Even with overcrowding, the largest class a graduating high school senior is likely to have encountered is about 40, so imagine how terrifying it probably is for most of those wide-eyed newbies. If only I had a do-over in Tim's class! Tim's tips are terrific and, as you'll see, supported by current scholarship, as well.

Tim's Tip Number 1:

> Remember that you are in charge. ALWAYS! You are not president of a democracy, but rather a benevolent dictator.

Michelle: Tim is giving great advice here, but it can be tough advice to follow. I totally agree with Frank Heppner, author of Teaching the Large Class: A Guidebook for Instructors with Multitudes, that the "one thing graduate school doesn't prepare you to do in academia is to be a boss" (Heppner, 2007, p. 55). Instructors, especially new teachers who may only be a few years older than the majority of their students, should avoid "[t]rying to assume the role of friend in their lives — either by your dress, or your interactions with them outside the classroom, or your correspondence with them" (Lang, 2008, p. 23). The problem with this dual role-playing is that it "is a disingenuous pose that obfuscates the nature of the real authority you have in their academic lives" (Lang, 2008, p. 24).

Also, large groups can be corrupted by the mob mentality, so if you're nervous, you'll need to fake the confidence. Be approachable, but the rule of thumb is to start tough, but friendly; you can always become more lenient as the course progresses, but it is difficult — if not nearly impossible – to do the reverse. You should "start like Attila the Hun, finish as Mr. Rogers" (Heppner, 2007, p. 10).

Tim's Tip Number 2:

> Write a clear and iron-clad syllabus with the grading policy very well-defined. Remind students of this often and that you do not and will not waver from its stated policies. There are NO EXCEPTIONS. This is really hard. Most of us professors are humans and can be easy prey for a well-told story, and, if tears are involved, well, it's game over. In my classes I do not round grades at all, for any reason. The example I give in class at the beginning of the semester is this: Say you have two students with the exact same 69.78 final grade. In my scheme this is a D+. Student A is a real sweetheart, asks good questions, tries hard, etc. Student B is a real pain, hardly comes to class, has an attitude, etc. At the end of the semester, who are you going to curve up? Student A, of course, and this is unfair, almost to the point of being capricious. Solve this problem by rounding no one at all.

Michelle: Regardless of the class size, the syllabus is your friend, your enforcer, your guardian. If you do have any problems or appeals, your syllabus will have your back, so to speak. Since many teachers now email or post their syllabi online or on Blackboard, there is no reason not to put everything, including the kitchen sink, refrigerator, and stove, in them. A well-organized syllabus that defines expectations, explains assessments, provides links between assignments and course goals "helps students discover at the outset what is expected of them and gives them the security of knowing where they are going" (Svinicki & McKeachie, 2011, p. 17).

I have two parts to every syllabus: The first part is the university protocols and guidelines, such as my disability and safety statements. The second section is specifically about the goals, protocols, and expectations of the course itself.

I treat my syllabus like a contract and, in addition to discussing the syllabus in class on the first day and throughout the semester as needed, I often have a syllabus quiz — administered on Blackboard and that students may take unlimited times before drop/add ends — with questions that highlight the most important aspects of the class, such as grading, attendance, and late papers. The last "question" of the quiz is a statement that the student has read the syllabus and agrees to abide by the policies. If they don't agree, they should drop the class.

Tim's Tip Number 3:

Lack of fairness is not an option. We owe it to all students to treat each one like all the others. My yardstick all these years has been to ask myself this question: Am I willing to go before all of my previous students, who worked hard and sweated to earn their grades, and explain to them why I made this decision for a single student? If the answer is yes, then I will do that for the student in question.

Michelle: Teaching would be wonderful if we could teach for love of the subject, and students learned for the joy of learning. But grade and administer consequences for infractions we must, and our students have the right to expect us to be consistent and fair about the process. It doesn't feel good to turn down students sometimes (OK, most of the time), but "[h]aving these anxieties does not mean you have done anything wrong; it means you wish along with the rest of us that grading would just go away" (Lang, 2008, p. 128).

Tim's Tip Number 4:

Related to the fairness issue is testing. Because of my high enrollments, my tests are about 60% one-best-answer multiple choice. But since this is college, I feel compelled to give written questions, as well. In either format, there arises on almost every exam a question or three that may have interpretations other than my own. Therefore, I have a test argument policy stated in the syllabus. It tells the students that they enjoy the same academic freedom that I do and, therefore, should exercise it when they feel they have a case. Once I have returned corrected tests, students have until the next class period to give me written arguments. Not a whine, not a rant, not a complaint, but a scholarly argument. They have to convince me that their line of thinking is logical and is a valid solution to the question in question. If the argument is backed up with documentation, then all the better. Few students actually pursue this because it requires some effort, but those who do are rewarded more often than not. This policy also allows grades to go into the bank as unchangeable grades, thus removing the inevitable point-grubbers from the picture at the end of the semester.

Michelle: Similar to Tim's argument about citations that build a case for a student answer marked incorrect, I often have students self-grade their papers according to a rubric. While my final grade designation stands, the students know, if they assess themselves fairly and accurately, they have earned the grade, rather than me arbitrarily assigning a grade. If there is a big discrepancy between my assessment and theirs, we have a grading conference and determine their final grade.

Giving students the opportunity to determine why the answer may be wrong and then justify their answer often will either allow them to see why their response is erroneous or — in some cases — convince the teacher that their answer is correct (Svincki & McKeachie, 2011). Students feel more invested in courses where they have a say in their grades and the ability to discuss or challenge the instructor, fostering an environment of mutual respect and trust.

Tim's Tip Number 5:

Speaking of tests, give no make-up exams. This is especially true if the students see you as an easy mark. Almost all of us have killed off a relative or two to gain extended time for a test or assignment. Make it a policy to simply not do this, and then be strong, brave, and resolute. In my case, I give a comprehensive final exam from which students may regain the points lost by skipping a regular test. In fact, a student may choose to take no exam but the final for their final grade. They may lay all their money on the table and roll the dice if they wish. This is a terrible idea, of course, but life is all about making choices, isn't it? This approach allows you to not give make-up exams, thus all of that heartache and effort, but it also gives a student the opportunity to retrieve their points. A sidebar to this policy is to allow students to take tests early, if the situation warrants.

Michelle: First, it may help you to maintain a strong position on making allowances when confronted with another dead grandmother, broken computer, or dead car battery excuse to know that in one study of 565 undergraduate students, 72% admitted to providing "fraudulent excuses" to their instructors (Roig & Caso, 2005). Regardless, the important element here is to create the makeup policy and state it distinctly in the syllabus. Tim essentially does have makeup tests inherently built into his comprehensive final. Makeup work is a burden on the instructor, whatever you decide, and you first must determine what you want students to gain from the makeup exam. Some instructors build in a missed assignment by dropping a lower grade, while others assign the makeup in research-based essay form (Sivinicki & McKeachie, 2011).

Tim's Tip Number 6:

> As much as we might like to deny it, some students cheat. In a large enrollment class, cheating may be so easily done that it almost can't be helped. Have you ever looked up from your test and seen a classmate's paper? I solve this problem by giving multiple versions of the same test. This takes some time and effort, but it is well worth it. I will reverse the order of the questions, re-order the answer choices, move questions to different pages, etc., but I always give the same questions. I never draw different sets of questions from a common question bank, since one version will likely be harder than another, at least in the eyes of the students. This goes back to the issue of fairness.

Michelle: Providing multiple versions of the test is an excellent deterrent for cheating, and there are also some other strategies to reduce the cheating. First, your syllabus should have a clear statement about what constitutes academic dishonesty and the consequences for infractions, and this policy should be discussed in class (Heppner, 2007). Since sometimes students cheat because they lack confidence, enhancing their self-belief is important. Yorke and Knight (2007) suggest that somewhere between 25% and 30% of all learners have fixed self-theories that could impact negatively on their environment. One way to build confidence is to provide practice tests or post practice problems on Blackboard that allow students to become familiar with the types of questions asked or how they need to think for the exams. Your feedback on the questions can not only further clarify the material, but it also help them become "test-wise" since students often don't know how to take tests (Svinicki & McKeachie, 2011). In addition, encouraging or requiring students to form study groups will both enhance engagement and foster learning relationships (Zepke & Leach, 2010). The better students know the material and are comfortable with taking tests, the less likely they are to cheat.

Tim's Tip Number 7:

Student anonymity is a problem in a large class. Students can be as invisible as they wish to be, but I want all students to feel as though I am teaching them directly and personally, even though there are 250 students in the class. You can pull this off by employing a few little tricks.

Students are very territorial. Once they have marked their space, they will stay there the whole semester. Untether yourself from the lectern and your notes and move throughout the lecture hall while giving forth. Pretty soon you will learn faces in different sections of the room, you will learn who is "in the game" in each class, and, in particular, you will learn which faces belong to the better grades. During each class, while moving about, identify those faces and look directly at them while speaking. It will appear that you are talking not only to that person, but to all the people in that section. No one gets to hide from you.

Print your class roster by their ID pictures. Study the sheets, work on the names, and write their grades longhand by their faces. You may never learn everyone's name, but you will quickly associate faces with performance. This will then allow you to recognize individuals when they come to your office or when you encounter them in the hallway or the sidewalk. You can acknowledge them and say something to them about their performance like, "You really did well on that last test." This says to the student that he or she is not invisible and that you are paying attention.

Always write a short personalized note on each test. An "attaboy" or a question mark speaks volumes and lets the students know you are concerned for them. As the semester progresses, I also incorporate their running average into the comment. Again, I know that they know that I know where they stand.

Michelle: Students love it when teachers know their name! Social psychologists report that anonymity makes people feel less "personal responsibility" and, therefore, less engaged (Svincki & McKeachie, 2011). My Chemistry 101 professor never left the stage, adding to the feeling of disconnect I felt to the subject; however, by the time I took French Novels in Translation as a senior at Chapel Hill, I exuded more self-belief and took more responsibility for my role in the class. I was also bartending until 4:30 in the morning and trying to make it to a 9:30 class, trying to find a parking place, and going to a class that was filled to capacity. More than once, I sat along the wall for the full hour-and-fifteen-minute class. Bravely, I went to the professor, explained that if I was late, it was not being disrespectful, that I was enjoying his class, and discussed my to-this-day-favorite No Exit. From that day forward, he would occasionally greet me by name if I came to class – me looking like something the proverbial cat dragged in – and once explained to the class if everyone worked as hard to show up, they, too, would also be making an A. I had never been so thrilled.

While teachers of large classes can't be expected to know all 250 students personally, students appreciate the effort. Even if they don't avail themselves of the ways you are striving to make them less invisible, such as offering to get coffee after class, having them complete biography cards with personal information (on which you can attach their pictures and make notes about their grades or performance), passing out observation forms to a few students that they complete during the class and then meet later to discuss, or offering to meet with a study group, students do find those gestures important (Svincki & McKeachie, 2011).

Tim's Tip Number 8:

> Maintain a presence. Never show up for class at the last moment and then fly away before your last words have stopping reverberating from the walls, unless you have a real emergency. The students are important, and they need to feel that they are as people. Go to class early, greet students, walk up and down the aisles, be personable, talk about non-class stuff. You aren't just a professor, you're also a human. Act like it! Linger after class. Answer questions. Encourage interactions. Some of the best teaching occurs during hallway discussions and may have nothing to do with class itself.

Michelle: Tim is right again. One of the most engaging and personable professors at Chapel Hill taught a large class titled something like Education in Society. He would roam the two aisles during his lecture, and, once, seeing me write with my fountain pen, stopped and asked me to hand it to him. "Ladies and gentlemen, this," he intoned to the class, holding up my pen, "is a real writing instrument. Well done!" He also would ask, "What do you think?" It has been, ahem, a number of years since I was an undergraduate, yet that very large class stands out to me because that professor related to me, person to person.

Tim's Tip Number 9:

Be accessible. Utilize your email. I encourage students to shoot me quick questions while they are studying. I check my in-box multiple times a day and respond as quickly as possible. This lets the students know you are accessible and approachable. A side benefit is that the students will stay out of your office for the little stuff. Think about it like this: If you have a class of 200, and 5% need to talk to you today, that's 10 students in your office. Email is easier, faster, and more conservative of your time. Do not, however, encourage emails and then ignore them.

Keep office hours and be faithful to them. Post those hours and make sure the students know you are available. Office hours are for the students. While it is OK to be doing mundane office work, this isn't a time to be deep in thought while writing a paper. You want to be able to meet with students, rather be dismissive of them. I have an open-door policy regarding office hours and require appointments otherwise. If you are consistently un-available, you will hear about it on student evaluations. Many problems can be solved during office hours before they blow up.

Michelle: A study conducted by Mearns et al. (2007) revealed that, when professors are "perceived to be approachable, well-prepared and sensitive to student needs," then "students are committed to work harder, get more out of the session, and are more willing to express their own opinion" (Zepke & Leach, 2010, p. 170). Further, Bryson and Hand (2007) concluded that students are more likely to engage if they are supported by teachers who "establish inviting learning environments, demand high standards, challenge, and make themselves freely available to discuss academic progress" (Zepke & Leach, 2010, p. 170).

Communicating in a large class can be daunting, but Laird and Kuh (2005) "found engagement with information technology is positively associated with academic challenge, active and collaborative learning, student-faculty interaction, and deep learning experiences" (Zepke & Leach, 2010, p. 171).

For example, Outlook allows you to email the entire class by typing in the course number and section. However, using a class Web site, such as Blackboard, to communicate 24/7 means that you can maintain contact with the class, especially if you are teaching more than one section of the same course, allowing you to merge the two rosters, and you can also email individual students, as well as the whole class. In addition, you can maintain virtual office hours, using Blackboard IM or some other asynchronous method (Svinicki & McKeachie, 2011).

Tim's Tip Number 10:

> Do not be boring! After all, your discipline is the most interesting in the world. You studied it because you were deeply enthusiastic about it. Tell stories, always point out parallels with current events, explain the relevance of minutiae. Explain why they should care like you do. This may not be automatically apparent to them. A few years ago, a student confided in me about another class: "I now have no need to go to hell. I spent an eternity there already." What a sad statement about a course. You are the expert. Make it fun, exciting, enticing, and engaging. Work as hard for your students as you expect them to work for you!

Michelle: Scholars of teaching could not agree with you more, Tim. Most recently, they are focusing heavily on active learning, which can be defined as simply as "learning experiences in which the students are thinking about the subject matter" (Svinicki & McKeachie, 2011, p. 36). After all, students "engage in disciplinary thinking … only when students are simultaneously engaged in reasoning about those facts (Bain, 2004). As a disengaged first-year student in my Chemistry 101 class, I took what Hockings et al. (2008) call a "'surface' approach to learning — copying out notes, focusing on fragmented facts and right answers and accepting those" (Zepke & Leach, 2010, p. 171).

Some instructors have the benefit of TA-facilitated breakout groups; however, instructors can organize large classes into small study groups. Again, technology can assist the instructor by creating small groups online, creating discussions on the online forums, or providing blogging opportunities. Creating prompts that explore real-world applications or controversies in the field allow students to "de-compartmentalize" the subject matter. Numerous studies identify "active learning in groups, peer relationships, and social skills are important in engaging learners" and positively increase the perception of their own investment in the course (Zepke & Leach, 2010, p. 171). All of these efforts point in one direction: Tim's Tip #10: "Do not be boring!"

Tim: So there you have it. My Top 10 hard-won tips for managing a high-enrollment classroom – or any class for that matter. Be honest, be open, be fair, be accessible, and have fun!

Editor's Note: So there you have it, indeed. Tim's hard-won tips check out beautifully with both the current scholarship in the field and with the experiences of his colleagues. If you're facing a large class, keep Tim's tips — and Michelle's endorsement — in mind as you take on the challenge. A bigger class may constrain many of the things you'd like to do, but, with a careful and informed approach like this one, it can also offer you the opportunity to reach many more students than you otherwise could. Thank you, Tim and Michelle!

REFERENCES

Bain, K. (2004). *What the best college teachers do.* Cambridge, MA: Harvard University Press.

Heppner, F. (2007). *Teaching the large college class: A guidebook for instructors with multitudes.* San Francisco, Ca: Jossey-Bass.

Lang, J. (2008). *On course: A week-by-week guide to your first semester of college teaching.* Cambridge, MA: Harvard University Press.

Roig, M., & Caso, M. (2005). Lying and cheating: Fraudulent excuse-making, cheating, and plagiarism. *Journal of Psychology, 139*(6), 485-494.

Svinicki, M., & McKeachie, W. (2011). *Teaching tips: Strategies, research, and theory for college and university teachers* (13th ed.). Belmont, CA: Wadsworth.

Zepke, N., & Leach, L. (2010). Improving student engagement: Ten proposals for action. *Active Learning in Higher Education, 11*(30), 167-177.

STEVE ELLIOTT
SCHOOL OF HEALTH AND APPLIED HUMAN SCIENCES

NANCY HRITZ
SCHOOL OF HEALTH AND APPLIED HUMAN SCIENCES

"Welcome to UNCW – You Have 100 Students in Your Class!"

Let us start with a disclaimer statement: We, as instructors of large classes, are prepared to do whatever it takes to engage our students in the learning process. Over the past seven years at UNCW, we have made a conscious effort to use teaching strategies that put the students at the center of learning. Some of the strategies we have utilized are quite traditional and can be found in most "Effective Teaching" textbooks. However, the focus of this essay is on some of the more non-traditional teaching strategies that we have found to be successful in our classrooms. This essay describes some of our efforts to create a positive, active learning environment and details the transformative journey we made (and are still making) from being lecturers to passive learners to creating a climate in which students learn from and with each other.

Up until recently, we had no idea what FTE's (full-time equivalencies), SCH's (student credit hours), and CIP codes (Classification of Instructional Programs) were. The economy was flourishing, faculty were receiving nice 5%-8% raises annually, and there were lots of opportunities to propose and teach interesting elective courses to small groups of motivated students. The recent economic crisis and subsequent cuts to Higher Education budgets have resulted in university administrators engaging in "fat trimming" exercises in an attempt to absorb substantial reductions in state funding. One of the outcomes has been the increase in class size in many majors, and especially in University Study (core curriculum) courses.

Many researchers have investigated the impact of increasing class sizes on teaching effectiveness, student learning, and retention of students. Not surprisingly, several negative outcomes have been associated with increased class sizes. Some specific deleterious outcomes included (a) instructors lectured more during class, (b) students were less involved during class, (c) the amount and quality of instructor-student interaction was reduced, (d) students engaged in less critical thinking, (e) students were less satisfied with the course, and (most importantly), (f) there were lower amounts of student learning (Cuseo, 2007). With this in mind, the challenge facing instructors of large-sized courses is pretty clear: Can you create an environment where students in your large class are actively engaged in the learning process?

Since the 1980s, an extensive research literature has investigated how instructors can enhance student engagement in their classes. After reviewing 93 research studies from ten countries, Zepke and Leach (2010) synthesized the findings to form ten propositions for improving student engagement in higher education courses. Many of the activities described in this essay are aligned to those ten propositions. For example, the use of case studies and team projects creates "learning that is active, collaborative, and fosters learning relationships" (p. 171).

The prospect of teaching a large class can be stressful! Many new faculty, already nervous about their "new preps" and gaining the respect of their students and colleagues, are now being challenged to teach large classes in their first semesters on campus. There are many resources for instructors to use in preparation for teaching a large class. We recommend reading Chapter 3 (Planning your students learning activities), Chapter 4 (Meeting a class for the first time), Chapter 5 (Facilitating discussion), and Chapter 6 (Lecturing) in McKeachie's (2013) book titled "Teaching Tips: Strategies, Research, and Theory for College and University Teachers." Another good resource is Unit 6 (Engaging all learners) in Kronowitz's (2012) book titled "The Teacher's Guide to Success." However, if the thought of reading more books isn't exhilarating, then you will be excited to know that the optimal resource for helping you improve any aspect of your teaching is all around you – your new colleagues and the friendly folks in the UNCW Center for Teaching Excellence! The best advice we can provide a new faculty member is to visit the classrooms of as many colleagues as possible and see how they guide students through learning activities. To encourage these types of mentoring interactions at UNCW, the Center for Teaching Excellence (CTE) helps new faculty partner with mentors across campus. You will find that many of the teaching excellence award winners at UNCW are no strangers to the services offered by the experienced staff at the CTE. Indeed, many of the active teaching strategies described throughout this essay were blatantly "borrowed" from other teachers or learned in CTE workshops.

Recently, we were asked to record a podcast titled "Active Teaching Strategies" for the High Impact Teaching program administered by the

Center for Teaching Excellence (you can listen to it here: http://uncw.edu/cte/HighImpactTeaching/index.html). In this podcast we discussed strategies that we have employed in large classes in an attempt to create and maintain an active learning environment. Although most of these strategies could be employed at any time during the semester or a specific class period, we have categorized them into active learning strategies that can be used, (a) on the first day of class, (b) at the start of a class period, (c) at any time during a class, and (d) at the end of a class period.

Active learning strategies for the first day of class

The first day of class is a chance to make a good initial impression and to set the tone for the entire semester. We have all seen the traditional approach for the first day of class: The instructor reads the syllabus word-for-word, answers students' questions, and then jumps straight into course content to show the students that this course is "all business" and that there is no time to be wasted. Alternatively, there are many things that you can do on the first day that will help you establish rapport with the students and show them that you care about them as individuals within a community of learners. This is not "wasted time" because we have known for many years that several affective factors are connected to student motivation (Forsythe, 2003).

We have found that first-day activities work best if the instructor is an enthusiastic participant and that every student is given the opportunity to speak. This is a perfect time to tell your students something about your personal and professional life – for example, where you went to university, why you are passionate about your field, and what kind of research you are engaged in. Two activities that we have used on the first day of class are (a) the "Kite," and (b) the "To tell the truth" game. Both of these activities serve as ice breakers, require whole class participation, and help establish a collaborative and respectful culture in the classroom.

The "Kite" is a non-threatening activity that gives the students a chance to learn a little bit more about each other and the instructor. It also enables the instructor to create several metaphors between the flight of the kite and the successful performance of students in the course. For example, kites soar when they are provided resistance just as students learn when they are challenged to think critically. The kite activity starts with the instructor providing each student with a blank piece of paper and instructing them to draw a kite with four quadrants and three ribbons on the tail. In the quadrants, the students have to draw (no writing is allowed!) their responses to the following four questions: (1) Where are you from? (2) What is your proudest moment ever? (3) Where is the best place you have visited? and

(4) What do you want to be doing five years after you graduate? Obviously, you can change these questions to get the information you want to know. On the three ribbons on the tail of the kite, the student has to write the three names of people (dead or alive, real or fictional) that they would invite to dinner. After 10-15 minutes, have the student partner up with someone else in the class and explain their kite to them. The final part of this activity is to invite students to introduce their partner to the rest of the class. Figure 1 is the kite drawn by one of the authors from a recent course.

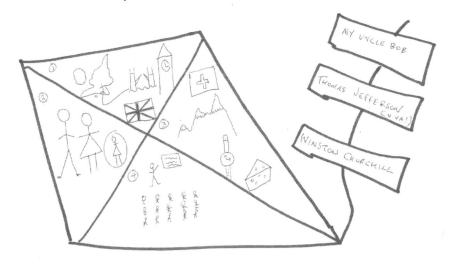

FIGURE 1. KITE ACTIVITY

The "To tell the Truth" game is a modified version of the popular TV game show, which features a panel of celebrities attempting to correctly identify a described contestant who has an unusual occupation or experience. In the classroom version, students have to make one true statement and two untrue statements about themselves and invite their classmates to guess the true one. This gives students a chance to choose what they wish to disclose in a fun activity and enables everybody to speak on the first day of class. Again, this activity works well when the instructor goes first.

Active learning strategies for the start of a class

The start of each class meeting provides the instructor with an excellent opportunity to interact with individual students and to reinforce the positive learning environment that has been established. Arriving 5-10 minutes before the class begins enables the instructor to sit amongst the students and talk with them. What you discuss sometimes isn't even that important, but the fact that you are amongst the students sends a strong message that you want to get to know them as individuals. In a large classroom, the instructor could mingle with a different section of the class each day to meet as many students as possible.

Some students are uncomfortable asking questions in a large-class format. We have helped these students by encouraging them to write any questions that they may have on a notecard or sent through email and pasting the question(s) on a PowerPoint slide, so that the whole class can see it. To promote active learning and critical thinking, a powerful follow-up strategy involves asking the students to think about the question on the slide, and then to engage in a "think, pair, n' share" activity. This challenges students to think about the question on their own, to turn to a partner to discuss it with them, and then to finally share their responses with the class. This activity (a) provides a review of previously covered content, (b) clarifies any confusion with specific course content, (c) encourages the students to think critically, and (d) requires students to communicate with classmates. Figure 2 shows a question that was emailed to one of the authors in a recent research methods course. The author used this question to create a partnered critical thinking activity to start the following class.

THINK, PAIR, N' SHARE

QUESTION:

- What is the different between a dependent t-test and an independent t-test?

ACTIVITY:

- Think about this question
- Turn and discuss with a partner
- Come up with a research question that would use each type of t-test
- Share with the class

FIGURE 2. THINK, PAIR, N' SHARE ACTIVITY

Short quizzes given at the start of a class meeting are effective in reviewing course concepts and finding out what content students may struggling with. This can be done in a "team quiz" competitive format in which students are grouped into teams at the start of the semester, and each team provides its answers to the daily quiz written on a notecard. The instructor can collect the teams' responses and keep a visual leaderboard that is displayed periodically throughout the semester. Team quizzes are generally popular with students and promote discussion related to the course content. Rather than tying the quizzes to a student's grade, we have rewarded winning teams with small gifts such as a bookstore voucher or a UNCW T-shirt.

Active learning strategies during any time in the class

Most large classes are held in theatre-style rooms with tiered seating. At UNCW, because effective teaching is at the fore of our mission, all of our large teaching areas have been equipped with the latest technology. Gone are the days when the instructor has to stand in front of the blackboard. Remote mouses and keyboards allow the instructor to "see all the students" by moving around the room and up and down the aisles. This basic strategy is effective at maintaining a positive learning environment and at promoting extended student talk whereby students respond to each other's comments.

Some of our favorite lessons have involved in-class demonstrations that enable learners to see concrete examples of abstract concepts. In a research methods class, bringing in a water tank and different objects and playing the "Will it float" game from the David Letterman show proved to be a bizarre, yet seemingly effective way, in helping students learn how to write research hypotheses. In another one of our classes, the instructor brought his 9-month-old daughter to class to provide a real-world example of motor behaviors that they were studying. In addition to discussing and reading about how infants transition from crawling to creeping to walking, the students were able to see an infant demonstrate what these movements looked like at the front of the class.

We encourage new faculty to be "Risk Takers" in the classroom. Perhaps the teaching strategy that we have employed to promote active learning that required the biggest leap of faith and highest subsequent risk has been the use of "Theme Days." The photograph below (Figure 3) is one of the authors dressed in outfit to help teach the concept of Gorilla / Guerrilla Marketing in a Tourism Management course. This was a particularly effective teaching tactic because not only did the costume represent the name of the marketing strategy, but it also demonstrated how guerrilla marketing is an unconventional system of promotions that relies on time, energy, and imagination rather than a big marketing budget. Student feedback has informed us that they really connect with activities that provide concrete examples and with instructors who are prepared to make themselves look a wee bit silly in an effort to bring the content to life for the students.

FIGURE 3. THEME DAYS

Another effective method of promoting active learning in large courses is to "Flip the Classroom" and use "Case Studies" to stimulate critical thinking and student interactions. Case studies can be distributed to students ahead of class in several different formats (e.g., journal articles, newspaper reports, online video clips, etc). Class time can then be used to discuss concepts, apply the knowledge, and do more practical work. This is a strategy that we have found results in students' spending more time interacting with the instructor and each other and less time passively listening. If you are planning on using case studies, then it is important to set the ground rules (e.g., one person talks at a time), so that a positive learning environment is maintained.

As we mentioned earlier, the best resource at UNCW will be your new colleagues. One of our most creative faculty members is Dr. Jeff Ertzberger, the Director of Technology in the Watson College of Education, who has created multiple whole-class participation games that are housed on his website "EdGames" (http://people.uncw.edu/ertzbergerj/msgames.htm). The games on this Web site are designed for use in a classroom setting where the teacher has his/her computer hooked up to a projector or large-screen TV, so that everyone in the class can view them at the same time. One of our favorite games is the "Big Board Facts" game, which is similar to the "Jeopardy" TV game show. This Web-based game allows you to put your "who, what, when, where" questions onto the board and have students try to answer them for points. This game also comes in a "with answers" version that allows the teacher to show the correct answer after the question. This game is particularly useful for reviewing content before examinations. Figure 4 shows a screenshot of a Big Board Facts game that was designed to reinforce concepts from a unit on rivers, bodies of water, continents, deserts, and planets.

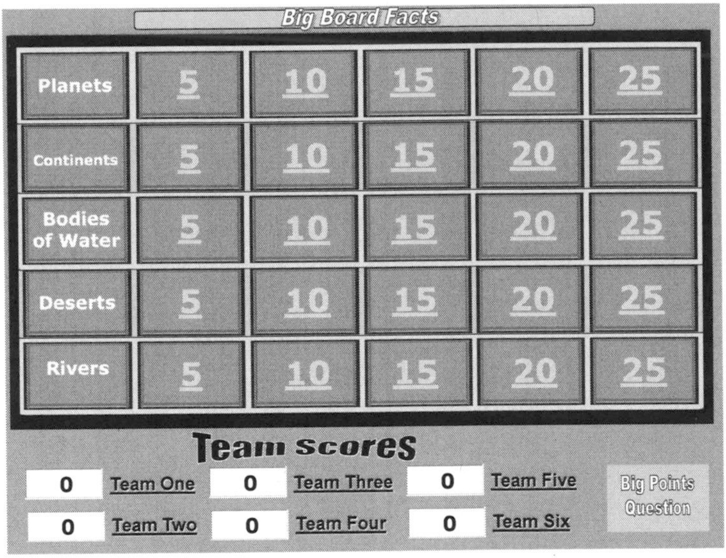

FIGURE 4. BIG BOARDS FACTS GAME

Active learning strategies for the closure and review

The last few minutes in a class provide an opportunity to review the content covered in the course and to prepare students for the upcoming lessons. However, many students, at the first sign of the class ending, will start unzipping their backpacks looking for a quick exit and, unfortunately, will miss any verbal review of content. There are several alternative strategies to the verbal review that engage students in the last few minutes of the class.

In some of our classes, we have required our students to purchase a pack of notecards and to bring them to every class. Periodically, we ask the students to take out a notecard at the end of the class and handwrite responses to a question, ask their own question(s), or to reflect on the lesson. This notecard serves as an "exit slip," which the students hand in on their way out of the classroom. Being that they come at the end of a lesson, unit, or segment of study, exit slips give teachers a snapshot of the overall student learning. This formative assessment technique requires student active engagement and enables them to (a) rate their current understanding of new learning, (b) analyze and reflect on their efforts around the learning, (c) provide feedback to teachers on an instructional strategy, and (d) provide feedback about the materials and teaching.

Another lesson-closing activity requiring the active engagement of students is the "two-minute free write." In this activity, students are instructed to put their pen to a piece of paper and to write for two minutes without their pen leaving the paper. As the name suggests, students can reflect on any aspect of the content and the course that they wish to. This can be a powerful reflective activity that provides some communication between the instructor and students in a large class.

Is teaching an art or a science? You will see this question asked in one form or another in most teaching effectiveness textbooks and workshops. As professional educators, we are all well-versed in the psychological and pedagogical principles that apply to learning. We have been taught by our mentors to root our own teaching behaviors in certain theoretical assumptions about our learners. However, an instructor can know all of the best educational theories and pedagogical methods, but applying them by relating to different types of learners, keeping students engaged, building relationships, and balancing curriculum is definitely an art, and it is an art that becomes a little trickier to master with large class sizes. We encourage all new faculty to be risk takers and try new things in the classroom in an all-out attempt to keep your students actively engaged in large class sizes. The chances are that you will experience the same things that we did ... that some of your well-conceived activities will crash and burn in spectacular fashion! But then, you get to dust yourself off, revise the activity, and try it again! And then you get to tell the rest of us about it, so we can learn from you!

REFERENCES

Cuseo, J. (2007). The empirical case against large class sizes: Adverse effects on the teaching, learning, and retention of first-year students. *Journal of Faculty Development, 21*(1), 5-21. Retrieved from: https://www.zotero.org/bcby/items/itemKey/A4UCTDDJ

Forsyth, D. R. (2003). *Prepping: Planning to teach a college class. The professor's guide to teaching:Psychological principles and practices.* (pp. 9-47). Washington, DC US: American Psychological Association

Kronowitz, E. (2012). *The teacher's guide to success* (2nd ed.). Upper Saddle River, NJ: Pearson Educational.

McKeachie, W. J. (2013). *Teaching tips: Strategies, research, and theory for college and university teachers* (14th ed.). Belmont, CA: Cengage.

Zepke, N., & Leach, L. (2010). Improving student engagement: Ten proposals for action. *Active Learning in Higher Education, 11*(3), 167-177. doi: 10.1177/1469787410379680

Contributors

Diana Ashe

Diana Ashe is Associate Professor of English and Associate Director of the Center for Teaching Excellence and Center for Faculty Leadership at the University of North Carolina Wilmington. The recipient of the 2010 Chancellor's Award for Teaching Excellence, the 2011 Board of Trustees Award for Teaching Excellence, and a 2011 Distinguished Teaching Professorship, she balances her work in faculty development with teaching courses in rhetoric and professional writing. She has published articles on writing program administration, academic mentoring, and environmental rhetoric, and is writing a monograph on the rhetoric of corporate greenwashing to be published by Teaxas A&M University Press in 2016.

Herb Berg

Dr. Herb Berg a professor of religion specializing in Islam in the Department of Philosophy and Religion and the Director of International Studies. His research focuses on Islam in its first few centuries and African American forms of Islam. For both, he examines how Muslims have understood, employed, and interpreted their scripture, the Qur'an. He is particularly interested in how groups who define themselves as "religious" construct their identities, perpetuate their groups, and legitimize authority structures.

Tim Ballard

Dr. Tim Ballard teaches human anatomy and physiology and other biomedical courses in the Department of Biology and Marine Biology, and serves as the UNCW Health Professions Advisor. He was received the Chancellor's Teaching Excellence Award, Board of Trustees Teaching Excellence Award, and has been a Distinguished Teaching Fellow. Currently, he is serving as a Bioscience

Education Network Scholar for the American Association for the Advancement of Science and the National Science Foundation.

Emily Boren

Emily Boren worked as a graduate assistant in the Center of Teaching Excellence (CTE) at University of North Carolina Wilmington for two years. She was the lead graduate student for CTE's AAC & U Bringing Theory to Practice Grant and the Designs on eLearning International Conference. She also created multiple faculty resources, such as the university-wide Chair's calendar. Emily completed her Master's degree in the general psychology program at UNCW in May 2014 and will begin her doctoral studies at George Mason University in August. She holds bachelor of arts degrees in both psychology and criminology from UNCW. Emily's research interests include psychological symptoms of victims and perpetrators of intimate partner violence, as well as personality traits in violent offenders.

Mark Boren

Mark Boren teaches literature and writing for the English dept. at UNCW. He's published on the work of Melville, Faulkner, James, and Wheatley, and on experimental teaching methods. His books are: *Sugar, Slavery, Christianity and the Making of Race* (Caribbean Studies Press 2013) and *Student Resistance: A History of the Unruly Subject* (Routledge 2001).

Robert Boyce

Dr. Robert Boyce is an associate professor in the School of Health and Applied Human Sciences at the University of North Carolina Wilmington (UNCW). He teaches Human Anatomy and Physiology and Exercise Physiology and conducts research in occupation physiology in worksites requiring high physical demands. He was awarded the distinction of "Fellow" in the American College of Sports Medicine for his service and research in Sports Medicine  and is distinguished at UNCW as a recipient of the Chancellor's Teaching Excellence Award.

Deborah Brunson

Dr. Deborah Brunson is an associate professor in the Department of Communication Studies where she teaches courses in communication theory, interracial communication, interpersonal communication and the discipline capstone. She has served as director of the Upperman African American Cultural Center, faculty co-chair of the Black Faculty and Staff Association, and coordinator of the Leadership Studies Minor. Deborah is co-editor on the books *Interracial Communication: Contexts, Communities, and Choices* and *Letters from the Future: Linking Students and Teaching with the Diversity of Everyday Life*. She has published in *Communication Education, Communication Teacher*, and *Journal of Leadership Studies*. Deborah is a recipient of the Chancellor's Teaching Excellence Award.

Katherine Bruce

Dr. Katherine Bruce is Professor of Psychology and Director of the UNCW Honors College. She teaches classes related to evolutionary psychology, animal behavior, and human sexuality, as well as Honors first-year seminars. She collaborates with Dr. Mark Galizio and several fantastic students to study comparative cognition, that is, learning in nonhumans from an evolutionary and functional perspective. She has served as President of the National Collegiate Honors Council, Southern Regional Honors Council, and North Carolina Honors Association, and she edits the state-wide undergraduate research journal, *Explorations*. Dr. Bruce is committed to mentoring undergraduates in applied learning experiences such as study abroad and research. For her individual efforts and for promoting campus-wide support for undergraduate research, she was named 2008 North Carolina Professor of the Year by the Carnegie Foundation and CASE (Council for Advancement and Support of Education.)

Larry Cahoon

Dr. Lawrence Cahoon teaches courses in biological oceanography, limnology, and coastal ocean science in the Department of Biology and Marine Biology, and directs graduate students in the marine Biology M.S. and Ph.D. programs and the Marine Science M.S. program. He is a Certified Senior

Ecologist with the ecological Society of America and was one of the first AAAS BiosciEdNet (BEN) Scholars. He has received over $5 million in external funding for his research and published over 90 peer-reviewed papers. He has won the UNCW Faculty Scholarship and Graduate Mentor awards.

Caroline Clements

Caroline Clements is currently Director of the Center for Teaching Excellence and Faculty Leadership at University of North Carolina Wilmington, a position she has held for ten years. She is a Professor in the Psychology Department. During her tenure as Director of the Centers, she has won the Distinguished Faculty Scholar Award and the J. Marshall Crews Distinguished Faculty Award. She edited the first edition of the *Best Practices in University Teaching* book for the purpose

of providing incoming faculty with a snapshot at teaching at its best from UNCW teaching award winning faculty. That book was picked up by Blair Publishing and was sold through Amazon and through a German publishing house. This second edition is designed with the same purpose in mind, to allow our newest faculty to be exposed to outstanding teaching from some of the best and brightest from our many outstanding faculty.

Steve Elliot

Dr. Steve Elliott is an Associate Professor and the Associate Director in the School of Health and Applied Human Sciences at UNC Wilmington. Dr. Elliott completed his undergraduate education at UNC Wilmington and received an MED and Ph.D from the University of Virginia where he was awarded the Outstanding Doctoral Student Award for the Curry School of Education. He teaches in the Physical Education and Health Teacher Education program and is committed to preparing new teachers to "make a difference in the lives of k-12 children." Dr. Elliott received the 2012

Chancellors Award for Teaching Excellence. He has published manuscripts in several Journals with his research agenda focusing on effective teaching strategies for the successful inclusion of children with special needs into regular classes.

John Fischetti

John Fischetti is the Head of School (Dean) of the School of Education at the University of Newcastle in Australia. He was Dean of Education at Southeastern Louisiana University and Department Chair and Professor at UNC Wilmington prior to that. John's research is related to effective pedagogy that promotes mastery and promotes equity, K-12 school reform and reinventing teacher education. You can reach John at fischettijc@gmail.com.

Tracy Hargrove

Dr. Tracy Y. Hargrove is Chair and Associate Professor in the Department of Early Childhood, Elementary, Middle, Literacy, and Special Education. Dr. Hargrove teaches courses in Elementary Mathematics Education in the Watson College. Her research interests include integrating mathematics and technology across the curriculum, teacher reflection, authentic assessment, and high-stakes accountability. Dr. Hargrove co-authored the book The Unintended Consequences of High-Stakes Testing with Dr. M. Gail Jones and Dr. Brett Jones. Dr. Hargrove was the 2006 recipient of the UNCW Chancellor's Teaching Excellence Award as well as the 2008 recipient of the UNCW Distinguished Teaching Professorship Award and the 2008 UNCW Board of Trustees Teaching Excellence Award.

Russ Herman

Dr. Russell L. Herman, professor of both Physics and Mathematics at UNC Wilmington, has a distinguished career in teaching, earning several teaching awards. He has directed dozens of undergraduate and graduate research projects. He is the Editor-in-Chief of *The Journal of Effective Teaching*, a peer reviewed journal devoted to teaching excellence in higher education, and has been a Faculty Associate for UNCW's Center for Teaching Excellence. Dr. Herman also has an established research record in several topics in physics and mathematics including the use of technology in classrooms. He has delivered a hundred lectures and published three dozen papers in these areas. He has recently published the textbook *A Course in Mathematical Methods for Physicists*.

Dr. Herman is the recipient of the UNC Board of Governor's Award for Excellence in Teaching (2006), UNCW's Distinguished Teaching Professorship Award (2005), the Chancellor's Teaching Excellence Award (2005), Carnegie Program U.S. Professors of the Year Nominee (2006), ITSD Research and Innovation Award for innovative use of technology (2005), Jack Charles Hall Award as "Recognition for nurturing students' enthusiasm for science and technology," (Science Olympiad, 2010), Chancellor's Discere Aude Award for student mentoring (2009), and a member of the James F. Merritt Million Dollar Club (2006).

Nancy Hritz

Dr. Nancy Hritz is an Associate Professor and Coordinator of the Recreation, Sport and Tourism Management program and a Certified Hospitality Educator with the American Hotel and Lodging Association. She earned her Bachelor and Masters degrees from the University of Missouri Columbia and Ph.D. from Indiana University Bloomington where she earned the Lebert H. Weir outstanding graduate student award. She is also the Coordinator of the Coastal Hospitality and Tourism Analysis research group and teaches courses in hospitality, tourism, marketing and research. She  has published in several journals, and her research interests' center around destination development, promotion and tourism market segments.

Patricia Kelley

Patricia Kelley parlayed an interest in dinosaurs at age 7 into a lifetime of studying and teaching about fossils. She received her BA in Geology from the College of Wooster in 1975 and her PhD from Harvard University in 1979. She taught at New England College, University of Mississippi, and University of North Dakota, and was a program officer at the National Science Foundation, before joining UNCW in 1997. She is a former president of the Paleontological Society and president of the Board of Trustees of the Paleontological Research Institution. Her research on evolutionary paleoecology of mollusks (not dinosaurs!) earned her the University of North Dakota Faculty Award for Outstanding Scientific Research  and the UNCW Distinguished Faculty Scholar Award. She received the

Association for Women Geoscientists Outstanding Educator Award in 2003, the AWG Professional Excellence Award in 2011, and the UNCW Chancellor's Teaching Excellence Award in 2012. In 2013 she received the UNCW Distinguished Teaching Professorship Award and the Board of Trustees Teaching Excellence Award. When not occupied with professional tasks, Tricia enjoys watching Johnny Depp movies and spending time with family, including watching Barney reruns with three-year old granddaughter McKenzie. (Someday Tricia will have to break the news that, unlike Barney, the real T. rex probably wasn't purple and may even have been covered in feathers, at least as a juvenile.)

Carol Pilgrim

Dr. Carol Pilgrim received her Ph.D. from the University of Florida in 1987 with a specialization in the Experimental Analysis of Behavior. She is currently Professor of Psychology and Associate Dean of the College of Arts and Sciences at the University of North Carolina Wilmington, where she has been honored with a Distinguished Teaching Professorship (1994-1997), the North Carolina Board of Governors Teaching  Excellence Award (2003), and the Faculty Scholarship Award (2000). She received the Chancellor's Teaching Excellence Award and the College of Arts and Sciences Excellence in Teaching Award in 1992, the ABA Student Committee Outstanding Mentor Award in 2006, and the UNCW Graduate Mentor Award in 2008. Her research contributions include both basic and applied behavior analysis, with an emphasis in human operant behavior, relational stimulus control, and the early detection of breast cancer. Dr. Pilgrim has served as editor of *The Behavior Analyst*, associate editor of the *Journal of the Experimental Analysis of Behavior* and *The Behavior Analyst*, co-editor of the *Experimental Analysis of Human Behavior Bulletin*, and as a member of the editorial boards of those and several other journals. She has served as President of the Association for Behavior Analysis, the Society for the Advancement of Behavior Analysis, Division 25 of the American Psychological Association, and the Southeastern Association for Behavior Analysis. Additionally, she has been Member-at-large of the Executive Council of ABA and Division 25, and member of the Boards of Directors of the Society for the Experimental Analysis of Behavior, the Society for the Advancement of Behavior Analysis, and the Cambridge Center for Behavioral Studies. She is a fellow of the Association for Behavior Analysis International and of Division 25 of the American Psychological Association.

Lisa Pollard

Lisa Pollard is a UC Berkeley alumna with BA, MA and PhD in history. She teaches modern Middle Eastern history, and is head of graduate studies in history. She writes about gender, race and social movements in nineteenth and early twentieth-century Egypt and Sudan. Her work has been funded by the Melon Foundation, the National Endowment for the Humanities and the American Research Center in Egypt. She has published in *Social Politics, Arab Studies Journal, Gender and History* and *International Journal of Middle East Studies.*

Michelle Manning

Michelle Manning is a full-time lecturer in the UNCW English Department, teaching both traditional and online classes in literature, teacher education, professional writing, and composition. She is the founder and coordinator of the English in Action Showcase, an end-of-semester event celebrating student work in the department. Michelle received a BA in English from UNCCH, as well as an English Ed degree, a MAT in English and a MFA in Creative Writing in Fiction from UNCW. She is the recipient of the UNCW Graduate Teaching Excellence Award, the English Department Outstanding Lecturer Award, the UNCW Lecturer of the Year Award, and the Excellence in Teaching First-Year Students Award.

Stephen McNamee

Dr. Stephen J. McNamee is Professor of Sociology and is currently serving as Interim Dean in the College of Arts and Sciences. He is a former department chair and former associate dean and recipient of the UNC Board of Governor's Award for Excellence in Teaching, the UNCW Distinguished Teaching Professorship Award, the UNCW Distinguished Faculty Scholar Award, and the North Carolina Sociological Association Contributions to Sociology Award.

Katherine Montwieler

Katherine Montwieler generally teaches courses in nineteenth-century British literature, contemporary women writers, and women's studies. Her scholarly articles usually focus on nineteenth-century British women writers, although she's also published on Charles Dickens and Claire de Duras. Her essay on Elizabeth Strout's *Olive Kitteridge* is forthcoming in the journal *Short Story*. She also enjoys writing for the popular press, and her essays have appeared in *The Wilmington Star News*, *The Raleigh News and Observer*, and *Integral Yoga Magazine*.

Meghan Sweeney

Dr. Meghan Sweeney is an associate professor of English at UNCW and the coordinator of the English graduate program. She teaches courses on children's and adolescent literature, critical theory, women in literature, and popular culture. Her writing has been published in the *ALAN Review*, *Children's Literature in Education*, and *Jeunesse*. She is working on a manuscript that addresses the ways that weddings are sold to American girls through books, costumes, toys, and games that help them feel connected to an appealing adult world but that also establish constrictive notions about consumption and gender identity.

Rick Olsen

Dr. Rick Olsen teaches in the department of communication studies with a focus on core courses including research methods, rhetorical theory, and debate. His research often focuses on the intersection of popular culture, values and rhetoric with cases studies as diverse as the NBA Draft, Sport Utility Vehicles and the "War" on Christmas controversy. He is also has been a consultant for a "train the trainer" program for the USMC which has help to provide great perspective on his own teaching practices.

KimMarie McGoldrick

KimMarie is active in faculty development programs, focusing primarily on mentoring and economic education. KimMarie served as a member of the American Economic Association's Committee on the Status of Women in the Economics Profession from 1999 through 2004. A major component of this committee's mission is to mentor young women in the discipline. In 2003 she was the co-recipient of an NSF ADVANCE Leadership Award: CeMENT: Workshops for Female Untenured Faculty in Economics (SBE-0317755). Her role in this project has been to develop and facilitate mentoring programs for female economics faculty in institutions which place emphasis on both teaching and research. KimMarie's focus  in economic education has led to the (co-) development of a number of economic education workshops including Service Learning in Economics, five Annual Teaching Workshops held in Wilmington NC, and she served as an instructor in the NSF funded Teaching Innovations Program (TIP).

Richard Ogle

Richard Ogle, Ph.D. is Professor and Chair of the Department of Psychology at the University of North Carolina Wilmington. Dr. Ogle is a clinical psychologist who teaches range of undergraduate and graduate courses. He is the recipient of a 2008 UNCW Chancellor's Teaching Excellence Award and a 2011 UNCW Distinguished Teaching Professorship Award.

Jessica Mesmer

Dr. Jessica Mesmer Magnus teaches in the human resource management concentration in the Cameron School of Business. Dr. Magnus has worked as a Human Resource Manager for a national consulting firm and is certified as a Senior Professional in Human Resources (SPHR). Dr. Magnus' research interests include team behavior and cognition, work/family conflict, and whistleblower retaliation. Her work has been published in a variety of top-tier academic outlets, including *Journal of Applied Psychology*, *Organizational Behavior and Human Decision Processes*, *Human Performance*, and *Journal of Business Ethics*.

Peter Schuhmann

Dr. Peter Schuhmann received his masters and PhD in economics from North Carolina State University and has been a faculty member in UNCW's Cameron School of Business since 1999. Prior to joining UNCW, he was on the faculty at the University of Richmond. He teaches a variety of classes including Principles of Microeconomics, Natural Resource Economics, The Economics of Growth and Development and Econometrics.

Dr. Schuhmann focuses his research on environmental and natural resource economics and also conducts research in the area of teaching methods and pedagogy. He has over 40 peer-reviewed publications to date. His work has been published in journals such as *Land Economics, Ecological Economics, Marine Resource Economics, Natural Resource Modeling, Marine Policy* and the *Journal of Economic Education.*

Along with Rob Burrus, Dr. Schuhmann has organized and hosted a regional economics teaching conference each fall for the past 13 years. Dr. Schuhmann has been recognized by the University with the following teaching awards: The UNC Board of Governors Teaching Excellence Award, the Board of Trustees Teaching Excellence Award, the Distinguished Teaching Professorship Award, the Chancellors Teaching Excellence Award, the MBA Outstanding Faculty Award, and the *Discere Aude* Award for outstanding student mentoring.

Dr. Schuhmann is a UNCW graduate, having received his bachelors degree in Business with a concentration in economics from UNCW in 1990.

Brad Walker

Dr. Brad Walker is an associate professor of language education at UNCW. Dr. Walker received his doctorate degree in reading education from Indiana University. He completed his undergraduate work and a Master's of Education Degree at Brigham Young University. Before coming to the university, Dr. Walker taught elementary school (3rd, 4th, and 5th grades) and worked as an elementary school principal.

Dr. Walker leads a summer study abroad trip to Japan each year. He has done this since 1999. The trip makes it possible for education students to interact with the teachers and students of Japan. Dr. Walker loves to learn and interact with others as they learn. He enjoys helping students take learning journeys that are exciting, productive, and motivating.

Michael Wentworth

Michael Wentworth joined the faculty of UNCW in 1983 when he was hired in the Department of English and later served as the first director of the Graduate Liberal Studies Program, the pedagogical and philosophical agendas of which adhere to the "continuing value and relevance of the liberal arts." Over the past thirty years Wentworth has taught nearly fifty-five different courses, including such interdisciplinary courses as Main Street U.S.A., The Contemporary American Workplace, Classic American Roadways, Academic Mayhem: College Life in Literature, Folklore, and the Popular Media, The Great Depression in American  Culture, and Hobo and Vagabond Traditions in American Culture. He has received a number of teaching awards, including the UNCW English Department Teaching Excellence Award (1991, 2009), the Chancellor's Teaching Excellence Award and the College of Arts and Sciences Excellence in Teaching Award (1991), the UNCW Chapter of Phi Eta Sigma Outstanding Educator Award (1993), the UNCW Board of Trustees Teaching Excellence Award (1995), a UNCW Distinguished Teaching Professorship Award (1996), the University of North Carolina Board of Governors Teaching Excellence Award (1998), and the UNCW Graduate Mentor Award (2006).